THE
THAMES HIGHWAY

A HISTORY OF THE INLAND NAVIGATION

BY

FRED. S. THACKER

Author of
The Stripling Thames

"*Heia, viri, nostrum reboans echo sonet heia!
Annisu parili tremat ictibus acta carina.*"

1914

Copyright © 2013 Read Books Ltd.
This book is copyright and may not be
reproduced or copied in any way without
the express permission of the publisher in writing

British Library Cataloguing-in-Publication Data
A catalogue record for this book is available from the
British Library

A Short Introduction to the History of the River Thames

The River Thames takes its name from the Middle English *Temese,* which is derived from the Celtic name for river. Originating at the Thames Head in Gloucestershire, it is the longest river in England, flowing a total length of 236 miles, out through the Thames Estuary and in to the North Sea. On its journey to open water it passes through the country's capital, London, where it is deep enough to be navigable for ships, thus allowing the city to become a major international trade port.

The earliest evidence of human habitation on the river is a Neolithic bowl (3300-2700 BC), found in the river at Buckinghamshire. Other Pre-Roman sites have also revealed watermills, navigations, burial mounds, and settlements along its banks. As with many geographical features of Europe, it was the Roman Empire that realised its strategic and economic importance. In the first century BC, under Emperor Claudius, they built many fortifications along the Thames Valley. They also established a trading centre at the river's lowest point on two hills, now known as Cornhill and Ludgate Hill. They built a bridge there and named the settlement Londinium, a settlement that would eventually become the City of London.

During the Middle Ages the river attracted great prosperity, being a hive of activity in the fishing, milling, and pottery industries. However, the success brought with it unwanted attention, and in 870 AD the Vikings swept up on the tide creating havoc and destroying buildings such as Chertsey Abbey. When William the Conqueror arrived in

1066 AD he was rightly concerned with protecting the Thames Valley. He built many castles along its banks, such as those at Windsor, Rochester, and the magnificent Tower of London. This cemented his strategic position and gave him a base from which to control the rest of the country. He was also responsible for giving us the Domesday Book (1086), a hugely detailed survey, which gives us great insight into the activities on the Thames in the Middle Ages.

In the 16th and 17th centuries the river became a hugely important tool for transporting goods such as timber, livestock, and foodstuffs, from Oxford to the capital. It helped the City of London grow with the expansion of world trade and the wharves became packed with shipping vessels. It was also during this period that the country endured a series of cold winters that froze the Thames. So solid was the sheet of ice that 1607 saw the first Frost Fair, where tents were set up on the river offering various amusements such as ice bowling. By the 18th century, London was the centre of the mercantile British Empire and the river became one of the busiest waterways in the world. Docks were expanded and locks were built, allowing for easier navigation and even greater method of trade.

Among the many uses of the Thames, unfortunately one of them was as a dumping site for the city's waste products. This had been the case since the Middle Ages, but the more populous the banks of the river became, the more it became an environmental hazard. This problem reached its zenith with the 'Great Stink' of 1858, when the stench from the raw sewage in the river caused the abandonment of a sitting at the House of Commons. A concerted effort was then made to clean up the river and the construction of massive sanitary sewers was undertaken. This was part of a great engineering drive in the wake of the Industrial Revolution that saw pollution decline, water sources become cleaner, and railway bridges reducing the congestion on the river.

Although the Port of London remains one of the UK's main ports, the growth of road transport has largely superseded the Thames as a medium of transport. There are also far fewer heavy industries utilising the river, and as a resulted it is cleaner than it has been in hundreds of years. The Thames has played a key role in the development of a nation. Its story, both geographically and with its human uses, is a long and fascinating one. As John Burns, MP for Battersea, said in 1929 'The Thames is Liquid History'.

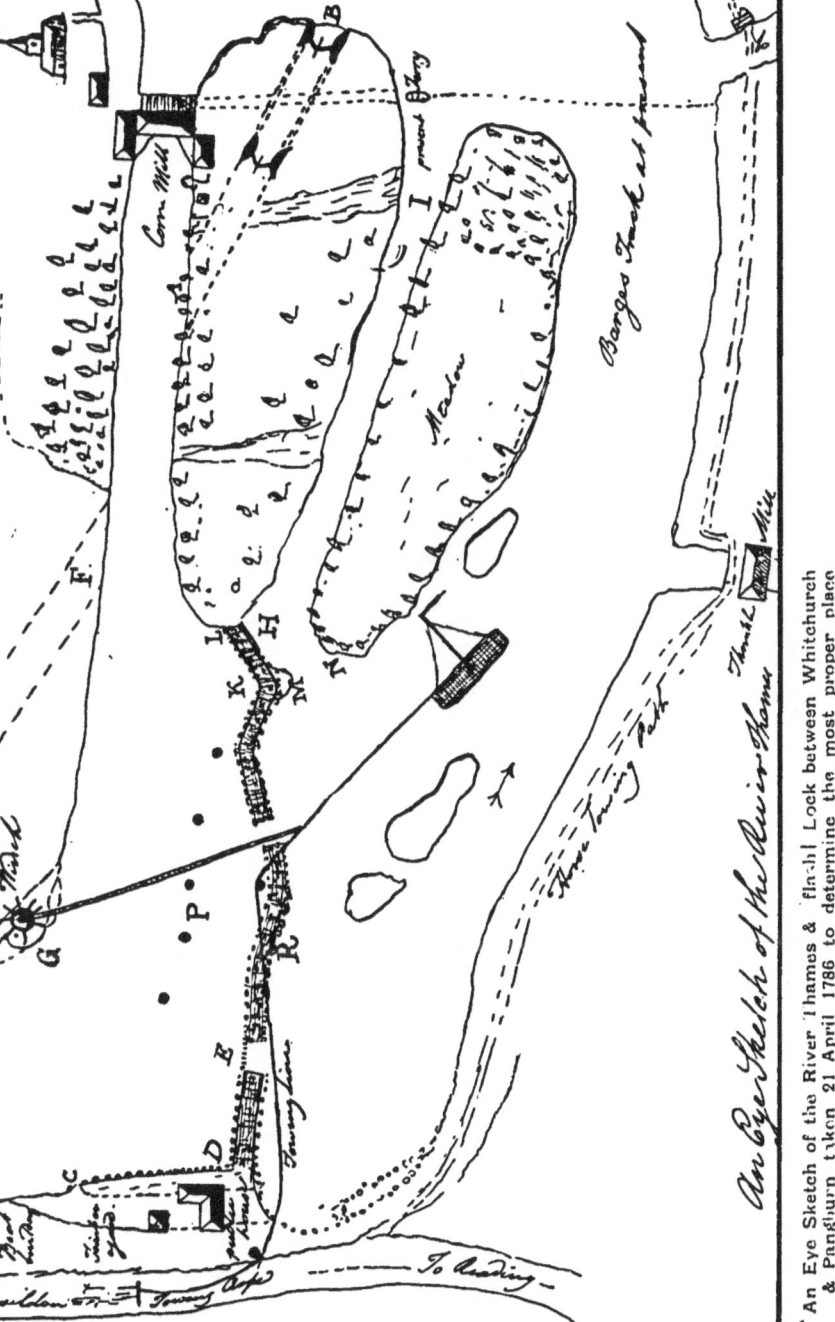

"An Eye Sketch of the River Thames & final Lock between Whitchurch & Pangbourn taken 21 April 1786 to determine the most proper place to erect a Pound Lock." Illustrating the contemporary method of ascending a weir. By kind permission of the Thames Conservancy.

Contents

Chapter			
I	Introductory		1
II	General History		12
III	Do. (*continued*)		37
IV	The Oxford-Burcot Commissions		62
V	General History (*continued*)		90
VI	The Thames Commissioners		122
VII	Do. (*continued*)		158
VIII	The City of London Jurisdiction		199
IX	The Thames Conservancy (1857)		236
X	The Thames Conservancy		239
XI	Conclusion		255

Appendix		
I	Table of Flashlock Tolls	261
II	Professor Thorold Rogers and the Navigation	268
III	Landing Places	274

List of Illustrations

Eye sketch at Whitchurch flashlock, 1786	*Frontispiece*
Weir tackle	*Page* 7
Kidels in Thames Estuary	23
Stride at Dedham lock, River Stour	133
Shiplake lock and paper mill, *circ.* 1811	136
Radcot weir, *circ.* 1811	251

THE REFERENCES to my "List," or "below," relate for the most part to the ensuing complementary volume : THE LOCKS AND WEIRS. The photographs alluded to on page ten herein will appear mostly in the same volume.

—

In preparation
THE KENNET COUNTRY

Chapter I : Introductory

TO THOSE in pursuit of pleasure, or more rarely of business, who navigate the pleasant reaches of the Thames above the tideway, the obstructions known as locks and weirs usually present themselves under a merely casual aspect. According to immediate circumstances you pass through and forget them: if of haste, as a nuisance whose necessity seems but slightly to compensate for the delay they entail; if of leisure and holiday, as a refreshment and cool relief for a little space from toil and the heat of the sun. At these beloved stations, set so often in the most alluring scene of their neighbourhood, it is no small pleasure to the simple voyager to be recognised and saluted by the keeper as a frequenter of the River, and shiningly to secure his spontaneous protection from some ill handled launch, or his permission to set the gates and sluices working.

Rarely perhaps does the spectacle of the locks, with their heavy sullen timbers, their terraces of whitened stone and shaven turf, their trickling water and frequent brilliance of flowers, bring to the remembrance of those who use them the persistent quarrel through long, slow moving centuries before the passage of the Thames achieved the easy and inexpensive facility of the present day. The quarrel indeed was drawing to a close when the modern locks, called at first for distinction pound locks, turnpikes, and sometimes even cistern locks, began so curiously late to be built towards the middle of the seventeenth century. For centuries earlier it had concerned itself with those much older institutions the weirs, themselves immemorially known as locks; locking or penning back the water as effectually as their successors.

It was justly urged against my *Stripling Thames* that it offered no considered study of the navigation under its historical and economic aspect; extending to the locks and weirs, like most Thames books, only an accidental and sporadic treatment. Upon this I proposed to myself to write a short sketch of the subject, so far as it affected those remote reaches above Oxford, to be incorporated into some later edition of that book. But I found this germinal idea so grow under my investigation, so much matter came to light never yet given to the world in any study of the River, that I determined to issue the fruit of my work in a separate volume upon the whole of Thames above the tideway. It has been a fascinating pursuit to trace in detail the history of the obscure but none the less real and important feud that lurks behind the white and peaceful framework of Medley weir, of King's and Eynsham and Eaton : sole and hardly surviving relics of many score of similar obstructions that once clumsily facilitated the navigation of the Thames.

The three main parties to the secular debate were, first, the riparian owners and the tenants of their mills and fisheries, who saw in the maintenance and increase of the weirs an easy and lucrative source of income; secondly the bargemasters, who desired clear navigation and good floating depths for as nearly nothing as they could compass; and, lastly, the dim Riverside populations, who perpetually and sullenly complained of many things, but chiefly of the floods caused by the continual heightening of the weirs, that drove them from their homes and ruined their precarious crops ; and of the wholesale, illegitimate destruction of the fry of fish, upon which they so largely depended for their livelihood, by way of either food or sport, through the illegal snares and engines commonly attached to the weirs. As I shall frequently notice, the fry of fish were destroyed of old time literally by cartloads, by no means solely for human food or even for bait, but as meals for swine, as manure, and for the sake of their scales which were sold to the beadmakers. The ancient value of this fry was a penny a bushel, say eighteen pence of our money; or I have seen it named at a bushel for six eggs. This third party had a further complaint which it shared with the second: that the difficulties and dangers in navigation caused by the mill and fishery weirs greatly enhanced the cost of the necessaries of life; but was for the most part crushed out of account by the two stronger and wealthier contestants.

Now if you consider the Thames in its navigable length, and compare it with itself above Lechlade or with other waters left to run at will, sometimes in deep slow pools, sometimes over shallows that cannot float a canoe, it will become evident that, properly placed and properly regulated, locks and weirs are in essence an advantage to water traffic. A navigator finds his passage frequently hindered at certain spots through lack of floating depth, and in the absence of mechanical means of increasing it is compelled to depend upon the rains for his assistance, or to resort to the cumbrous and expensive, and necessarily often repeated, process of dredging. In course of time it would occur to him to choose the lowest of a series of these shallows, and there to erect a dam across the current, which would result in raising the height of the water some appreciable distance above, the benefit varying with the fall of the channel: the slighter the gradient, the more extended the advantage. Hereupon the trouble of the floods would

General History 5

become more acute; for not only would the dam cause, possibly, a novel and immediate overflow in its vicinity at normal times, but it would prove also a barrier to ordinary floods in their season. And besides this aggravation of floods, it would not be long before the convenience of these stations for fishing, regular and illegitimate, would become too manifest to be resisted; and many more would be erected for this sole purpose, not in aid but directly obstructive of the navigation. Thus many abuses would and did gradually creep in to spoil their essential benefit.

I have here presented the navigation as the original motive for weirs; but I believe, though it is occasionally disputed, that they were primarily built by the millers, who needed them to keep up a head of water for their mills. The two interests, indeed, required the dams in identical positions: wherever sharp, shallow falls of the River bed caused a rapid stream. It was stated in 1884 that out of twenty-six pound locks below Oxford, placed just where the bargemasters most required them, and adjacent to ancient weirs, only five were without a neighbouring mill. But not only the navigation and the milling interests have been put forward as originally responsible for the weirs; frequently, and for example in an anonymous four-page folio of just subsequent to 1791, the theory is advanced that "the fishery originally suggested the use of dams and weirs, to intercept and catch fish in large quantities. So much water penned to different heads, naturally led to the erection of mills at the falls. The improved depth of water above the dams suggested the idea of carriage by boats, and the boatowners came justly under the tax of a contribution to the owners of old weirs." Thus at the very outset of the enquiry you are met with obscurity; the mills, the navigation and the fisheries being each in turn presented as the originators of the weirs.

Mr. C. J. Cornish in his *Naturalist on the Thames* says: " Fish and flour go together as bye-products of nearly all our large rivers. The combination comes about thus: wherever there is a water-mill, a mill cut is made to take the water to it. This mill-dam holds the biggest fish. When the old mills were first founded, and for eight centuries onwards [it would be interesting to know at which century the eight are to begin], it was as a source of power, a substitute for steam, that the river was valued. The times will probably alter, and the Thames currents turn mill wheels again to generate electric light for the towns and villages on its banks. The chance of this is enough to make any one who owns a mill right on the water keep it." I think this transformation had actually begun when Mr. Cornish wrote; the Whitchurch mill, for example, has I

WEIR TACKLE at Boveney lock.

To face p. 7.

General History

believe long been such a generating station. And so now is Goring; and perhaps others.

The primordial water pen was no doubt a solid bank of stakes, filled in with chalk and stones, set across the stream, over which the water fell, and in whose construction very little or no provision was made for regulating the flow or for passing barges. When however the traffic began to assert itself a central span from ten to twenty feet wide was filled with moveable tackle: paddles and rymers; and it was to this opening that the term lock was originally applied. The tackle was held in position by fitting into a sill or beam under water at the bottom of the river, and towards the top on to the weir bridge. Such were the flash locks; the term flash or flush denoting the rush of water let through, by removal of the tackle, whenever required for the passage of a barge. Eaton weir was the last survivor so used for small boats; and here, and at Medley and Eynsham, barges and launches still have to be flashed through: King's has an arrangement like a single pair of lock gates. When a vessel desires to pass a sufficient number of the paddles and rymers are hauled out (no light work: *crede experto!*) and stood handy on the bridge or just ashore. This allows the water to rush through the opening in great volume, which continues until the water above the weir is reduced nearly to the level of that below, and the rush is considerably quietened. Then the vessel is dragged up through the opening; the old classical method being by means of a rope and winch stationed above the weir, the only surviving specimen of which is the garlanded relic at Hurley. Other means were to pole her through, or for the crew or horses themselves to haul upon a line. The craft while passing up presents the appearance of ascending an incline. Going down the same rush is relied on of itself to carry the barge through. It will be quite evident that this operation is attended with an enormous waste of water; the level of the whole upper reach for perhaps a couple of miles being lowered a considerable number of inches, needing perhaps several days to recover its normal depth.

The immemorial mills were, as I said, great offenders in the matter of erecting these weirs, whether convenient to the navigation or not. And as barge traffic increased, they were allowed gradually to acquire a prescriptive right to levy toll (*consuetudo*) on passing vessels, in compensation for the loss of water power they suffered at each passage; thus subjecting themselves to the obloquy of being "sellers of water." Flashes were required, not only at the weirs, but very frequently also to float barges over distant shallows. The miller would then, for a fee and at his own grudging choice of time, let down a flash for this purpose. Even so all trouble was not necessarily at an end for the much enduring navigator. For it often happened that a second mill intervened, whose owner would cheerfully divert the welcome abundance to his own wheel and rob the bargemaster of the accommodation for which he had not only paid, but walked perhaps many miles to arrange. These and other amenities naturally caused much friction between the millers and the barge traffic.

From the date of the earliest records down to 1350 the general jurisdiction over the River Thames, and over the three or more other royal rivers, was a Crown prerogative exercised through mere special, temporary commissions, constituted chiefly by letters patent. In 1350 Parliament passed its first Act against obstructions of the navigable highway of the River. The execution of this and of subsequent early Acts was also entrusted to similar commissions. The earliest approach to a permanent public control, the Oxford-Burcot Commission inaugurated in 1605 and strengthened in 1623, was confined to its own district, and its membership was limited to eight connections of the University and City of Oxford. Under it the first building of modern locks upon the Thames took place. The first general public Authority was constituted in 1695; and from that time downwards there has been an almost unbroken succession of commissions.

There must be reserved, between 1197 and 1857,

the jurisdiction of the City of London : strict as far westward as Staines, vague and doubtful beyond.

No locks, in the familiar modern sense of the word, were built upon the Thames between those of the Oxford-Burcot Commission, whose works were completed about 1635, and 1771, nearly a century and a half later : an interval very surprising and very difficult to account for.

The interesting but obscure subject of local jurisdiction exercised by the larger riparian communities over their own districts of the River should not be forgotten. The aforesaid Oxford Authority, of which I present the first detailed printed account, is a clear and shining example ; and it may safely be assumed that, in some more obscure and unrecorded fashion, other powerful corporations such as Windsor and Kingston once exercised a more or less exclusive control over their communication by water with their neighbours and with London. The bare fact that there were towns on the banks, between which the water would often be the quickest and easiest communication, presupposes some immemorial, decentralised jurisdiction, or prescription, in support of local navigation against encroachments.

—

My photographs have been taken very frequently after a long day's sculling ; sometimes in driving rain or an iron wind, sometimes from my unsteady boat, in waning light or beneath cloudy skies. They are simply records, secured often under unfavourable circumstances, of interesting and sometimes little known features of Thames topography. It is upon such an understanding that I present them.

Chapter II

I NOW turn to a particular account of the long history of my subject. And as with the origins of many primitive institutions, I am met at the outset with some obscurity as to when this dispute between Thames traffic on the one hand, and Thames mills and fisheries on the other, first compelled State intervention. For the ostensible date of the supposed earliest general reference we possess, the Edward the Confessor proclamation, is not admitted. It is printed in *Ancient Laws and Institutions*, the twelfth article under this sovereign, contemplating the King's Peace. "Pax regis multiplex est .... quam habent aque quarum navigio de diversis partibus deferuntur victualia civitatibus et burgis," and the rest. It was promulgated professedly in 1066, during the final days of the Confessor's life: he died on January 5 in this year. It proceeds, being interpreted: "If mills, fisheries, or any other works are constructed to their [the four royal rivers'] hindrance, let these works be destroyed, the waters repaired, and the forfeit to the King not forgotten." Here the navigation is

General History

presented as the paramount interest on these rivers : the Thames, the Severn, the Trent, and the Yorkshire Ouse. The difficulty is that at its professed date Edward was seriously ill, indeed within a few days of his death.

A still earlier localised note of actual traffic is fully established. It is contained in the chronicle of Abingdon Abbey. Translated from the Latin it reads: "Abingdon monastery has the Thames flowing along its southward parts, up and down which navigation is conducted. In the days of Abbot Ordric [1054-1066], beyond the precinct of the church, at a place called Barton, next the hamlet of Thrup, the wide bed of the river used to cause rowers no little difficulty. For the land below being steeper than that above often made the said channel slack of water. The citizens of Oxford, therefore (having most traffic there), petitioned that the course of the river might be diverted through the church's meadow further south, so that ever after by all their vessels a hundred *allecia* [herrings in English, though I think the French more daintily construe it anchovies] should be paid as toll to the cellarer of the monastery. While their tribute is duly paid, as agreed, the said undertaking is performed to this very day." Further notes of detail upon this incident will be found under the heading of the Swift Ditch, below.

The pleasing rider that the man actually handing

in the toll was to receive back five fish for himself, together with a meal of bread, cheese and ale, while quite characteristic of the hospitality of those ancient houses, is not in Stevenson. Wood, however, mentions it; adding that the contract was infringed under Henry I (1100-1135); and thereupon confirmed by royal decree.

The next reference to regulation of the Thames highway is the second charter of Richard I, dated by Birch July 14, 1197, vesting the care of the River for the first time in the Mayor and Corporation of the City of London. The Crusader had returned from his wars in an impecunious condition, and in the said year, it is stated for a consideration of 1,500 marks, quite £20,000 of our money, signed this charter:

"Know ye all that we, for the health of our soul, our father's soul, and all our ancestors' souls, and also for the common weal of our City of London, and of all our realm, have granted and stedfastly commanded that all weirs that are in the Thames be removed, wheresoever they shall be within the Thames: Also, we have quitclaimed all that which the keeper of our Tower of London was wont yearly to receive of the said weirs. Wherefore we will and stedfastly command, that no keeper of the said Tower, at any time hereafter, shall exact anything of anyone, neither molest nor burden, nor any demand make of any person by reason of the said weirs. For it is manifest to us . . . . that great detriment and inconvenience hath grown to our said City of London, and also to the whole realm, by occasion of the said weirs."

General History

This is the highly important document upon which the ancient authority of the City of London over the River reposed, until within living memory ; and which has often been launched against offenders with irresistible effect. It is noticeable that it prescribes no limits for the jurisdiction. Probably the whole River was intended ; but its "loose expressions," as Birch describes them, allowed the City's authority to be so strongly assailed that it ultimately dwindled to covering only the portion of the River from Staines downward : from Colne Ditch to Yantlet Creek. I have however met with the reverse theory in some obscure, mid-Victorian book : that the charter was intended to cover only this lower district ; and that the City had ever since been making frequent and unsuccessful attempts to push its jurisdiction further west !

The charter was confirmed almost *verbatim* by John, on June 17, 1199, adding only a penalty of £10 against offenders ; and by Henry III, on February 18, 1227. The dates are Birch's.

A letter patent was granted by John in 1205 to "William son of Andrew our servant that he might have while he lived one ship going and returning upon the Thames between Oxford and London with his property and merchandise free and unmolested by any toll and exaction which belongs to us ; and that he might freely and without hindrance load that vessel wherever on the Thames he desired between Oxford and London." The governors of Wallingford and other River ports were forbidden to interfere with him. Madox, in his *History of the Exchequer*, explains that there were at that time duties payable to the Crown on Thames borne merchandise. "The duty paid for trafficking along the Thames, or at least one sort of that duty, was called *Avalagum Thamisiae*." He quotes John's earlier patent to Andrew of the Exchequer, probably the Andrew above mentioned, to have a ship carrying *blada* and victuals, and other necessaries for him and his, from Abingdon to London, unmolested by any toll going and returning as long as he remained at the Exchequer.

And so I arrive at the classical twenty-third clause of Magna Charta in 1215 : " *Omnes kidelli deponantur :* all weirs from henceforth shall be utterly put down by *Thames* and *Medway*, and through all England, except only [*nisi*] by the sea coasts." It is a highly interesting speculation whether the term *kidelli* was intended to cover all weirs and dams of every sort. My own view is that it was not so intended ; there is abundant evidence that kidels were an engine devoted and limited entirely to the catching of fish : mere screens of stakes and hurdles set usually only partly across the current, thickly woven with bushy twigs and wickerwork. If all sorts of weirs were aimed at would not some

General History

other word: *gurgites* perhaps, have been substituted, or added? The *Penny Encyclopaedia* has a description of brushwood weirs, which are kidels. Seebohm states that the Saxon *wera* denotes any structure for entrapping fish. He has some interesting information and sketches, notably from Tidenham-on-Severn. Boydell, or Coombe his ghost, is of opinion that all kinds of weirs were not prohibited by Magna Charta. It was never contemplated, he thinks, that there should be no weirs whatever upon navigated streams. The complaints were directed usually, he says, against such as were in unsuitable positions, or laid down or enlarged solely for gain. " Dams or weirs," he writes, " were then necessary, as they now are [1794], to facilitate and quicken the passage of vessels; and their construction, support and repair were attached to particular estates, tenures and districts." In proof he cites, perhaps from Wood, the indictment of John Drayton, knight, 5 Henry IV, 1403, " because he did not keepe up, at Rotherfield Pypard [near Henley], in the water of Thames there, locks and winches for the necessary conduct of vessels from London to Oxon": an early reference, doubtless, to the weir at Marsh mills.

(I may add here that the word kidel has been used to denote also a species of net. In the City of London *Letter Book A*, under date 1313, seizure is noted of a "Net, called a kidel," as "too close and insufficient for fishing, *pro destruccione riparie*... Adjudged that the said kidel be burnt in Chepe." The kidel destroyed the bank and captured undersized fish; it is not alleged that it obstructed the navigation.)

In 1227 Henry III issued a patent "to his well beloved and faithful Wilfrid de Lucy and others," appointing them justices to inspect and measure all weirs which to the hindrance of vessels passing through them had been heightened or increased in the counties of Oxford and Berkshire, etc., "since the last return of our lord King John our father from Scotland into England," perhaps about 1209; that they were so placed that vessels could pass over them without hindrance or damage, as before that date; and to enquire diligently on oath of the knights and freemen of the several counties what men had taken toll from vessels passing through their weirs without good warrant.

It seems arguable from the foregoing that there were weir owners at this date whose right to toll was admitted. Concurrently both the Richard I charter, and the clause of Magna Charta, were confirmed, as I have said; the latter expressly "for the advantage of the City." A contemporary incident is recorded in the Close Rolls, wherein Henry forgave Haweis daughter of Wilfrid son of Peter the 20s. in which

General History

she had been amerced by the justices for the inspection of Thames weirs in Berkshire; though she was to amend the erection to the liking of the justices. The exact site does not appear.

In 1235, in the same reign, it was ordered that weirs should be made to stand at that height, and width of opening between the posts, as in the reigns of Henry II, Richard I, and John.

In 1274, 3 Edward I, an allusion to engineering or dredging seems implied. The "water of Thames" was "to be so widened that ships and great barges might ascend from London to Oxford, and descend, without hindrance from any weirs; as the Thames was so narrowed in divers places that ships could not pass." The mention of the whole extent between the two cities proves that the River was regarded as a continuous highway, and not used in local sections merely.

Four years later a commission issued to Geoffrey de Pycheford and John de London to enquire by jury of the counties of Bucks and Berks what men were setting kidels in the River to the destruction of small fish. Subsequent orders admitted a prescriptive right in all weirs that had existed previous to the end of the reign of Edward I : 1307. But it lay with the owners to keep them within specific dimensions.

In 1281 Stephen de Pincestre was commanded to cry down kidels in Thames and Medway. Five years later de Pycheford was again instructed to enquire touching those persons who were so straitening and obstructing weirs, and attaching such nets to them, that ships, and small and other fish, by reason of their excessive narrowness, could no longer pass as they had been wont.

The date 1285 upon Staines Stone comes in here. I have not discovered any salient incident which might explain its erection this year.

In the Year Book of Edward I, 1294, occurs an interesting legal note: "If one have common in another's water, although that water be turned into another channel, or by overflow run through other lands, yet he may always follow the water wherever it run, in order to enjoy his common."

In 1294, also, Robert Malet and William de Bereford were appointed to view the gorces and weirs in various counties, as divers lords had erected them in fresh places, and had straitened and heightened others. They were to remove all made contrary to the assize. Eleven years later de Bereford and others were re-appointed; and for the first time it is expressly declared that there had been complaints from bargeowners and other citizens navigating the Thames. "Magnates and others have made weirs, mills, and divers enclosures, without licence, or raised those already higher than they used to be, so that ships and fish cannot pass as accustomed."

General History

I think this patent may have been consequent upon the following petition :

"A nrē seignr le Roi & a son conseill monstrent les coēs marchandz passantz p̄ eau entre la cite de Londres & Oxonford Q come en leau de Thamis entre la dite cite & la ville auantdite seient plusurs gortz les queux dussent estre issuit reparilez q̄ batz poeiont passer illoeqs et les queus sont ore si estopez restreintz & barres p̄ bars & loks p̄ ceaus qˡ les dement q̄ nul bat ne put passer sanz ceo qil done gñt somme a ceaux qi dement les ditz gortz p̄ qei les marchantz passanz illoeqs gisent souentefeth deux iours ou treis auant ceo qil punt passer tanq il eient fait rannceon ou gree pr lur passage & issuit p̄dont lur avantages le ble encherist & autres vitailles aussint & plusurs autres damages veignent au poeple de quele chose auant ces houres Justices nrē seignr le Roi vut estre assignez de sʳuer les defautes & de mettre remedie & vncore nul amendement est fait prient les ditz marchantz a nrē seignr le Roi & son conseill pr dieu qil voillent cōmander q̄ remedie & amendement se facent sr les choses auant dites pr le coē p̄fit de son poeple." *Endorsed* "Sient suffisants gentz q pront a ceo entendrᵉ assignez de sʳuer les gortz entrᵉ Londr̄ & Oxñ & a hoster les estupures & les nusances issuit q̄ batz puissent passer sollom ceo qil deuient de reson et auncienement solleient."

It is quite evident that decrees and investigations concerning nuisances were quite as ineffective then as they sometimes are today ; that ancient magnates, like our present legislators of both complexions in respect of the motor pest, were themselves too deeply interested in breaking and evading the laws to interfere heartily in upholding them. Indeed, another petition of some uncertain year of Edward I or II confirms this impression :

"The merchants who frequent the water [*ewe*] between London and Oxford are disturbed by gortz, lokes, mills and many other nuisances ; that William de Bereford and the rest have been so occupied *en le svice du dit nostre Seignour le Roy* [felicitous euphemism !] that they could not give the matter proper attention." And the petitioners besought less preoccupied justices : " to wit, the Constable of Windsor," and others.

In 1316 occurs a complaint against a specific offender. A commission issued to William de Monte Acuto to enquire into a charge from Oxfordshire and Berkshire that "the abbot of Abindon and others, who have weirs on the river Thames between Oxford and Wallingford, have reconstructed them of such a height that the lands on each bank are flooded ; and have constructed certain obstacles on the weirs, called 'lokes,' by which ships and boats are obstructed." I do not understand the gravamen of the complaint against the "lokes" added to the weirs, unless the latter had previously been short fishing hedges, past which, along the part of the channel left open, navigation could be conducted ; which weirs had now been perhaps extended completely across from bank to bank, and flash locks built into them, entailing a fresh delay and toll upon the barges.

General History

In 1327, 1 Edward III, occurs a complaint of more explicit detail: " Divers men of riverside counties have kidels along the banks of the River; have made weirs in the same River; and fixed piles and pales along its course, and tied the cords of their nets athwart the stream, contrary to divers charters of the citizens, and more especially to Magna Charta ... to enquire ... and to punish offenders by fine and otherwise." Herein it is very noteworthy that an undeniable distinction is made between kidels and weirs. The kidels were "along the banks"; short hedges or rows of hurdles, set sometimes zigzag but only partly across the current, in some cases several rows deep, and intended always, not to hold up heads of water, but to snare large quantities of the fry of fish. I think it doubtful that these rows of brushwood screens, two or three deep, were confined, as Seebohm states, to the Severn and the Wye. Here are plans of three in the estuary of the Thames,

On Whitstable Flats

Opposite Swale Cliff

copied from an Ordnance survey published early in 1819, and actually in position on that date. As I am not dealing with that part of the River I may mention here that there was much complaint at this late date of kidels at the mouth of the Thames, and allegations of cartloads of fry snared and carried away as manure and pigs' food.

At some uncertain date under Edward III, 1327-1377, occurs a complaint on the other side of the question, of which I give details below, under Shepperton: a riparian owner petitioning to be upheld in his claim for towpath toll, and succeeding.

By the same king in his first year, 1327, a commission was granted; perhaps connected with the first charter of the reign, dated by Birch March 6, 1327. The charter issued "by consent of Parliament." It gives authority to the citizens of London to "remove and take away all the weirs in the water of Thames and Medway." In 1337 arose a fresh complaint and command for redress:

> "Fishermen in the river Thames, and keepers of weirs, sluices and piles fixed across the River, and millers of mills, take fish great, small and young by nets made with too narrow meshes and other engines .... and the weirs made for mills are so raised and obstructed that the adjoining lands are often flooded." To take various steps, including the reduction to the proper height of weirs and mill pounds raised above measure.

This order was entrusted to the de Beches, and amongst others to de Worth, "parson of the church at Fifhide." Was it the Fyfield near New Bridge?

General History

The de Beches were doubtless of that family whose curiously named effigies are still in the church of Aldworth near Streatley.

Instructions to various persons in 1338 are interesting in two small details. One is that salmon are mentioned among the kinds of fish illegally destroyed in the Thames; the other is the occurrence of the word *stank* as a kind of dam, which puzzled me once as a field name at Cricklade. I believe that in the form of *stanch* it is in common use today upon East Anglian navigations.

A brief note in the Patent Rolls in 1344 is noteworthy as seeming to imply that at that time the tides were felt as high as Staines: a subject I discuss more fully below, under this head. During this same year is noted, in the City of London *Letter Book F*, a letter patent " appointing Roger Hillary, Walter de Chestehunte, William de Langford, John de Braye and Roger de Louthe to be commissioners for the removal of piles, hurdles (*cleyas*) and other engines from the Thames, so as to afford a free passage to vessels carrying victuals and other merchandise between the vill of Westminster and the bridge of Stanes."

The next record is embodied in a common petition of Parliament in 1348. More detailed than earlier complaints, it seems to contain a note almost of suppressed anger:

"Whereas the four great rivers, Thames, Severn, Ouse and Trente, from ancient time have been open for the passage of ships and boats, for the common profit of the people, of late ... there are so many and so great obstructions ... building of wears and mills and fixing of piles and palings athwart the rivers by every lord against his own estate that ships can pass to London and other good towns of the realm only in time of extreme abundance of water [*outrageous cretin de ewe*]; and divers ransoms imposed at will are exacted ... at the wears, and so the common carriage of victuals by ship is greatly impeded and victuals daily grow dearer." This complaint was specially directed to the district between Henley and London.

In 1350 the first Act of Parliament, 24 Edward III, was launched against the abuses. "Whereas the common passage of boats and ships in the great rivers of England be oftentimes annoyed by the inhancing (*le lever*) of gorces, mills, weirs, stanks, stakes and kidels, in great damage of the people, it is accorded and established: That all such gorces, etc., which be raised in the time of King Edward the king's grandfather and after .... shall be out and utterly pulled down without being renewed (*soient oustes & nettement abatuz sanz estre relevez*). And that no man take for passage by water, going or coming, beyond what is rightful, under fixed penalty."

As early as the following year a further commission was issued, interesting as containing mention of a place above Oxford. John Golafre and others were "to survey all gorces, mills, stanks, etc., in the water of Thames between London and the bridge of Rodecotbrigge." It is not at all improbable that Golafre himself possessed a weir or two in the upper reaches of this district.

There were two subsequent pretences at reform: in 1364 between Oxford and London; and in 1369 between Henley and Radcot. The next important occurrence however was in 1371, when another Act, 45 Edward III, was passed, entitled "The Penalty of him that setteth up or enhanceth Wares." After rehearsing the Act of 1350 it proceeds:

> "And now at the grievous complaint of the great men and the commons" that the said Act is not duly executed nor kept, "it is accorded and established that the said statute be holden and kept . . . and he that shall repeat the said annoyance shall incur the penalty of an hundred marks to the king; and the like law shall hold of annoyance made by enhancing of such weirs, as by the new setting up."

The City of London *Letter Book G* mentions the issue of a writ in 1372 to the Mayor and Corporation of the City, forbidding the casting of rushes, dung and refuse into the Thames, and ordering the removal of all obstructions. As a consequence, appointment was made under the mayor's seal of several collectors of the sum of 12d. to be thenceforth levied on all boats coming into the City with rushes; the said toll to be appropriated *pro mundacione locor. ubi discarcantur.*

A petition was presented to Edward III in 1376 regarding the fishery in tidal waters, in which salmon are again mentioned, as having their fry destroyed in great quantities and given to swine to eat (*porcs au manger*). In the same year the king's subjects who had "shouts" and other craft upon the River complained that although they had been granted statutory free passage without disturbance from " Lokes, Weres, Stages [Stakes], or Ponds," a certain lock called Hamelden had been rebuilt, "whereat boatmen had been in great peril of their lives, and badly hurt ; and one had lately perished. Also vessels had been in great danger of foundering if they ventured to pass." An invidious distinction for this breezy and beloved station ! A writ of survey and reform was issued. An interesting sequel is discovered in the Close Rolls. On June 10, 1377, Edward interfered in favour of Hambledon, as only three weeks earlier he winked down another writ to please the Dominicans of Oxford. A letter close was addressed to the Buckinghamshire sheriff to desist from meddling with the weirs, etc., of old time set "in the town of Hamelden" by Richard le Scrope.

The slow, inexpugnable importunity persists ; and seems gradually to infuse a more vigorous sincerity into the relief commissions. There was a further effort made in 1388, under Richard II; and another in 1391 presents an appearance of greater strictness. Thomas Barentyne and others are appointed, not merely in a general sense to inspect and punish, but to discover the names of actual evil-doers who had by stealth recovered and removed certain illegal nets placed under arrest.

Eight years passed; and in 1399, under Henry IV, a new Act recites that "the common passage of ships and boats, and also meadows and pastures, and lands sowed adjoining to the said rivers, be greatly disturbed, drowned, wasted and destroyed by outragious enhancing and straitening of wears, etc., whereof great damage and loss hath come to the people of the realm, and will come." The usual order follows for abatement and penalty: "saving always a reasonable substance of wears, mills, etc."

Three years later the Commons petitioned that as by various kinds of obstructions in the Thames and other great rivers navigation was hindered, several people drowned, and small fish destroyed and wasted against reason and given *a porkes a manger* against the will of God and to the great detriment of king and Commons, they desired all to be removed and not rebuilt; and that the party suing in this behalf might have twenty marks from the guilty person, and everyone be allowed suit who would move in the matter. An arresting plea: "against the will of God"! But religion and civic life were still one; men still used one architecture for their churches and their houses; they were still ignorantly steeped in the devotion which a one and undivided Church inculcated, if it did not too greatly practise; a devotion which our opened eyes regard as the daughter of that very ignorance. Still, as in the magnificent peroration of Catullus:

> "ante domos invisere castas
> heroum et sese mortali ostendere coetu
> caelicolae nondum spreta pietate solebant."

And the Commons therefore felt nothing incongruous in preferring the will of God as their first reason against using the fry of fish as food for swine.

Stow prints, under the year 1405: "Maior Iohn Wodcocke, mercer: this maior caused all Weres in the river of Thames, from Stanes to the river of Medway, to bee destroyed and the trinkes to be burned." Concerning these trinks, I have not been able quite satisfactorily to define them to myself. A classical allusion, perhaps intended to be descriptive, is in 2 Henry VI, c. 9, entitled: *No man shall fasten nets to anything ouer rivers.* "Standing of Nets and Engines called *Trinks*, which be and were wont to be fastened and hanged continually Day and Night, by a certain time in the year, to Great Posts, Boats, and Anchors, overthwart the

River of Thames, be wholly defended for ever." They were nets of perhaps 1½ inch mesh, and not narrower. In the City of London *Letter Book A* I find a note of at least a century earlier: "Another maner of nettes that is cleped Treinkys, of the largeness of two ynches and ynche and an half large and no lasse."

The fishery dispute is inextricably involved in the navigation history; and I make no apology for an occasional, inevitable digression into it. It is evident that huge nets fixed with cables across the fairway for months together must have interfered very considerably with water traffic. My impression is, however, that this particular obstruction was not found to any appreciable extent above bridge.

A little instance of human resentment against the law breaks through the series of charters and enactments in 1407. The *Acts of the Privy Council* relate that on February 19 John Sampson and others were haled up for resisting Alisaundre Boner, the City's officer, so that he could not exercise his function touching *kydelz reys et autres engins pour pessons prendre en les eawes de Tamise et Medeway.* According to the City *Letter Book I*, John Sampson, having recaptured the nets, " with many others from the counties of Essex and Kent, to the number of 2,000, assaulted the said Alexander with bows and arrows while he was on the Thames, and pursued him to Barking." The owners were treated so leniently as almost to suggest a censure on Boner's zeal. They were ordered to bring the *reys* before the mayor *Dimanche prochain*; and were allowed to weave new ones "according to the standard of London" for inspection and approval by the mayor before use. Boner had been involved in a similar dispute about eleven years earlier.

Another interesting and important incident arose, still under Henry IV, in 1411. On December 3 there was issued a "grant to Thomas Holgill and Elizabeth Lasyngby [a name of piquant association] to make a weir on the king's soil across the Thames where they pleased between the town of Stronde [doubtless Strand-on-the-Green] and the town of Mortlake, saving a reasonable passage on the Surrey side for all vessels." The claim of the Crown to the bed and soil of the River at this point is noteworthy. This "Holgyllys Were" was actually built, and persisted for some decades, from "Paternoster Lane in the County of Middlesex on the west to the east part of the same place called 'le gardyn' or 'Hokehawes' in the same county." I have enquired in vain in the locality for any traces of these old place names. The sequel is remarkable. In connection with a proposed renewal of the weir about half a century later the City of London took its first recorded definite action in support of its

General History

charter of conservacy from Richard I, then but little short of three centuries old. "October 12, 1468; 8 Edward IV. The king's kinsman, William, Earl of Pembroke, was permitted by the king 'to make a weir across the Thames called Overithwart-were in the place where a *weir called Holgyllys Were* used to be, and to take fish in it, rendering to the king 20s. yearly. And for this 20s. 4d. to be paid.'" In the following April, however, the grant was cancelled by direct interference of the City. Edward apologetically explained that he had granted the patent because he was informed that he was entitled to a weir called Holgilles Were, now broken and utterly destroyed. "But William Taillour, the mayor, and the aldermen have shewn that they have the conservance of certain statutes within the said river from the bridge of Staines to the said city; *and the rebuilding of the weir would be contrary to the same and to the liberty of the city*." Thus spake the City; and the City was obeyed: probably its merchants had raised many loans, and might raise others, for royal necessities.

A few minor incidents intervene. About 1415 *Letter Book I* mentions an order "that no officer connected with the water of the Thames keep an hostel." This is interesting in that, four centuries later, the Thames Commissioners made an identical order in connection with their lockkeepers.

In 1421 the fishers of the Thames presented a petition to Parliament against the grievous and long continued mischief arising from gorces and stakes fixed in the River, covered at times by the water, amongst which several persons and vessels had been drowned and lost. The ancient and even now unremedied complaint was renewed that huge quantities of fry were destroyed for swine's food. "Covered by the water" is an arresting point. It is intelligible that the stakes should sometimes be so concealed; but by gorces I understand water pens, or flash locks, and is it implied that these upstanding erections were themselves under water on occasion?

In 1439 a grant for life was made to John Penycook, yeoman of the robes, of the office of searcher of nets in the "river of Thames, its streams and members between the bridge of Stanes and the town of Surcestre, and in all weirs, lokkes, marquettes, and other engines belonging thereto." "Surcestre" is Cirencester, whereby no Thames water ever yet ran; but it is arguable from the terms of the grant that the Churn, the connecting link between this town and the River, was regarded at this time as part of the Thames: a piece of evidence I freely present to the Seven Springs enthusiasts.

A note occurs in October, 1454, of the presentment and fining of weirkeepers at Merton, Kayowe (Kew), Kyngeston, Septon (Shepperton), Walton,

General History

Hampton, Ditton, Wykewere (Hampton Wick), Peresham (Petersham), Todyngton and Istilworthe. The site of the first-named I do not identify.

The next salient event after the City's success at Strand-on-the-Green is the Act 12 Ed. IV, c. 37, of 1472, into which seem compressed all the accumulated force of previous charters and decrees, all the characteristic denunciation in the name of religion, and all the grotesque names the different forms of weir had acquired through the centuries and upon different parts of the River. It recites " the laudable statute of Magna Charta" and "the great sentence and apostolick curse pronounced against the breakers of the same"; and the subsequent proclamations. It ordains that the Great Charter be duly observed and kept; "adjoining thereto that if after the feast of St. Michael, 1475, it be found that any such weirs, fishgarths, locks, ebbing wears, kedels, becks or floodgates be made, levied, enhanced, straitened or enlarged" the offender "shall forfeit to our lord the king one hundred marks if not abated within three months, and one hundred marks for every month thereafter the nuisance be not abated, half to the king and half to any of his liege subjects which in this behalf will sue for the same."

Stow, quoting perhaps from a Lansdowne MS. which I discuss later, states that at the time of this Act "there was no common passage for barges so far as Marlow and Bisham." I do not think this statement can be accepted without qualification. Something turns, perhaps, upon the meaning due to the word common; the implication may be only that the passage was uncertain, or difficult. Or "so far as" may mean so far as these places were concerned; and that when the undoubtedly large and frequent traffic had arrived so far it could only with difficulty proceed further. The facts that there was a winch at Marlow in 1305, doubtless still in being, and that there were such bitter complaints of the difficulty and danger of ascending the great rush of water at the local flash lock, seem to prevent the acceptation of the statement under its superficial meaning.

Down to the end of the fifteenth century charters and statutes applied generally to the four royal rivers.

Chapter III

SO FAR the aspect of my history has been chiefly legal, confined largely to royal decrees and to Acts of Parliament perhaps never seriously expected to ensure the free navigation of the Thames. Up to the close of the fifteenth century, and considerably into the sixteenth, I have discovered very few original complaints, accounts of disturbances and of definite and localised encroachments and reprisals. But with the later sixteenth century the subject begins to glow with more human warmth ; names of places appear in the petty histories and quicken one's interest ; and above all observers begin to publish chronicles of what they have noticed and experienced as they voyaged up and down the River.

The first note of the century occurs in the spring of 1519, when the University of Oxford complained to Wolsey that their neighbourhood was regularly infested with plague at every return of warm weather. The city drains, they said, could not be cleared because the Thames was dammed up by various obstructions. A piece of evidence, this, of that ancient regard of the River as a common sewer which led to the terrible state of the Thames three and a half centuries later: now so happily remedied.

In and about 1535 a ferocious crusade against weirs was waged all over the country, instigated apparently by the king himself: a piquant little parergon in the intervals of harrying the monasteries; to which, and to private Catholics, it is notable that many of the weirs belonged. The Severn, the Wye, the Thames and many smaller rivers were searched by visitors; and Lady Lisle endured much trouble and vexation from the destruction of a weir she owned upon the river Exe. Sir Walter Stonor wrote to Cromwell, more to my purpose, that he had pulled up the weir of Water Eyton, belonging to the little house the Godstow minchons had there.

"The king has certain weirs in Oxfordshire and Berkshire, which I have commanded the hundreds to pluck up, but they want to know who shall give them meat and drink and wages. They desire that certain barges and bargemen may be at the locks, to the intent that such 'gynnys' as must be used may stand on the barge to winch up the great timber. On Monday they will be at one of the king's weirs, called North Stoke. I beg I may be excused from plucking up every weir, for every owner who ought to pluck them up at his own charge now waits to have it done at the charge of the country."

The "certain weirs" alluded to as belonging to Henry were indubitably those which had fallen to

General History 39

him through his suppression of their owners the monasteries: at Eynsham, Abingdon and elsewhere. As regards North Stoke, this may always have been Crown property. It stood probably on the little stream that enters the Thames there; not on the main River. The mill was certainly of royal ownership under Elizabeth.

A "remembrance" of Cromwell's in 1536 foreshadows "An Act that never weir nor watermill shall hereafter be erected or made within this realm."

In 1535 the Act 27 Henry VIII was passed, prohibiting the casting of rubbish and pollution into the Thames. It recites that the River has been most commodious unto all the king's liege people for "conveighance of merchandises," till now of late divers evil disposed persons had habitually cast in dung and filth, and carried away shore piles and other timberwork, by reason whereof "great shelfs and risings have of late growne in the farway of the said river," and floods had ensued on low lying ground, and the Thames was like to be utterly destroyed for ever, if speedy remedy were not taken. For amendment whereof, if anyone thereafter should do anything "in the annoying of the stream of the said river of Thames" similar to these offences, he should pay 100s. on each occasion, half to the king and half to the city: connoting a present day value of perhaps £100.

About 1547 a dispute arose between the Admiralty and the City over the conservancy of the River: a piece of history often alluded to, but as to the details and conclusion of which I have not come upon any clear and satisfactory account. A Lansdowne MS. gives notes of a debate held between the parties before the Privy Council on July 3 of this year. The immediate result was indecisive: the Council, in a spirit and sly phraseology indicative of the pawkiness that was descending upon us at this period, "thought not convenient sudenlie to geve absolute sentence, for that in time there might percase arise some other just matter for the more full mayntenance of either of their claymes; and that alsoo the citie not having at the first the full of ther demaunde would be the more readie to reforme th'abuses in places limited unto them wherbie to deserve enlargement of their graunte." Meanwhile the City officers were to maintain their jurisdiction between London Bridge and Staines; and officers of both parties were to act below bridge as they had been accustomed. The ultimate effect was in 1596 the more strongly to confirm to the Lord Mayor his whole ancient jurisdiction.

I derive from a Lansdowne MS. of 1572 what I believe is the earliest suggestion o a public perpetual office of Conservancy. It is entitled, in Cecil's characteristic style: "Cõmodities arising by her

Māties graunt of the office of Principall conservator and surveyor of freshe waters to any one person"; and proceeds to the following effect, in modern spelling.

"The fry and spawn of fresh fish shall be generally better preserved:

The water better scoured and cleaned to the great amendment of sundry highways, marshes, meadows, and low grounds:

The Queen's revenues by a yearly rent (never before had) increased:

Offences shall with more speed and ease to the subjects be reformed, by granting this office to one person than to leave it at large unto the Informer:

The principal cause of the great havoc and spoil which is now so generally made of spawn and fry of fish, and the not cleansing of Rivers and Waters and also the not speedy repairing of the Water banks and shores (by means whereof sundry highways, marshes, meadows, and low grounds are overflowed) grows (as I do take it) by reason that such persons to whom commission is granted for the reformation and survey thereof are remiss and slack in putting their authority in execution; which they omit to do because it is a thing altogether to their great charge, and nothing tending to their benefit or profit:

Therefore the special care hereof being now committed to one, if reformation hereof be not had and found, the said one person is then to be admonished as well of the matter or misdemeanour, as of the place where; and if within reasonable time it be not reformed the said one person for such negligence is to be pained either by fine, amercement, or otherwise, as shall seem good to the Lord

Treasurer, Chancellor, and Baron of the Exchequer: which in short time must of necessity bring speedy and general reformation:

It is very like that when the Commissioners of Sewers and lords in their leets shall perceive, if they will not seek the redress thereof, that the same shall be done by a stranger, it will cause them to put their authority into execution, whereby reformation must needs ensue either by them or the other:

The offences of unlawful engines and meshes of nets and the secret selling of unseasonable fish are very hardly to be found out and proved otherwise than by the oaths of the neighbours. Informers are over suspicious and discredited with the subject:

And to the end that her Majesty's subjects shall be no way hardly dealt withal, the Conservator is contented to covenant that neither he nor his assigns shall take above the third part of any penalty; nor set any fine above 7s. 6d., and that not without the assent of six honest persons dwelling near the place where such offence shall be committed:

It is to be remembered that by granting this to one person there is no greater authority given than very many subjects have at this instant, namely, all lords which may keep leets, the Clerk of the Market throughout England, and the Lord Mayor of the City of London for the time being in the River of Thames."

It is quite possible that this very important document may have been of Cecil's authorship. It was his well known habit to draw up similar schedules of arguments for and against various projects; and he certainly took a personal interest in the affairs of the

General History 43

River. Whoever its author was, it is the earliest extant suggestion for a public Conservancy Board; to supervise, it will be noticed, all the "freshe waters"; and not yet the Thames distinctively. That the scheme contemplated a board, or at least a chief surveyor with a plenipotentiary staff, is evident from the mention of assigns. Such a purposely created, permanent Authority would be an immeasureable improvement upon the old, casual authorisation of self-interested justices and local gentry encumbered with a hundred more congenial duties.

One or two details are noticeable: The better scouring of watercourses would prevent damage through floods to the highways, so much scarcer and softer then than now; and the insouciance complained of on the part of the landowners appointed to effect improvements is brought into prominence. The limitation of fines is also noteworthy. Nothing, however, was yet to result from so admirable a proposal.

The same series affords another interesting document, dated 1574, and, as I have said, probably used by Stow, or Strype; entitled: "A Declaration of what is to be said and proved for the maintenance of mills, locks and weirs within the River of Thames." I content myself with its general tenour. The first clause urges their immemorial existence in favour of these obstructions. It contains the statement quoted in Stow, and commented on above, that in 1472, a century earlier, "there was no common passage for barges so far as Marlow or Bisham"; adding that at that time there were not above seven barges that ascended so high, and that now in 1574 there are about three score. It is next declared that, in desiring the abolition of the weirs, navigators were compassing their own ruin, seeing that they were often compelled to seek the aid of the millers for flashes; and that if the weir banks were dismantled the stream would become more than ever choked with hills of chalk and rubbish from the washing down of the materials; the blocking of the channel would hinder the conveyance of provisions; mills were necessary for the grinding of corn; no Commission of Sewers had ever placed the mills under penalty; and finally the mills and weirs were the property of her Majesty's subjects, and if there were any disorder amongst them a remedy existed at law.

In this same year, 1574, certain members of the Court of Aldermen were appointed to be "humble suters to the quenes ma^{ties} moste honorable pryvye counselle that ordre may be taken for the reformacon of certein abuses done within the ryver of Thamyse, in castynge of trees into the same ryver and stoppynge of the passage of bargemen travelynge unto this cyttye above the Towne of Stanes." This is the only instance I find of this particular complaint;

General History 45

was some attempt being made to float lumber rafts downstream?

And so at last I arrive at the broad history of the subject added by Strype to Stow's *Survey*; and at the earliest of the personal chronicles promised at the beginning of this chapter. " About the Year 1578. or 1579. there were Three and twenty Locks, Sixteen Mills, Sixteen Floud-gates, Seven Wears between *Maidenhead* and *Oxford*." (The number of the mills is surely an under-statement. Omitting the two or more at Maidenhead and Taplow I think over twenty must have existed: Cookham, Bourne End, three at Marlow, Temple, Hurley, Frogg's, Hambledon, New, Marsh, Shiplake, Sonning, Caversham, Mapledurham, Whitchurch, Goring, Streatley, Cleeve, Benson, Sutton, Abingdon, Sandford, and Iffley: all close upon the main River. I doubt if research would indicate the necessity of removing any of these from a contemporary list.)

Strype proceeds:

"Whereof one *John Bishop* made a Complaint to the Lord Treasurer *Burleigh*. To whom he shewed, how by these Stoppages of the Water, several Persons, to the Number of 15 or 16, in four Years only, had been drowned, and their Goods lost; having been Persons belonging to Barges and Vessels using the River. But notwithstanding these Complaints, about the Year 1584 or 1585. there were above Seventy Locks and Wears (that is, Thirty more at least than there was but Six

Years before.) And whereas before there were not above Ten or Twelve Barges employed to and fro, now the number was encreased to Fourscore; and were of much greater Bulk and Bigness than before was used. Some of these Locks were extraordinary dangerous in passing. The going up the Locks were so steep, that every Year Cables had been broken that cost 400*l*. and Bargemen and Goods drowned. And in coming down, the Waters fell so high, that it sunk the Vessels, and destroyed Corn and Malt wherewith they were laden."

The passage follows about Marlow which I quote below under that head. And here I will remark that, in reading old descriptions of the Thames, it is necessary always to picture it to your imagination entirely divested of the whole of the present lock cuts. Up to nearly the middle of the seventeenth century not one of these existed; you had perforce to navigate along all those long circuitous weir streams which you are now spared by the locks. The whole River was so different in detail. Here at Marlow, for instance, in coming downstream you would not skirt the churchyard wall and wait at the boom for any lockgates to open. That course would have taken you, then, only to the millwheels; as in a certain contemporary adventure upon the river of Ebro. What actually occurred was that you came under the bridge, then some yards lower than now, and turned immediately to the right over the weir, through its flashlock of moveable tackle, opened for the most

General History 47

part only at the miller's leisure. The Thames in those days can have been no place for holiday folk in a hurry, unless they were prepared to carry over almost everywhere. A fortnight's leave, if such a privilege then existed, might easily have been spent in waiting, in a dry summer, to pass through any one of the "seventy locks."

Before proceeding with the Bishop history it will illuminate the contemporary attitude of high officials if I present an excerpt from the *Acts of the Privy Council.* "September 4, 1580. The Lord Mayor was required to send an account to the Lords of the Council how many wears there were between London Bridge and Staines; how many there have been of ancient times; and how many had been erected within the last seven years: her Majesty being given to understand that by the multitude of wears the river is like to be choked and made unnavigable; and is disposed to have some present redress taken therein"; her hostile interest having been aroused, I learn elsewhere, by certain stops insolently erected within direct view of her palace of Richmond; and also, perhaps, by such documents as those of 1572 and 1574 just quoted. Four days later the report was presented to the Council; no doubt the Lord Mayor was glad to obtain royal countenance for his prerogative, and quite conceivably delighted to get in a sly reference to Majesty's own delinquencies. For amongst other obstructions he indicates fifteen "hatches" and six "stoppes" commanded by letters from Mr. Comptroller to be erected for the supply of "lampreyes and roches" to her Majesty's own household. The queen gravely commanded that so many of the said "weares, stoppes and hatches" as were illegal should be defaced; as "her Majesty's gratious intent is not to take the benefit of any thing which by lawe is not allowed to her Majesty." I am afraid, however, that in this small domestic affair, as in matters of much more comprehensive importance, something of Elizabeth's constitutional duplicity appears. For in September 1578, exactly two years earlier, the Lord Mayor had been summoned to Richmond to answer for weirs erected "directly over against her Majesty's house of Richmond to her great displeasure." On this occasion also he had pleaded his inability to suppress them, being "for the taking of lamprons by the purveyors of the household from the beginning of the preceding month until All Saints Day." The pleas and proceedings occupy very many pages of the records; and include, not only about a dozen small stops or hatches between Richmond and Staines, but also "Four great wears maintained under colour that they be her Majesty's and that her Majesty hath rent therefor." These four erections are thus particularised:

General History

One great wear at Isleworth built by the late Duke of Somerset in 2 Edward VI. Yearly rent £10., paid to Sir Francis Knoweles by Thomas Honyball and William Knight farmers thereof and dwelling in Isleworth.

One at Twickenham builded by the monks of Sheen in 2 Mary; yearly rent £6., paid to the Marquess of Winchester by William Whyte farmer thereof, of Twickenham.

One at Kingston built by Thomas Benson and Oliver Wood, with others of the same town, in 2 Mary; yearly rent £6 : 5/-, paid to the bridgewardens by the builders and by George Gold and Richard Jennyngs, all of Kingston and farmers thereof.

The fourth and last at Hampton, built by the late Lord Treasurer of England, the Marquess of Winchester, in 8 Elizabeth. Rent £6. 8. 4, paid into the Exchequer for the queen's use by Thomas Reddnapp [a well known River name] and John Upton, farmers thereof.

These were not only very hurtful to the fry of fish, but also a lett and hindrance to the common passage by reason of the driving in every year of "newe great pyles or postes with great hurdells into the grounde within the said wears."

So that Elizabeth knew very thoroughly about the matter; and her assumption of concern for the law has something of an artificial appearance.

It was to such doubtful sympathies in high places that Bishop made his first appeal in 1580, preserved in the Lansdowne MSS., endorsed "6 Sept[br] 1580 name & number of y[e] Locks & wears upon y[e] River

50 The Thames Highway

Thames"; which after an inscription to Sir Wm. Burleigh proceeds to the following lengthy title, and list; much of both being now illegible, and being also, probably, only a rough draft of the later and fuller list of 1585 : also presented below.

> "Hereafter followeth the names of the Locks and wea . . . . . he | Queenes Maties Ryver of thames from a towne . . . . . | Maydenhedd unto another towne called Abington . . . . . | unlawfull Anoyzuncs wch stoppe the course of t . . . . . | Ryver and are noysome and daungerous for . . . . . | that are passengers one the same ryver . . . . . | or other vessells and the names of the . . . . . f | the said locks and weares and of the keys of the . . . . . | wch sell the Queenes Maties watter in the said ryver.

1 In primus Rea Locke being th . . . Harry Merry one of the Queenes Ma^t y . . . her highenes chamber and kepte by Robert . . . . .
2 Marlowe locke being the locke of Thomas . . . . gentelman and kepte by Georg Westcott
3 Temple locke being the locke of John Brynty gent & kept by Richard Mathewe
4 New locke being the locke of Mr Bowde and Mr Lovelace being kept by Harry Tailor
5 Hambledon Locke being Mr Scropes loke and kept by Thomas Butler a seller of water [It is very notable that this lock is in the same family as recorded in 1377.]
6 Marsh locke being the lock of ffrauncis Ston . . . . and kepte by Richard Heywoode a seller of water
7 A weare called Bowney weare being kept by Mr Anthony Elmes & k . . . by John fforde

General History

8 One Weare called waregrowes weare . . . . . Robert Ilande
9 Shepelacke weare kept by Richarde C . . . . .
10 Sunnynge Locke being Mr Michaell Blu . . . s Locke being kept by Robert ffrewen & Joh Wydm . . e
11 C . . . . . ke being kept by one Richarde S . . .
12 C . . . eare being kept by one wyllys
13 Ma . . . durham locke being Mr William Blu . . . . . ke kepte by Roberte Byrde
14 Wh . . . urche locke being one Hareknappes Locke . . . . . by Nicolas Wylforde
15 One lock called Harts lock kept by Hughe Whysler
16 Gooringe locke kept by William Whisler and Ric Smyth
17 Cleve Lock being the Earl of Darbies locke & kept by William Roberts
18 Wallingforde locke being the locke of Raphe Pollingtons and kepte by Georg Banckes
19 Bearsone locke being Roberte Georges locke and kept by Robert Brodewater and Jacobe Buisshoppe
20 Little Whitnam one lock . . . . . . res one locke and a weare kepte by one M . . . ffettiplace and one weare by one Mr W . . . . se and all kept by . . . .
21 One weare at . . . . being the weare of one Wyddowe Sa . . .
22 One locke called Th . . s Trullocks locke dwelling at Appleforde
23 Two locks called Sutton locks and one myll kept by John Elson and Richard Justice
24 One Weare called C . llombe weare being Edward Wilmotts
25 One locke called Abington locke being Mr William Blackmannes locke and kepte by Thomas Tisdale.

Finding this complaint unavailing Bishop renewed it on October 13, 1585, in verse, direct to the queen herself. The document contains forty-three quatrains, of very rich and curious reading. Here are four:

<dl><dt>The names of the wrongs</dt><dd>

Mylls weares and locks men do them call
that doe annoy that worthy streame
Against the lawe they doe stande all
but still the drownde those symple men
</dd>

<dt>A Locke of great Murther (Marlow)</dt><dd>

One ffarmer hath a Lock in store
That hath made many a Child to weepe
Their mothers begg from dore to dore
Their ffathers drowned in the deepe.
</dd>

<dt>Swine and dogges do eat mens fleshe</dt><dd>

Then being drowned they bury them there
where doggs and swyne then do them finde
their fleshe they eat and all to teare
which is contrarie to mankinde
</dd>

<dt>Four murthers of late don att farmers Lock</dt><dd>

At ffarmers lock foure men be loste
of late I putt yo^u out of doubt
three were drowned the streams them toste
the fourth he had his braines knocked out.
</dd></dl>

It is not to be expected that vested interests of that day, any more than of this, should allow such an attack to proceed without retaliation. Strype relates their natural counterstroke in terms curiously like an amplified version of the document of 1574 on page 43.

"Those concerned in these Locks, Wears and Mills,

the very day after this Complaint, *Octob.* 14. gave in a Note by way of Petition, of Reasons for the Maintenance of them upon the River; with the Causes of the Danger thereof, and some Account of the Persons lately drowned there: (1) That the Mills & Locks were of as great antiquity as the towns & villages to which they adjoin; and as ancient evidence to be shewed for them as any man hath for any land he held within the realm of England; That they were a necessity (*a*) for grinding corn and (*b*) for passage of barges; That within the Banks & Wears were contained infinite loads of chalk & other rubbish which if loosed it would be the next way to choke the River: (2) The causes of the increased peril of the passage was that the Barges were become of greater burthen; almost double what they used to be; that they laded them beyond reason; that they used partly to unload below the lock and reship again above, even when they used to bring but seven or eight Loads. Now they came with twenty they would unload nothing; they employed people of no skill; they travelled so late & so early as to be unable to see what they were doing; they commonly spared neither the Sabbath Day nor others. And lastly it was likely there would be more accidents, as the number of Barges was increased from ten or twelve to fourscore: (3) As touching the accidents at *Marlow*, one was drowned by manifest negligence, partly that the barge was overloaded, partly that it wanted Washboards on the Sides. Another was drowned, but not at the Lock. Another by his own negligence. Another came up the said Lock in Winter so late as he could not discern what he did. And it was no wonder the cables parted; they were often made of ill stuff, and the barges so great and so heavily laden."

Bishop's second list, attached to his metrical petition of 1585, is ampler than that of 1580. The parishes to which the locks belong are noted in the MS.; for the sake of brevity I omit them except where necessary for identification.

"1 Rea Locke belonging to Harry Merrye one of the yomen of her Mat^s chamber and in the keping of Roberte Weston.

2 Item one weare called Hedgworthe Weare belonginge to Hughe Cottrell. In the parishe of Cowcombe. [Probably Hedsor; "Cottrells of Cookham" is noted by John Taylor.]

3 Marlowe Locke belonginge to Thomas . . . mer gent & kepte by George Westcotte. The lock in the pishe of Byssham, the myll & floudgate in Great Marlow.

4 Temple Lock belonging to John . . . rinkys gent & in the keping of Richard Mat . . we.

5 Newlock [Hurley] belonging to Mr. Bowde & Mr. Lovelace & kept by Henry Tayler.

6 Hambledon Lock belonging [still] to Mr. Scrope & kept by Thomas Bulter " a seller of water."

7 At the marshe two mylles havinge one Locke & one weare. One lock & myll belonginge to ffrauncis Stoner

8 gentleman. Thother kepte by one Roberte Wolley yeoman.

9 Bowney Weare kepte by John fforde and belonging to M^r. Anthony Elmes. In the parishe of Waregrove. [Evidently something in the Bolney backwaters that has disappeared.]

10 Wargroves weare kept by Robte Ilande. In the parish of Wargrave. [Probably near the head of the Hennerton backwater; where it is said was once a mill.]

General History 55

11 Shiplack weare kept by Richard Cottrell. The Quenes mat^{ie} the owner *smeared out.*

12 Suning Lock belonging to Mr. Richard Blunte kept by Robte ffrewyne & John Wydmore being sellers of watter. The Quenes mat^{ie} the owner *deleted.*

13 An old Ruynous Weare in the pish of Suninge. [I do not indentify this, unless it be what came to be known as Breach's, discussed below.]

14 Cawsam Lock and Cawsam weare, the lock kepte by Richard Barton and the weare by one Salt^r. In the pishe of Redinge.

15 An old weare called Chawsey being kept by one Wyllys. In Cawsham. [Either immediately, or a long mile, above Caversham Bridge.]

16 Mawple Durham Lock belonging to Mr. Michaell Blunt & kept by Robert Blunt.

17 Whitchurche Lock belonging to Harry Knappes and kept by Nicolas Wilford.

18 Harts Locke kept by Hewe Whisler. In the pishe of Bassledon.

19 Goringe Lock kept by William Whisler & Richard Smyth.

20 Two weares and one Mill kept by the same Whisler And Smyth. The two weares myll and floudgate in the pish of Streatley.

21 Cleve Lock belonging to the Earle of Darbie and kepte by Willm Roberts.

22 Sowthmill Weare. In the parish of Chowlsey. [This may have been the ancient obstruction at the islands against the railway bridge; or at Cholsey Mill Brook, 23 miles below Oxford.]

23 Northstock weare kept by Raphe Pollington of Wallingford. In the parish of Chowlsey.

24 Wallingford Lock belonging to the same and kept by George Bancks. The lock myll and floudgate in the parish of Alhollowes in Wallingford. [I cannot locate this; some notes on Pollington's enterprises appear below, under Wallingford.]

25 Benson Lock and Weare belonginge to Robte George & kepte by Robte Brodewater & Jacob Buisshope.

26 One other weare above Bensons lock. In the parish of Sutton. [I do not trace this.]

27 Little Witnham one lock and ij weares the one weare and lock kept by Edmunde Fettiplace, thother wear by Mr Will$\overline{m}$ Dunshe. One lock and a wear in Dorchester, the other wear in little Witenham. [Doubtless Day's.]

28 One weare at longe Witnam belonginge to wyddowe Sawyer.

29 Thomas Trullocks lock, in Sutton parish.

30 An old ruynous weare being one Clement Dabnet. In Sutton parish.

31 Two Locks & one myll kept by Richard Elstone & Richard Justice. In Sutton.

32 Collombe weare belonging to Edward Wilmot gent. In the parish of Collombe. [Doubtless halfway along the Swift Ditch, *q.v.*]

33 Abington Lock kepte by Thomas Tysdale. [The Abbey flash lock, part of the present weir.]

34 Three Locks at Newnam kept by John Mollyners. All in said parish.

35 Samfords Lock kept by John Ovens. The locke in the p̃ish of Kennington.

36 Ifle Lock kept by one Mrs. Pitts.

Euery one of these being most perrillous for all Passengers and the keping of euery locke making sale of the water keping the same seuerall wch ought to be comon to all

General History

her Ma^{ts} subiects and wherunto in truth they have noe right...... The nombre of the Anoyzuncs I sawe them my self."

Lists follow of the persons drowned and of the witnesses: "maisters and owners of Barges." I print the surnames of the latter as indicating some of the River carriers of that day: Hill, Chilburye, Gnill, Sawde, Collyer, Browne, Greye, Welshe, Lynche, Bonde, Wyllyams, Gvylden, Cutler, Wynter, Coddesdon, Larchyn, Bowthe, Warde, Collet, Myddleton.

This, then, is the oldest extant personal survey and description of the River Thames. It is very interesting to observe that three fourths of the weirs named have survived nearly three and a half centuries down to the present day.

A few isolated incidents project my history into the seventeenth century. In September, 1584, there were issued "Orders for the conservation of the River Thames." They concern the fishery chiefly, but the following are pertinent. "First that there be no Purprestures, encroachmentes, Wharfes, Bankes, Walles or buildinge of howses in or uppon the Thames to the stoppinge of the passage thereof. Item that noe Donge Robish or other filth be cast into the Thames. Item that noe postes or stakes be fixed in the thames. Item that the faire waye be kept as depe and lardg as heretofore it hath bene."

An Oxford note of 1586 reports a decision "That the weeds in the ryver and the Sandbedds and Flaggsbedds downwards from the Castle Mylls to Chilswell poole and upward from the said Mylls up to the stone beneath Godstowe bridge the Ryver shalbe moven [mowed] at the Citty charges. Overseers appointed." I do not identify Chilswell; there is a Childsworth farm southwest of S. Hinksey, two miles from the River.

The *Acts of the Privy Council* mentions in 1590 that the Thames, between Kingston and London Bridge, "by reason of the wayres, stakes and picthes [pitches], is soe shallowe in divers places as boates and barges doe sticke by the waie." Ordered to be plucked up "that the river maie have yt's course, being of yt self shallow by reason of great droughtes." And I suppose that as many of the obstructions as did not belong to the councillors or their friends were plucked up; certainly no more, probably fewer.

The same chronicle alludes to a dispute at Walton in 1592-3. Details are given below under this head; some comments are more fitting here. The first point is the mention of towing by horses, a custom whose earliest statutory record is in the Act of 1623. The second is the term "Westerne barges," or West Country barges, still a phrase in quite common use; meaning, a lockkeeper told me, all barges that come down, except canal boats, without entering tidal waters. Hall notes an earlier reference; adding "the larger barges, sometimes carrying ninety tons, are still [1859] used in the district above Oxford, although rarely; and are called West Country barges. The next size are called trows [there is a Trowlock Ait in Teddington], and average 50-60 tons. The least, called worsers, are of thirty, or rather less." He states that worsers first came on to the River from the Coventry Canal. This is borne out by what a jolly great Reading man told me in 1911: that worsers are two canal boats lashed together side by side. The last point is the mention of the towpath as "an ordinary way." Possibly the particular length of towpath in question happened to be also a public highway; but a public right of way along towpaths in general in those days, and parochial responsibility for their maintenance, may perhaps be implied in the phrase.

In the Hatfield Papers, under the date 1597, it is recorded that the Attorney General, in reply to a petition regarding metage of coal presented by the Lord Mayor, mentioned a "verdict of twelve men in Surrey in 42 Henry III (1257): *Quod nullus aliquid juris habet in Thamesia usque ad novum gurgitem nisi civitas London.*" And that in 46 Henry III the river of Thames was allowed to belong to the City *usque ad newe Were.* In 29 Edward I

(1300), upon a similar controversy touching salt, it was found by inquisition and jury that no measure from London to Lechlade should exist except those of Queenhithe. Where was this New Weir? The Lechlade neighbourhood seems indicated; but the only place near there to which this title to my knowledge was ever attached was the old flash weir, Day's or East, that preceded Grafton lock. It was of old often called New Lock wear. The group of statements form an interesting commentary upon the obscure subject of the ancient westward limit of the jurisdiction of the City of London.

About 1604 Thomas Wildgoose wrote to Viscount Cranborne that his first work was to be a boat of pleasure "for his Majesty [James I] and his fair queen to sport up and down the Thames, and no man perceive how it goeth." He desired a patent to build further similar craft.

The first charter of James I, dated by Birch August 20, 1605, confirms the conservancy of the River to the City of London, noticeably only "from the bridge of Staines" downwards. It was directed chiefly to the metage of Thames borne merchandise, in the exercise of which right the City had been hindered.

In a Common Council *Acte for the reformation of diuers Abuses used in the ward mote inquest*, printed in 1617, I read :

General History

"4 Also, ye shall inquire and truly present all the offences and defaults done by any person or persons within the River of Thames, according to the intent & purport of an Acte made by our late Soveraigne Lord King Edward the sixt, in his high Court of Parliament, and also of divers other things ordained by acte of Common Councell of this Citie, for the redresse and amendment of the said River, which as now is in great decay and ruine, and will bee in short time past all remedy if high and substantiall provision and great helpe be not had with all speede and diligence possible."

This pessimist report hardly bears out John Taylor's praise of the City's vigilant care of the River printed only fifteen years later, which I present; but perhaps he had his reasons for desiring to stand well with the Corporation.

Chapter IV

The Oxford-Burcot Commissions

ALL THE ensuing part of the seventeenth century is full of important and interesting history. In spite of the complaints of their size ever larger barges were employed, requiring so great a minimum depth of water throughout the River that the fourteen and a half miles between Burcot, just below Clifton Hampden, and Oxford acquired the reputation of being impassable; the important traffic to the latter place having to proceed thither by road from Burcot, at great additional expense. It was indeed of old time always an arduous stretch of Thames. At its very entrance, for the upward voyager, there was the hard rock bed at Clifton, difficult to deepen and full of half sunken ledges. Then (and pray forget the locks and cuts; there were none!) he reached the expensive obstructions at Sutton, and the bad shallows through and above Abingdon and between Nuneham and Sandford. It resulted that this district, quite early in the seventeenth century,

The Oxford-Burcot Commission 63

attracted so much attention to itself that special legislation was enacted for its improvement. In the preamble of 3 James I, c. 20, it is recited that the River is (1605) "from the Citye of London till within a few miles of the Citye of Oxeforde verie navigable and passeable with and for Boates and Barges of great Contente and Carriage"; and it was thought that by the "remooving of some fewe Letts Impediments and Obstruccons" it could be made passable to Oxford also, and beyond. The Act, however, provided only vague powers; and notably omitted to empower the building of pound locks by the commissioners created under it.

I find two or three allusions to their transactions. In January, 1606, the recorder of Gloucestershire writes to the vice-chancellor that he will further the projects of James Jessopp for making the Thames navigable from Burcot to Oxford, "and thence to Crockley-in-the-Edge, Gloucestershire."

I also find a MS. report of what, judging from its tenour, seems to have been the first meeting of the commissioners, held on July 7, 1607, and including Henry Ayray the vice-chancellor, Richard Good the mayor, Sir Henry Hyde, Edmund Fettiplace, Edmund Dunch, and about half a dozen others. They resolved to divide themselves into groups, each group to survey a separate section of that part of the River to be improved: defined, it is notable, as "from Clifton ferry unto Cricklade"; noting all impediments and obstructions, and considering not only the method but the cost of rectifying them. At their next meeting they would thus be in a position "to direct a counsell" for effecting the alterations, for "the indifferent Leavy" of necessary charges, and for the "amende" to be allowed to the encroachments "to be damnified." The sections and survey thereof were thus arranged:

1. From Clifton ferry to Oxford: to be inspected on July 20.
2. From Oxford to Radcot: on July 27, beginning at Oxford.
3. From Radcot to Cricklade: "at Radcot on the 30th and end at Cricklade on the 31st."

The three groups were to take with them such "assistants of the better sort of their cuntryes" as they thought fit; "Jonius Stone and James Jess" were to attend upon the whole proceedings; and the next general meeting was fixed for August 6.

I think this body must have done its destined work pretty thoroughly above Oxford, since in the preamble of the subsequent Act, devoted to the district below the city down to Burcot, it is distinctly declared that westward of Oxford the River is already navigable for boats of good burthen. The only other note I possess of the history of this commission is that on May 3, 1611, the Lord Treasurer wrote

The Oxford-Burcot Commissions 65

ordering certain timber to be delivered to Sir Thomas Bodley for enlarging the library at Oxford, "which timber was to have been employed for making the Thames navigable to Oxford, but that work does not proceed."

This Act remained in force for eighteen years, and was repealed in 1623 in favour of 21 James I, c. 32. Towards the end of this period, on January 20, 1620/1, Convocation ordered that Roger Jones should be sent to London entrusted with the promotion of the Bill. Accordingly Roger Jones "set forth towards London" three days later, "in manibus 5^{li}, touchinge the passage for boates." His detailed account of travelling expenses is still in the university archives, by the favour of the Keeper of which I am enabled to present much unpublished matter concerning this commission. Jones made a similar journey the following month. In November, 1621, Mr. Styles the proctor travelled on the like errand; and the archbishops, peers, members of both Houses and the burgesses of Oxford were approached by letter in favour of the measure. On February 3, 1623/4, Convocation heard that the Bill had been read and approved by the Lords, but its further progress had been delayed by a sudden rising of Parliament. On April 29, 1624, it was announced that both Houses had passed the Bill, and that only the royal assent was now required.

Its preamble is interesting : "Whereas the clearing a passage by the river of Thames to Oxford will be very convenient for conveyance of Heddington stone to London, and most profitable and necessary to Oxford in respect of conveyance of coals and other necessaries thereto And whereas the said passage will be very behooveful for preserving highways now so worn and broken, that in winter season they are for travellers dangerous And whereas Thames for many miles westward beyond Oxford is already navigable for boats of good burthen and contents, and likewise is already navigable for barges from London to Burcot And whereas the passage is easy to make by removing some lets and impediments : " It is enacted that the Lord Chancellor shall appoint eight commissioners, four from the University and four from the City of Oxford, to have full power to cleanse and make navigable the said river of Thames between Oxford and Burcot, and amongst other things to open, prepare or make all weirs, locks and turnpikes for the said passage. Provision throughout the district was made for a towpath "without hindrance, trouble or impeachment of any person"; and in consideration that barges "must of necessity in some places and at some times be haled up by the strength of men, horses, winches and other engines," it was made lawful to instal such winches and other engines at requisite places. The University and City

The Oxford-Burcot Commissions 67

of Oxford would reap the principal immediate benefit of the improvements, and were therefore to be taxed for their erection and maintenance. Authority was bestowed to make bye-laws and rates of freight.

Under, though not expressly by, this Act "the navigation was made to pass at about a mile distant from the town of Abingdon, and turned out of the main river under Culham Bridge: the navigation, however, was perfectly good from the said bridge to the wharf at Abingdon." This statement is a reference to the rehabilitation of the Swift Ditch effected by the 1623 commissioners; and was made in 1794 in support of a contention that engineers (like plumbers) "created difficulties in the management of the Thames."

But the shining distinction of this Act is that it inaugurated the system of modern locks upon the Thames: "turnpikes," as they were at that time most usually called. These pioneer stations were three in number: Iffley, Sandford and Swift Ditch: the last not much known today, but still discoverable in that beautiful, lonely haunt of reeds and herons, just below Nuneham railway bridge. A fourth, at Sutton Courtenay, may very dubiously be added to the company. Even so they were, I think, a belated introduction. If I read rightly, pound locks were in use a century and a half earlier in Lombardy. They were not even the first in England. Westall, in his

Inland Cruising of 1908, devoted to the interests of the execrable motor craft, asserts that the first pound lock in this country was built upon the Exeter Canal, excavated in 1563.

On January 18, 1625/6, the university ordered that the 2,000 marks left them by Sir Nicholas Kempe, of Islington in the county of Middlesex, should be employed for the benefit of the new works; which money was, in Wood's translation, "to be collected again out of Wharfage or the like profits, and put together into a chest and kept till the same sum was made up again." The first half of this 2,000 marks, £666 : 13 : 4, was paid out during the year ended July, 1626. A second instalment of £537 : 0 : 2 went on August 6, 1632; and on August 6, 1635, the final balance of £129 : 13 : 2 was counted out to Dr. Tolson, one of the university commissioners. I have closely searched the Register and the Accounts of Convocation, and the Book of the Chest, but have discovered no details of the spending of this money: nothing but the bare note of the issuing of the three instalments. I shall present a few details of sums spent on maintenance, but they begin some time subsequently to the date of the latest of these issues, and were evidently additional expenditure. In all probability the commissioners kept a separate account, at any rate of Kempe's legacy; of the existence of which no-one is at present aware. Nor

The Oxford-Burcot Commissions 69

did my search reveal the repayment of any of the legacy "into the chest."

The commissioners appear to have set to work very promptly surveying for the improvements. At some date before July 26, 1624, there was paid to Mr. Thimble "cum aliis secum proficiscentibus ad perlustrandum Thamesin [not Isin] de aquae ductu, 18s. 6d." A total silence ensues of five years' duration, from the date of the first instalment of Kempe's legacy in July 1626 until a series of small incidents recorded in the State Papers Domestic, beginning in August, 1631. On the eighteenth of this month Charles I, who seems more intimately than any other sovereign to have interested himself in the well being of the River, and even somewhat severely in the dealings of the Lord Mayor therewith, addressed a commission of survey to various peers. A body appointed the previous year had dealt very successfully with the districts below Staines; and Charles proposed that the same persons should proceed to act between Staines and Oxford, devoting special attention to

> "the impediments of the navigation between Bircot (belowe Abingdon) and Oxford .... according to the intent of an act of Parliament made in the 21th year of our blessed father. In which particular, because we doe find that small effect hath followed hetherto upon the care and provision then taken, our further will and pleasure is, that you inquire what course the Commissioners author-

ised and employed in that worke have held for the execution of the trust committed to them to the end you may report unto us. Whereupon we are resolved to give further directions for the perfecting of so good and necessary a worke."

Quite evidently there had been some culpable hitch or slackness in the procedure of the Oxford Commissioners; and indeed the six or seven years that had now elapsed since their Act might appear sufficient for the completion of the work.

On the seventh of September Charles, in disposing of some timber from Shotover and Stowood forest, instructed that the verderers "were to furnish at reasonable prices for making navigable the river of Thames by means of Locks and Sluces to the place from Oxford downwards where barges and other boats of burden doe already passe so much thereof as found necessary."

Some intention seems to have existed of appointing an independent surveyor, as I find a letter dated the previous day, September 6, from one Hugo Spiering to Mr. Secretary Dorchester, apologising for having missed an appointment to meet him at Oxford "to take view of the River there and the same to make navigable." One of his many excuses is that he had "taken charge of certain Sluces and a Sasse [an old word for a lock I have never met elsewhere] through the which boats and vessels do passe in and out."

The Oxford-Burcot Commissions 71

He dates from Thorn ; and adds that "Oxforth is distant from this place about 200 miles." He hopes the secretary "will houlde me exscheused"; and promises "at towe wecks" notice to keep any further appointment. He had been introduced to Dorchester as a "gentelman of understanding in such like affairs."

On October 10 the mayor of Abingdon wrote Lord Dorchester that he had been engaged with the Oxford Commissioners, and had heard that Charles had given special charge that the interests of Abingdon should not be neglected ; "but that wee might receive the benifitt thereof by bringinge them by the waye to our said Towne." For which "voluntarie care and love" they were much beholden to his Majesty. But "the passuage of the Barges is already clear unto Abingdon, and so hath bene for these 4 years past"; the town therefore anticipated no further benefit from the works, and seemed indifferent what course the commissioners took with the district above them, though Abingdon would always assist to the uttermost its "neighbour towne and Universitie." They seem strangely content with the clear passage made up to the town wharf; and with the fact that the channel reopened for upward traffic to Oxford passed along the distant Swift Ditch, avoiding Abingdon.

A reminder to Lord Dorchester, dated November 4, 1631, of his continued existence and anxiety to be employed on the works, is the last I hear of Spiering.

In the absence of official records, my earliest witness to the completion of two of these locks: Sandford and Iffley, is John Taylor's *Thame Isis*, published in 1632, eight years after the passing of the Act. His comments upon them will be found below in my quotations from his book. Next M. F. Madan, in his *Oxford Books*, vol. II, quotes that "the Thames was made navigable up to Oxford itself" in 1635; "and the first barge reached the city on August 31, 1635." In the Convocation accounts for the year ended the fifth of this month there is evidence that this completion had not been effected in time for a good deal of special traffic. The Schools were being built, and the new channel being still imperfect all the timber and other materials could be brought upstream as far only as Burcot, and had to be carted thence into Oxford. The locks were almost certainly built, but the dredging and clearing was probably still incomplete. Thus I find:

"For bringing the timber from Reding to Burcott and for bringing the dealeboardes & Tackle from London to Burcott   34 : 8 : 10

For a Ginne to loade ye timber at Burcott, etc.   6 : 18 : 9

For carriage of the deales from Burcott, for the wharfage of timber and deales there, etc.   8 : 8 : 10'

The Oxford-Burcot Commissions

No similar reference to Burcot appears subsequently, so that after August 31, 1635, it may be assumed that the new channel was in active use; though it was not until August 2, 1638, that Convocation could congratulate the commission upon having "brought their undertaking to a happy ending."

The Authority now considered putting their works under responsible management; and establishing some revenue therefrom. I find accordingly in the summer of 1638 the following order:

Wee doe constitute and authorise Richard Farmer forthwith upon the date of these presents to enter upon and hold our Wharfe at Southbridge togeather with all those our Turnepecks erected upon the Thames at Yflie and Sandford and that other in Swiftditch and also to demand and receive for us at the Wharfe by Southbridge for the whole passage thence to Culham bridge downwards and at the Turnepeck in Swiftditch for the whole passage upwards such summe and rates of money of all persons whatsoever passing that waye with boat or barge as usually heretofore hath been payd at the said wharf and Turnpecke; and also of such as shall take in or unlade their carriages at any other place then at the Wharfe at Southbridge or then from beneath the Turnpeck in Swiftditch and yet nevertheless shall make theire benefitt of passing through our turnpecks or any one of them to take the like rates in proportion to their carriages. Provided always that the said Richard ffarmer when he shall be thereunto by us required shall make a just accompt and payment to us of all sums of money by him so received. And alsoe that the authoritie and power by these presents to him by us given shall utterlie cease and become voyde at what time wee or our successors shall require him to forbeare and desist from further executing the same.

Given under our hand 15° Junij 1638
Ric Baylie Vicecanc. Oxon."

Adjoining this order appear the following

"Condicions required by Mr. Farmer March 21 1637/8
In primis that such as loade not att the Wharfe but at Leachlad doe pay at the 1st turnepike both for their passage and also more as other in proportion pay for wharfage

2 that suites arising from such as shall resist the orders sett downe by the Commiss^r be followed ex officio and not at the charge of the wharfeman

3 that all repairs above 5^{li} be borne by Universitie and Towne but soe that if the Wharfeager bee found negligent in informing the Commiss : of the decays that hee submit to their censure and obey it

4 that all things be set in full repaire before hee enter upon the wharfage : or in convenient time after

5 that wee provide a crane in present out of his wage and hee bound to leave us when he leaveth the Wharfage another crane equall to this newlie made

6 that a turnpike be made neere Culham bridg

7 that the Wharfe be pitched and he bound for to leave it soe

8 The rent to be 50^{li} per annū by eeven portions at Mich and Ladie day beginning at the Ladie day 1638

Mdm. The Cill at Newnam must be removed Wharffinger."

Not all Farmer's conditions were embodied in the

The Oxford-Burcot Commissions 75

order; and the latter was itself reshaped before being finally agreed upon. Its first effect would seem to be, from several obvious indications, the appointment of Farmer merely as a servant, or agent. He was to account for his takings, his "wage" is referred to, and he was to be subject to dismissal without notice. He succeeded in obtaining more responsible terms. I find the final lease granted to him on the sixteenth of July, 1638. It includes the wharf at St. Aldate's, "lately erected," wherein one Christopher Stringer had recently dwelt; the wharfage thereat, and at the locks and weirs between Oxford and the "weare at Sutton," *viz.*, Iffley, Sandford and Swift Ditch locks, and "the weare erected or to bee erected at or neare unto Culneham Bridge"; all subject to the orders presented below. The annual rent was to be £60. If any station needed repair of more than £5, the commissioners were to pay it. Farmer was to erect a crane on the wharf before Michaelmas 1639 at his own cost; also before the same date to "build or repair" a sufficient lock or weir and winch in some convenient spot in Swift Ditch in Culham, and to furnish it with tackle to pen up the water there and to winch up passing vessels; also to repair generally.

The orders alluded to above, dated two days earlier, are to the following condensed effect:

    1 A register to be kept at St. Aldate's wharf of all

downward and another at Sutton of all upward vessels.

2 On account of the many former misdemeanours of the bargemen, for prevention thereof and for other causes a record was to be kept in these registers of the barge-owners' names, "what number of servants doe therein worke, what day and as neare as Cann bee the howre of the day or knight when they passe and the quantitie and kinds of their ffraight."

3 Bargeowners to make good all injuries and trespasses; but if the owner responsible be not discoverable, all barges passing within six hours before and six hours after the damage to contribute towards reparation. . . .

5 Mr. Debois, his farmers and tenants, and the lords, farmers and owners of Sutton mills, "whiles they shall repaire and mainteyne the passage and turnepickes there," to receive to their own use the fees and profits for the passage of vessels through that lock, "in regard that he hath at his Charges hetherunto repayred the same soe that there bee not taken there for passage upward or downeward of or for any flatt Bootham boate above the some of six pence or for a barge above the some of twoe shillings for any one passage."

6 At every other turnpike, for each passage up or down, for every "fflatt bootham" boat 4d., and for a barge 20d.; and at every "weare or Locke" 4d. and for a barge 6d.

7 For wharfage and carriage of every "Loade or Tunne" of merchandise, 2d.

8 The registrar at Sutton to collect the wharfage, carriage and passage of all upward vessels; and the St. Aldate's registrar of all downward.

9 The Sutton registrar to render a signed "Cockett or ticket" for a fee of one penny, which ticket to be a

The Oxford-Burcot Commissions 77

sufficient pass at all the upward stations. The Oxford official to do the like, his ticket to pass at all locks " except at Sutton Milles as aforesaid." . . .

11 Anyone attempting to pass without such warrant to be stopped by the lockkeeper, who may take " for his care fidelity and paines such further recompence as shall be reasonable."

12 If any keepers at stations where no dues were payable chose to keep a private record, by means of which frauds might come to be detected, they to receive 2s. 6d. for each discovery due to their help. . . .

I have shewn that on John Taylor's contemporary evidence Iffley and Sandford locks were already in being in 1632. It will now be observed that Swift Ditch and Sutton locks are spoken of as in existence in 1638. From the latitude given to Farmer to "build or repair" a "sufficient lock or weare" (synonymous in this case, I think) at some convenient site in the Swift Ditch, it may be presumed that there had, perhaps immemorially, been a weir about halfway along this channel, that it had fallen into decay and that the lessee had the option of repairing or of entirely rebuilding it. It is not quite obvious why this weir was required, in addition to the pound lock at the head of the Ditch and, probably, the mainstream lasher.

Clause 5 is particularly interesting in the light, or half light, it throws upon the pound lock underneath Sutton mill. The miller had evidently been in the habit of repairing it: an act of ownership; and it was moreover apparently coeval with the three turnpikes indubitably built by the 1623 commission. The utmost authority over it the latter seem prepared assert is to regulate its tolls, while renouncing all claim to them both on their own and their lessee's parts. I present below other history of this curious station under Sutton mills. One isolated statement will be found there that it was originally built chiefly at the commissioners' expense; but it is never enumerated amongst their works or property. Most probably it was a private speculation of the miller's. It will be noticed how small its original charges were, compared with subsequent extortions.

If it be just to judge from their sole survivor in the Swift Ditch, which has not, so far as I can discover, been touched for at least one hundred and twenty years, these original locks were of solid and beautifully joined masonry, far more substantial than their first successors: often mere timber skeletons. A note of 1783 says "they are too contracted to pass a barge more than 75 feet including its rudder; therefore are an impediment to the increasing size of the barges."

In the archives occurs a power of attorney dated 1639, under which the commissioners resumed possession of Sandford lock from Edmund Powell, jr., whose father had been in charge and had just died.

The Oxford-Burcot Commissions

The following is the promised series of payments in connection with the various works, extracted from the Convocation accounts. Most of them cannot be dated more exactly than the financial year in which they occur. As I have said, Sir Nicholas Kempe's legacy had doubtless already been entirely spent, and these were later subsidies which would have to appear in the general accounts. A note attached to one of them: "the University part," should I think be understood of the whole; doubtless the City paid its share separately.

"1637-8.	To Dr. Pinke for making the River navigable	60 : 6 : 0
1638-9.	For Charges in renewing the Commission of waterworks	2 : 14 : 0
1639-40.	Dr. Pinke for expences in y^e business of opening y^e River	3 : 10 : 0
	Mr ffarmer by his bills	9 : 17 : 7
1640-1.	For renewing y^e Commission	2 : 0 : 8
1643-4.	To Robert Panting Wharfinger towards y^e mending of the Turnpikes by the Lords C$\bar{\text{r}}$s order	10 : 0 : 0
July 14, 1647	Laid forth at Abingdon for a dinner for y^e C$\bar{\text{r}}$s for y^e Waterworks 25s. 8d., and a boatman 3s. 4d. White a carpenter 2s. 6d.	1 : 11 : 6
1647	Delivered to Mr. Ball at severall times for repair of Sanford mill turnpike	155 : 0 : 0

> To Mr. Ball in discharge of his account for repair of Sandford and Swift Ditch 1647   11 : 15 : 11
> Purchases of timber   6 : 7 : 8
> To George Bury of Culham in full for a cut formerly made in his Meadows by Swift Ditch and for a bank upon which a house is now built (the University part)   15 : 0 : 0
> To the River Commissioners at several times for repair of the turnpike at Swift Ditch, and for the building of the house there   105 : 0 : 0
> 1648-50 Adams and Rancklyn Smiths for work about the Turnpike   20 : 0 : 0
> Another payment for the same   10 : 0 : 0
> Sir George Stonehouse for timber used about the Turnpike   7 : 0 : 0
> 1652-3 Towards the house at Swift Ditch   10 : 0 : 0."

Up till 1666 no further payment appears in the Convocation accounts; although elsewhere I discover one item:

> "Aug. 9, 1661 to Sep. 18, 1662. To Mr John Houghton towards y⁰ maintaining of y⁰ Waterworks for making y⁰ Thames navigable   20 : 0 : 0"

In "the yeare of our Lord according to the Computacon now used in England, one Thousand

The Oxford-Burcot Commissions 81

Six Hundred ffifty & Two," I find an indenture made between the commissioners and George Bury, lord of the manor of Culham. It was agreed between the parties that a two-roomed cottage (alluded to in the above payments) should shortly be built "upon the Wall of the Southside of the Turnepike at Swift Ditch" for the accommodation of the lockkeeper, who was to be a single man, and to lose his job if he married. He was not to make use of the house to sell "Ale or Beer or any kind of victual" to bargemen or others. He might not open the gates for flashes, but only for the passage of barges; in order that the banks of the channel might not be undermined. And in going to and from his cottage he might use no path but the one called Boatman's Way, or such other ways as had anciently led past the site of the house.

In July of the same year some further bye-laws were made by the commissioners, to remedy the increasing complaints made by the traffic between Oxford and London of oppressions and exactions by the millers of Sandford, Abingdon and Sutton. Here are the more interesting:

    1. Concerning Sandford, whenever the water is under grinding head at the lock belonging to Sandford mill, the miller shall receive for every two hours' flash 10s. and no more; and when above grinding head 6s. 8d.

    2. If a boatman draw a waste gate in order to pass Sandford, the miller not to demand more than 1s. for a

F

single boat, 1s. 6d. for two boats, 2s. for three, and 6d. for each additional boat.

3. If millers, when their mills are grinding and they have sufficient grist to continue, shall upon the approach of an upstream boat shut down their mills on purpose to lay such boat aground and force her to buy water to bring her up to the turnpike, upon proof the party so offending shall forfeit 10s. for each offence. . . .

5. Whenever the water at the lasher by Swift Ditch is under grinding head the Abingdon miller to receive 13s. 4d. and no more for two hours' flash ; when above grinding head 6s. 8d.

6. Whenever upward boats from Culham cannot reach the stop below the Swift Ditch turnpike without drawing that turnpike, they shall pay to the Abingdon miller as to Sandford in clause 2.

7. Concerning Sutton : Whenever the water is under grinding head at " Sutton-Howse Lock," the miller may receive 20s. and no more for two hours' flash ; when at or above, 13s. 4d. . . .

9. Obstructions to bargemen towing by strength of men, horses, winches, engines or other convenient means between Burcot and Oxford, they doing no other harm than peaceably passing along the banks, to be punished with a fine of 6s. 8d. for each offence. . . .

Dr. Plot has an allusion to these works in his *Oxfordshire* published in 1677.

"The Locks & Turn-pikes made upon the River Isis, the 21 of King James, when it was made navigable from Oxford to Bercot to keep up the water & give the vessels an easie descent. For the first whereof, a [flash] lock will suffice, which is made up only of bars of wood called

The Oxford-Burcot Commissions 83

> Rimers, which must be all pulled up at [the barge's] arrival before the boat may pass either down or upwards; which with the stream, is not without violent precipitation; & against it, at many places, not without the help of a Capstain at Land; & sometimes neither of them without imminent Danger."

He then proceeds to describe, and to name, the three new upper pound locks; and adds the comment about the reopening of the Swift-Ditch, which, with his other remarks, will be found under this head below. Owing, doubtless, to the quite intelligible selfishness of the millers, the doctor was compelled, nearly half a century after these first locks had been built, to add also that, in spite of improved possibilities: "the River Thames is not made so perfectly navigable to Oxford, but that in dry times, barges do somtimes lie aground three weeks, or a month, or more, as we have had experience this last summer." He suggests locks, or dams, in the Cherwell, Kennet, and Loddon, to afford flashes when necessary to replenish the Thames.

Anthony à Wood comments adversely upon the district on March 23, 1685:

> "Some little raigne fell; none from 7 March to this time—a dry Feb. and March. Waters low, & the boatmen can not [" scarce " scored through] goe from Oxon to London but take boats at Bircot..... A drie winter; waters very low; not portable."

Ten years later, in 1695, I find a petition in which Sir John Somers is besought

> "to put in execution an Act made in the 21th yeare of the late King James the first for makeing the River of Thames Navigable for Barges Boats and Lighters from the village of Borcott unto the Citty of Oxon. And alsoo One other Act made in the last Session of the present Parliament [discussed below] to prevent exactions of the Occupiers of Locks and Weares and for ascertaining the rates of Watercarriage there being none in force."

Similar remonstrances occur in 1722, 1723, and at irregular intervals down to 1838. With reference to the first clause of the petition quoted, is it allowable to suppose that the Oxford Authority had, in three quarters of a century, found the millers and landowners too much for them ; and had, by 1695, subsided into mere toll collectors and remained no longer reformers?

Whether or no : at a meeting of the commission on May 12, 1712, it was ordered in effect, and with reference solely to Sutton lock :

> 1. That every barge passing down from Oxford or Abingdon (except such as come from above Oxford) shall at every passage pay at Sutton lock 27s. 6d., to include all necessary assistance. (The huge increase upon the 1638 rate, and the reason, or excuse, for it will be noticed.)
> 2. Provided that if any boat in its return upwards shall make use of the "s d" lock (probably Swift Ditch is

The Oxford-Burcot Commissions 85

meant) between the said lock and Sandford, it shall pay 2s. 6d. over and above the sum previously mentioned.

3. If any boat returning to Abingdon, Oxford or Lechlade shall make use of the said lock "for an Up-Stream water" to get into Sutton Pool, it shall pay to the lockowner as follows: If the upstream water be wanted at Wallingford Bridge, 10s.; if at Day's lock, 6s.; Clifton ferry, 4s. 6d.; "Wittenham Maddy or Down Mead," 3s. 6d.; Culham wharf, 2s. (An "up-stream water" I conceive to mean a flash from above.)

4. Barges from above Oxford to pay 22s. 6d. for passage and assistance.

The following seems to be a case presented, about 1739, for counsel's opinion upon the point that, in consequence of the Act 3 Geo. II not perpetuating the powers and rights of the commission, bargemen were defying its jurisdiction. The case runs:

"Nothing has been done by the commissioners made by this Act of 3 Geo. II relating to the Locks or Turnpikes between Bercot & Oxford, Nor any other Locks or Turnpikes, for five or six years last past.—this Act being thought ineffectual for the ends designed by it, and it continues only in force for one year longer.

"On the 8th Septr 1737 The Commisioners appointed by the 21 of James I made an order which was signed and sealed by every one of them, and also by the vice-chancellor of the university and mayor of the City of Oxford.

"In contempt of which Order several Boatmen have at several times broken through the Turnpikes belonging to the said commissioners before two credible witnesses.

"Q. Which is the proper method of prosecuting these offenders?"

The opinion given, if any, does not appear. There is no doubt that the Act referred to, while generally continuing the Act of 1695, expressly excepts the proviso in the latter upholding the commission. How such a "salvo" (to use the contemporary term) could be suppressed, with such powerful interests to support it, I do not understand. Possibly it was intended that the two Authorities should exercise concurrent jurisdiction between Oxford and Burcot. The traffic quickly discovered and exploited the ambiguity.

From the Commissioners' Cash Book, "Began in May 1767," I gather that at this date a man named Tomkins held one of the locks, probably Swift Ditch, at an annual rental of £42. The same amount, but for two years, was paid by Danby, probably for Iffley; £42 for one year by Mrs. Hill, probably for Sandford; and the same rental by one Edward Mayow, perhaps for the Oxford wharf. £30 was paid by Wyatt for three years' rent. The premises paid for are not expressed in any case.

In 1775 one Hatt was prosecuted for damaging Iffley turnpike. Sandford and Iffley profits for the year ended June 30, 1775, amounted together to £43, and to £48 two years later. Several small payments occur for "getting the stones out of the turnpikes." In 1780 there is a reference to repairs

The Oxford-Burcot Commissions 87

to "the Dwelling House" at Swift Ditch turnpike. This year one Beckley appears as the tenant at Sandford. In 1783-4 Swift Ditch weir, "the old lock," was extensively repaired: in July, 1783, the commissioners had surveyed it at a cost of £4. 11. 3½, surely a large sum; perhaps it included a dinner at Abingdon; the cost of the actual work amounted to £157. In September 1784 occurs an item of 10s. 6d. for "Horsehire & Expences Attending Meeting at Abingdon 7th Novr last of Promoters of a Canal from Lechlade to Abingdon & acquaintg. them that if no Provision was made to the Univ^y & City as a Compensation for Loss of Trade the Univ^y & City wou'd oppose the Canal." In 1785 a man named Collins pays £46 for a year's rent of the "old Lock at Culham"; and in 1789 a rope for the same station cost £1. 17. 6. This year an omen of the end of the Authority's jurisdiction appears in an item of horsehire and expenses, 10s. 6d., for attending the Commissioners of the Thames Navigation (the 1770 Authority) "to receive the purchase Money for the sale of Iffley and Sandford turnpikes Locks and house adjoining, when the said commissioners were not prepared to pay the Purchase Money"; which indeed, £600 in amount, expressly for the aforesaid premises and "Culham" (Swift Ditch) turnpike, was not paid till April 26, 1790.

Meanwhile, on May 23, 1780, some further

orders had been issued, contained in a Ledger Book beginning in 1754. All the earlier contents of this volume consist of leases to successive tenants of the St. Aldate's wharf. The more interesting of the orders are as follow. A fine of 6s. 8d. was set upon the obstruction of boatmen in their "just Liberty of Towing upon the banks of the River." The wharf or loading charge at St. Aldate's was fixed at 6d. per ton except for coals and timber; and barges loading at any other wharf in Oxford were to pay the like charge to the commissioners' wharf: an effective piece of protection! No vessels loading at any alien wharf in Oxford might pass Iffley lock without paying 40s. to the tenant thereof for each passage; and if loading between Iffley and Sandford they were to pay a like sum at the latter station.

Several minute books of this commission are preserved; but the earliest begins in 1783, only seven years before all the works except the wharf were sold. The only item I gleaned from them is that in June, 1784, the letting of the tolls at Swift Ditch turnpike and "old lock" was ordered to be advertised.

The negotiations for the sale of the works to the 1770 Commission opened in 1787. In 1789 it was stated that the tolls at Iffley, Sandford, Swift Ditch and Nuneham (which last is vaguely included, though it is uncertain that it was a work of this commission, and was in any case only a flash lock) produced in tolls about £77. 10s. annually, subject to a maintenance charge of about one-third that sum. The Oxford Authority offered to sell for £1,500, but as has already appeared was ultimately satisfied with £600. In 1843 the University and City of Oxford obtained statutory authority to dispose of the wharf to make room for local improvements.

Chapter V

IT WILL be fully evident what an immense economy of water and of time might be anticipated from the modern locks that had now begun to be built upon the River. Under the old system barges on arrival at the weirs had often to wait as much as several days before the grudging miller would draw his paddles. Then it would take some considerable time, perhaps an hour or more, to remove the tackle and reduce the upper water level to something near the lower. Lastly, at the expense of much drudgery, at more or less risk of life and property against a headlong and plunging current, the vessel would be hauled up through the opening. The waste of water was enormous: a fall of several inches, or even of two or three feet, along perhaps three or four miles of River, being sometimes requisite. Now, under the new system, whenever the millers were reasonable, a great economy would appear. The contents of each modern lock lower the upper level an inappreciable inch or two for a very little distance, and the time occupied need not be more than a quarter of an hour for a single barge. Another frequent inconvenience in the old system was that after two or three vessels had passed the water might have fallen to such shallowness on the groundsill of the weir that nothing further could pass, and waiting barges would be compelled to delay many hours, or even days, before the River could recover itself. Nowadays a whole string can be pounded through without seriously affecting the floating depth above.

Charles I, who, as I have said, strongly interested himself in his earlier and happier days in the welfare of the River, ordered on August 6, 1630, that when the Lord Mayor went his next survey he should advise his Majesty, so that some of the Council might accompany the party, "on account of past neglect." The Lord Mayor, Sir James Cambell, overlooked the command, and wrote on September 9 apologising to Secretary Dorchester, and mentioning that there was "a double going yearly," naming an approaching inspection. On November 25 the Lord Mayor again wrote : " For removal of stakes in the Thames, the waterbailiff had been continually abroad, to the great danger of his life, among that rude sort of people, and had taken up all their stops, and drawn up stakes that by the report of neighbouring inhabitants had stood beyond any of their remembrances. Only some few short stakes are yet remaining at Isleworth, which are hidden under water and cannot be removed until the tides grow lower." The *Remembrancia* adds that "the petermen, who destroyed the fry, had promised to forbear their unlawful assemblies and operations." (A note of September, 1584, in this volume defines a peternet as a net two inches wide in the mesh. Allusions to peterboats are very frequent. Mr. C. J. Cornish, in his *Naturalist*, speaks of the "last of the Peterboat men" being about Putney or Chiswick in 1902.)

Half a century after Bishop, John Taylor the Water Poet, the Cobbett and the Taunt of his age and of the Thames, affords the earliest personal description of the River subsequent to the building of the Oxford-Burcot locks. His little book *Thame Isis* was published in 1632; and is a long tirade, like Bishop's in verse, against the obstructions on the River.

> And for the good to England it hath done,
> Shall it to spoyle and ruine be let runne?
> Shall private persons for their gainfull use,
> Ingrosse the water and the land abuse?

Conditions are satisfactory, he declares, below Staines:

> Nor is the river wanting much repaire,
> Within the bounds of Londons honourd Maior,
> Which limits all are cleare from stakes and piles,
> Beyond Stanes bridge (thats more than forty miles).

But he complains that there are many wrongs

General History

between London Stone and Oxford, which he proceeds to publish :

> Not doubting but good mindes their powers will lend,
> T'endevour these abuses to amend.

The following substantial excerpts will, like Bishop's list, prove more interesting assembled than scattered piecemeal over my own List.

At Iffley, he begins :

> a new turne pike doth stand amisse

and another at "Stanford." His mention of these two pound locks fixes 1632 as the earliest year to which, without further evidence, I can attribute them. Below Sandford, where now the high bare bank lines the right shore, heaped up, perhaps illegally, after Taylor's age to preserve the meadows from flood, he found

> Weeds, shelves, and shoales all waterlesse and flat.

At Nuneham he complains of a fishing weir and a gravel hill that caused a shoal. At Abingdon the shallows were worse, so

> That Swift ditch seemes to be the better course.

It is noticeable that he does not allude to a pound lock in this channel ; it may not yet have been in existence, or perhaps he battled along the shoals through Abingdon weir and bridge. He seems, however, to imply that the Ditch had already been recut and scoured. At Sutton Courtenay

> there are left
> Piles that almost our Barges bottome cleft;
> These Sutton locks are great impediments,
> The waters fall with such great violence.

It may be a fair inference from the last couplet that the pound lock beneath the mill had not yet been built, and that Taylor shot one of the several weirs here, three of which are still in existence falling into the beautiful pool.

The "Weare of Carpenter's" he thought "sans fault." Where was it? It was perhaps identical with No. 29, 30 or 31 of Bishop's later list. There was more trouble at Clifton, where he found

> rocks, and sands, and flats,
> Which made us wade, and wet like drowned rats.

He mentions neither Day's nor Benson, which were certainly in being. At Wallingford piles were "plac'd unmeet": possibly against the bridge, or possibly connected with Ralph Pollington's mill. Another curious omission is Moulsford; though I have no proof that it was as early as Taylor's period, except, doubtfully, Bishop's No. 22. "Cleave," Goring, and Hart's follow without comment.

> And next to Whitchurch locke which must be mended,
> Because the waters turne so swift and various
> And gainst our wils to dangerous courses cary us:

a rhyme Robert Browning may have envied. Passing another, unnamed weir, which must have been near Hardwick, he declares it

> Should be well lib'd, or else removed quite.

What is "lib'd"? There has always been a local family of the name of Lybbe: certainly a Lybbe at Hardwick in 1722; and a Lybbe Powys in 1868. Is it some obscure pun of Taylor's? He then comes to Mapledurham:

> Where stands three faulty and untoward Weares.

Near Caversham bridge was

> One Welbeck's Weare, fit to be mov'd I wis:

identical perhaps with No. 15 of Bishop's second list. Below Caversham he found the River "very foule." Near Sonning was "Breaches Weare," now utterly gone. "Sunning locke" had its "groundsill too high"; perhaps other craft had just preceded him and run the water low. Then

> Haules Weare doth almost cross the river all,
> Making the passage straight and very small,
> How can that man be counted a good liver
> That for his private use will stop a river?

—a veritable Stevenson whimsy! This may have been the weir I mention below at Buck Ait, just below the outfall of the Patrick stream; it is noteworthy that a Thomas Hall was the first lockkeeper at Sonning about 1772, and that the large island below Buck Ait is known as Hallsmead Eyot. "Shiplocke" or Cottrels was very near, and not far below was Elmes "his fishing weare": doubtless Bishop's No. 9. Marsh and "Hambleton" follow: then another now vanished obstruction occasions a good epigram :

> Next Mednam Weare doth speedy mending lacke ;
> It puts the Thames, and Thames puts it to wracke.

This (a mere guess) may have been at Magpie Island, where are still eelbucks blocking navigation through a very lovely backwater. If so, it may possibly be inferred that the present channel to the north of the island either did not then exist or was impassable. "Froggs-mill," on the right bank below the abbey, opposed "two paltry stops" to Taylor's passage. He then mentions "Newlocke" at "Harley"; and a weir below "almost a stop": there seems scant room for this last anonymous obstruction in that tiny reach. Next comes Temple :

> Beneath which is a Weare somewhat amisse :

another riddle, unless it be an ancestor of Rosewell's effort in 1783, just below Bisham church, discussed later.

> Then Marlow locke is worst, I must confess,
> The water is so pinched with shallowness.

General History

(Again I exhort you that you dismiss from your mind all the pound locks and their cuts, if you would bring home to your imagination the River Taylor knew, and all its risks and difficulties.) An unnamed weir below "should be defac'd"; and Cottrells of Cookham be displaced. Then follow Holderness's: a name that recurs in my Cookham matter below; a stop against Taplow warren; Boulter's; a stop above and one below Maidenhead Bridge; and against Bray mill and church three more

> Indifferent bad as any were before.

These "stops," doubtless short fishery hedges or scouring dams, below Boulter's should be noticed in view of later legislation prohibiting for a long time the erection of modern locks below that station. Another stop occurred at Water Oakley, possibly against Queen's Ait; and "gravel hills" too high at "Rudlespoole."

> Near Boveney church a dangerous stop is found
> On which five passengers were lately drowned.

Was this Gill's bucks; or was it that weir anciently crossing the head of the Clewer stream? Needless piles below Windsor Bridge; and a stop and weir near "Eaton" college, probably at Black Potts.

> A stop, a weare, a dangerous sunke tree
> Not far from Datchet Ferry are all three:

perhaps Newman's bucks. He next indicts a gravel

G

bed, and two stops and stakes, near Old Windsor church (I myself saw barges in trouble at this spot in 1910, nearly three centuries later); two stops near Ankerwyke; and the like near London Stone: perhaps Bell's fishing weir.

> From Stanes we past to Lallum gulls, most shallow,
> Whereas five Barges fast aground did wallow;
> And such a trowling current there did set
> That we were vildly puzzled by to get.

And so he ends, for my purpose, with a parting shot at old skewwise Chertsey Bridge; which must, he declares, have been built by a lefthanded man. One difficulty has certainly not been greatly ameliorated: the "trowling current" at Laleham, which has assuredly "vildly puzzled" one solitary navigator of these degenerate days "by to get." It may be observed that Taylor mentions none of the seven present stations from Penton Hook to Richmond; except as partial stops in one or two cases none of them then existed, either as lock or weir.

In 1633 the department charged with obtaining timber for the navy yards complained of the difficulty they experienced with the Upper River traffic. "Every barge coming from Burcot fetcheth water at 19 locks between Burcot and London, the charg thereof is to each of them 42s. 2d., whereof the locks above Wallingford Bridge receave 28s. 8d. The usuall rate allowed by his Ma^{ty} for watercarriage

General History 99

from Burcot to Deptford is 8s. 6d p loade, at wch rate, ye owners affirme, they loose in every freight 5*l* & sometimes 6*l*." These nineteen flash locks are to be reckoned from Day's to Boulter's inclusive; and are noticeably fewer than Bishop's later list. The toll named is considerably less than the nearest in date in my Table: the incomplete schedule of 1681. The large proportion paid above Wallingford is not easy to account for; there were probably only two weirs levying toll between there and Burcot: Day's and Benson; neither of which was ever extortionate.

Amongst the long catalogue of Taylor's other books there are several about the Thames, but only one to my purpose: his *Carriers Cosmographie* of 1637. Herein he printed some very interesting details (would they were more!) of the carrying trade on the River; indicating more vividly than any general description what a real everyday convenience the Thames was in those days of no railways and scanty, ill kept roads. The book is a sort of little *Bradshaw*, or conveyance directory; and the following is the whole of the Thames matter, but little condensed.

"To Bull Wharfe (neere Queenhithe) there doth come & goe great boats twice or thrice every weeke betwixt London & Kingston; also thither doth often come a Boat from Colebrooke.

Great Boats that doe carry Passengers & goods betwixt London and Maydenhead, Windsor, Stanes, Chertsey, with other parts of Surry, Barkeshire, Midlesex, & Buckingamshire do come every Munday, & Thursday to Queenhith, & go away upon tuesdayes & thusdaies.

"The Redding Boat is to be had at Queenhith weekly."

In 1638 one Rd. Bagnall procured a "deputation" to make saltpetre in certain River and other counties, and asked that his produce might be barged to Broken Wharf "at the usual rates for his Majesty's carriages," *viz.*, between London and Wallingford and Burcot 5s. per ton, Reading 4s. 2d., Henley or Windsor 3s. 4d.

It is a curious fact that for the next twenty-two years, a period covering the civil wars and the Commonwealth, the history of the River is, except for a vague complaint or two, a complete blank.

Humpherus points out, in his *History of Watermen*, that into the original Bill in 1660 for a General Letter Office a clause was inserted: "That this Act shall not extend to take away the profit belonging to the barges of Windsor and Maidenhead for the carriage of letters and pacquets, but that they shall carry the same as formerly." The clause was dropped; but it is a piquant little ingredient in the navigation history I have not seen noticed elsewhere: the function of barges as letter carriers.

Pepys has the following note on May 14, 1669; it may be added to my previous allusions to West Country barges. "By water with my brother as high as Fulham, talking and singing, and playing the rogue with the Western bargemen about the women of Woolwich; which mads them." I may comment here upon the word bargemen that I have not found in any of the innumerable books and manuscripts I have read for the purpose of this history one solitary instance of the use of the modern "bargee." Ackerley in 1834 calls the Western barges "monkeys."

In *The Travels of Cosmo III* of 1669 it is stated: "On the Thames, all the way from Windsor to the Fleet, there are ten thousand small boats, to take persons up and down the river, or to ferry them over from one side to the other."

My next piece of history is extracted from Yarranton's *England's Improvement:* published in 1677 with the object, amongst several others, of demonstrating "the Advantage of making the Great Rivers of *England* Navigable." So he laments:

> "There is no notice or regard taken of the great defects that are in the Navigation upon the River *Thames*, from *Oxford* to *London*, which River would be the best Servant the City hath, if compleated as it ought to be. *London* is as the Heart is in the Body, & the great Rivers are as its Veins; let them be stopt, there will then be great danger of death. I having this Summer surveyed the River *Thames* from *Oxford* to *London*, & my Son twice, we find the Water-men much abused, being forc't to pay several Taxes, at several Sluces betwixt *Oxford* and *Burcot*, that part of the River being made Navigable

in the 21. of King James, & by that Law all People and Barges are to pass & repass without Tax. [This is not the case; the Act expressly empowers the commission to make " rates for carriages by the said passage."] It is a misery that the Barges should lye on ground a Month or six Weeks, as they did this [Dr. Plot's] Year, & the poor Barge-Masters should be forc't all that time to maintain so many men, as of necessity they must; besides, the Tradesman in *London* wants the Commodity to sell."

The text follows of a petition he has in hand for submission to Charles II. It recites the Act 21 James I; suggests a scheme for " carrying Commodities down the Severne, up the Avon, and thence to Oxford by land, and so to London by water." The point is made, as so frequently in those days, that improvement of the navigation will ensure that " the Highways & Bridges will be preserved." And, following Plot, the author suggests three " holds " for water in the Cherwell, to be let down in drought; a lock at Swift Ditch and a pair of gates at Sutton; a " turnpike " a mile below Sutton, two flushes out of Kennet and sites for two others: one near Windsor and the other near " Chersey." Yarranton finally urges the necessity of inspecting the River for these and other improvements; and nepotically proffers his son as surveyor.

Why does he suggest " a lock at Swift Ditch " ? The document quoted on page 73 seems conclusive that the " Turnepeck in Swiftditch " was in being,

General History 103

and levying toll, in 1638. Was it in "sheer ignorance" that he proposed it? If so, it is difficult to accept his next suggestion, of "a pair of gates at Sutton," as evidence that the lock had not already been built under the mill there.

In the course of a dispute in 1678 between the university and the city of Oxford, it is related that "a proproctor in his night walk seizes a townsman and demands 40s. for noctinavigation."

Under the date of April 6, 1695, occurs the following retrospective note, embodying the earliest definite schedule of River tolls I have discovered. It is a reference, apparently used during the discussion of the Act of 1695 alluded to below, to a transaction fourteen years previous.

"Order of the Court of Sewers for Berkshire and Oxon, held at Abingdon on 26 May 1681 before [fourteen named] Commissioners.... Upon the Petition of John Tomkins, Philip Lockton, Nicholas Culley, John Rush and Nicholas Hooper, Boatmasters trading on the Thames between Abingdon and Staines Bridge, shewing that the Thames had been freely navigable time out of mind from Birket to London, and for over 50 years from Oxford to Birket, and the Court of Sewers had kept the river cleansed and fixed the lock dues; and that divers millers and occupiers of locks, etc., have been too exacting in their charges, the Court finds that the lock dues fixed by former Courts are the following:

Whitchurch Locks and Turnpikes	2/-	Cleeve Lock	,,	3/-
Mapledurham Lock	1/8	Goring	,,	3/4
Caversham ,,	2/-	Sunning	,,	1/8
New Mill ,,	-/6	Hambledon	,,	1/-
Little Witnam ,,	1/-	Hurley	,,	-/8
Bensington ,,	-/10	Marlow	,,	-/8
		Boulter's	,,	1/-

and these it confirms, with a penalty of 40*l.* for any overcharge."

An interesting note indeed; with one tantalising riddle. What were "turnpikes" doing at Whitchurch at this date? Nothing built, as I believe, between the Oxford-Burcot group of 1623 and the revival in 1771; and yet this intermediate reference to one there! New Mill is perhaps Hurley or at Marsh.

There is an entertaining outburst in T. H[ale]'s *New Inventions* published in 1691.

"*I know a Gentleman, who charging a late* Water-Bailiff *with taking of* Money *from* Encroachers, *was answer'd,* That he did no such thing, but would not deny but that some of his followers might do so. *What unsafe anchoring do all our great* Trusts *in this World find, while we trust our* Bodies *to* Apothecaries Boyes, *our souls to poor* Curates, *and our principal* Royal River *to a* Water-baily's Followers!"

A small legal matter arises in October of the same year. The Corporation of London petitioned that the conservacy was vested in them, and the fines imposed in their courts were their own property; but of late many offenders, in order to delay the course of justice, had removed the presentments by writs of *certiorari* to the King's Bench, and had thereby often escaped punishment. In May, 1692, it was suggested that, as the King's Bench fines had recently been of little value, and the grant thereof to the City might encourage them to bring more offenders to justice, their petition should be allowed; a rider, however, being added that the Corporation had perhaps been remiss in pursuing cases removed to the King's Bench, having no interest in the fines.

Notwithstanding this cloud of witnesses, notwithstanding Bishop and Taylor and the Law, matters had not very greatly improved during the century. The Oxford-Burcot pound locks found no sequel elsewhere on the River for a hundred and fifty years; and meanwhile the exactions of the weir owners, and the alleged ruffianism and obscenities amongst the bargemen, were clamouring more and more insistently for further legislation. And at length, in 1695, the Act 6 & 7 Wm. III was passed: " To prevent exactions of the occupiers of locks and wears upon the river of Thames westward, and for ascertaining the rates of watercarriage." It recites that the Thames has been navigable from time immemorial from London to Burcot, and for " divers years last past" from Burcot westward, " somewhat farther than Letchlade"; that there have been and are various locks, weirs, bucks, turnpikes, etc., on the River, the tenants of which anciently took, and still ought to take, a moderate and reasonable price from all passing vessels; that the owners had lately so raised their prices that freights also had necessarily advanced; and then with an allusion to the bad behaviour of the bargemen proceeds to enact that the justices of the peace of the Riverside counties, and they only, shall be commissioners for the regulation of the navigation, with authority to settle rates and put down abuses. They were not to supersede the commission of 1623 between Burcot and Oxford. Bargeowners were to be held responsible for damage done by their vessels or servants to weirs and other property.

(It should be remarked, with reference to these not infrequent charges against bargemen, that this class once included large numbers of labourers beyond the crews. Old views of the River often shew horses and gangs of men waiting to take up the towing. Almost within living memory barges were towed by successive gangs of men. One gang would haul on the line until the towpath ended on their side; and the rope was then passed across to another gang on the opposite bank, who took up the work. These hauliers are not seldom described as a terror to the Riverside communities.)

This Act was ordered to remain in force for only nine years. It fell into desuetude, as will be seen immediately; and was not revived until 1730; although, in addition to what follows, I find in the Oxford city papers an address in March, 1716, to Lord Abingdon, stating that the university and city "had agreed to endeavour this Session to get the said last Act revived with some necessary additions much to the advantage of the navigation and of the Inhabitants of this place and parts adjacent."

In November, 1698, one Francis Barry of Kensington petitioned for employment under a scheme of his own for preventing "the frauds practised in the Thames above bridge westward as far as Wallingford in Oxfordshire" (sic). It unfortunately does not appear what these frauds, and the preventive scheme, were. The latter, however, included "An Inspection of the River of Thames, and a correspondence settled in All the Most Convenient Places, Which may be Performed by makeing a Quarterly Visitation to all the said Places above Winsor."

An example follows, a little condensed, of what must have been the numerous complaints and petitions for redress. It is a four page foolscap folio, printed in 1720, evidently the work of a harassed bargemaster, and contains evidence of the desuetude of the Act of 1695.

"By Length of Time Impositions were laid on the

Navigation, by Persons, Owners and Renters of private Wears, Locks, Bucks, Gates, Winches, &c., which were a very great Hardship attending the Navigation, & of Ill Consequence to the Carriage of Goods upon the said River of *Thames*, which Abuses were regulated by an Act made in the 6th & 7th *W*. III which Impower'd the Justices to settle the Rates for each Barge or Vessel passing through; which Act was Temporary, & continued only for Nine years, although during the Continuance thereof, the Navigation of the R. *Thames* was carry'd on with Success, and was at a Certainty."

But thereafter things grew worse; finding themselves unchecked the riparians gradually and grievously increased their charges; so that at Day's the rate leapt from 1/6 to 5/-, and at Goring from 6/- to 15/-. And towing charges were imposed at several fresh places. "Formerly there were none of these charges attended the Navigation of the River *Thames*; the Locks, Wears, etc., having been erected for the Use of Mills near them; and are only an Obstruction to the Navigation; which before used to be free." The concluding prayer is that the rates shall be settled out of the power of the weir owners to increase them at their pleasure.

The declaration that mills were the original begetters of the weirs is interesting, and probably well founded. The claim, however, that, anterior to the existence of the mills, the navigation was free, while very plausible, is capable of neither substantiation nor disproof.

In 1728 an Act was passed "For punishing such persons as shall wilfully and maliciously pull down or destroy turnpikes [on land or water], locks or other works, erected by authority of Parliament." Evilly disposed persons had been banding together to destroy them, incited thereto without doubt by the wrongs alluded to in the petition just presented. A second conviction was to constitute a felony, punishable with transportation for seven years. In 1733 the statute was re-enacted for five years, a provision being added that the felons, if they returned during banishment, should be liable to death. The Act was renewed periodically; and made perpetual in 1754.

Meanwhile the Act of 1730, 3 Geo. II, c. 11, had been passed; reviving the statute of 1695. It begins by declaring that the latter had proved useful to the trade and navigation of the River while in force; but that since its expiry the weir owners had been exacting such exorbitant tolls as tended to the discouragement of the traffic, and to the increase of the cost of water carriage. Several persons also were taking money for towing paths, "which paths used to be free for men to tow." Owing almost certainly, though not expressed in the Act, to the huge enlargement of the barges, "towing requires such numbers of men as renders it very chargeable, and it is found much more convenient to tow with horses." Thereupon landowners were compelling bargemasters to pay for the passage of the horses such sums as if not moderated would lessen the traffic. The preamble includes a trifle of some freshness: that "upon sudden summer floods" the lockowners had exacted great sums from the landowners above them, before they would open their flash locks to let down the flood.

The ineffective remedies ordered in 1695 were revived, adding that towpath dues obtaining since then, for thirty-five years that is, were to continue.

In 1746 an octavo was published by Roger Griffiths, the water bailiff of his day, under the title "An Essay to prove that the Jurisdiction & Conservacy of the River of Thames etc. is committed to the Lord Mayor and City of London," etc., etc. The contemporary morals of authors, or of publishers, or of their confederacy, may be estimated from the fact that before I lit upon Griffiths I had already read the whole of his matter, misprints and all, in a precisely similar octavo put out by one Robert Binnell in 1758: twelve years later; the only variations being an insignificant alteration in the title, a different dedication, and an ambiguous passage in the preface which may or may not be intended as a veiled acknowledgement of the original author: "The following Description was begun by a Gentleman, who had many Years the Honour to serve the City in a Station, which gave him the greatest Opportunity of being perfectly acquainted with the Subject, and as he has been pleased out of kindness, to indulge me with the Presentation hereof, I hereby offer them to the public." The inference is invited that the "Gentleman's" notes had so far reposed in manuscript, which is not the case. Except for these trifling matters, the volumes are identical.

One third of each book is devoted to "Fish: their Nature, Element, Cloathing, Wars and Sensations"; from which section I do not hesitate to extract that, at that date: "though some of our Northern Countries have as fat and as large [Salmon] as the River *Thames*, yet none are of so exquisite taste."

The topographical account of the source of the River is a most extraordinary jumble in both Griffiths and his plagiarist. Kemble is printed as Hemble, and is placed in Cubberley parish: "a little to the southwest of Cirencester"; instead of actually some ten miles due north. It is evident that the author was bemused by the ancient rivalry between Thames Head and Seven Springs. This, he explains, "to be sure is the most distant stream. But others have rather chosen to place its fountain near *Siddington* where the *Isis* springs." I think Griffiths was conscious of some ineptitude, for he shruggingly suggests that the point is, after all, of extremely small importance; and Binnell smirks in sympathy.

There is nothing in the book regarding the earlier history of the subject which I had not already discovered elsewhere. The contemporary information is, however, both full and interesting in three respects : a list of flash locks and tolls of which I have made use in my own List and Table; a schedule of watermen's fares to different points on the River, also incorporated in my List; and a carriers' and travellers' guide or time-table, rather ampler than Taylor's, as follows :

"To Abindon, Newbery & Reading from the Bull by Brook's Wharf Queenhithe every Week.

To Windsor from Queenhithe, Tuesdays & Fridays.

Stain's Barge; from Queenhithe Tuesdays & Fridays.

Shepperton, Sundbury and Hampton-Town Boats Tuesdays, Thursdays and Saturdays in Summer, Tuesdays & Fridays in Winter.

Oxfordshire from Brook's Wharf by Queenhithe [no day given].

Chertsea and Weybridge. Barges from Queenhithe Tuesdays and Thursdays.

Walton-Boats from Queenhithe & Hungerford Stairs, Tuesdays, Thursdays and Saturdays in Summer, Tuesdays and Fridays in Winter.

Guilford Luggage Boats : from Queenhithe & other places."

The author is anxious once more to prove, what cannot be disputed, that the jurisdiction between Staines and the sea was in the Lord Mayor, Commonalty and Citizens of London, "with an absolute

General History

power to inflict Punishment for all Abuse of his Authority." He speaks very meagrely concerning the navigation westward of "London-Mark-Stone." The method of flash weirs, the old locks, is once more and clearly presented.

> "To remedy the want of water the use of Locks was happily invented, which are a kind of wooden machines placed quite a-cross the Current, and dam up the water. By this artifice the River is obliged to rise to a proper height till there is Depth enough for the barge to pass over the shallows, which done, the confined Waters are set at liberty. This Method is attended with great charge to the Navigators or Bargemen, for they are obliged to pay in the Voyage near £14 if they pass thro' all the locks in their passage to or from [Lechlade and] London. This is chiefly owing to the Locks being the property of private persons who raise a large annual income therefrom if we consider that 300 Barges pass and repass at least six times in a year."

The passage reads like nothing more than a modernised paraphrase of the Norman-French petition of four and a half centuries earlier; so slight were the changes that had been effected, and so unalterable the instincts of humanity. There is but little else in the book except the piscicultural section already alluded to; and I am "no fisher," though a "well wisher to the game."

Matters now begin to advance more swiftly. In 1751, under the Act 24 George II, c. 8, a wider body

H

than that of 1695, and perhaps it may justly be said the first permanent general Authority, was appointed to watch the interests of the navigation westward of Staines, on the pattern of the Oxford-Burcot Commission. It was a most unwieldy body, including no less than about six hundred members. Everyone who possessed landed estate of over £100 in annual value in the seven upper riparian counties, representatives from Oxford University, and the mayors of all Riverside towns, were given seats on the board. This was the original of the body which became more generally known, twenty years later, as the Thames Commissioners: direct ancestors of the Thames Conservancy of 1866. They went a very little way under their inaugural constitution, which gave them no power to instal pound locks or do anything but settle rates, patch things up, and correct abuses. They might not lay out new towpaths without the consent of the owners both of the old paths and the new. Bargemasters, as in 1695, were to be responsible for the torts of their employés. In cases of flooding of meadows through too high penning of water they were not to intervene directly, but might send a warrant to the parish constable to warn the offender, and on refusal to compel him to lower the head. In the case of overloaded barges lying aground, and blocking the way of craft of less draught, they were authorised to compel the ob-

General History 115

structing vessel to unload sufficiently to float her out of the way. Part of the Kennet, from its mouth to "the common landing-place at Reading," was placed under their control. The Act almost epitomises its own want of effectiveness in its provision not "to take away any jurisdiction, power or authority of any other body or persons whatsoever." Twenty years after their constitution they were compelled to seek new powers; of which history I present a particular account in its chronological order.

I have searched with but slight success for records of the transactions of this commission of 1751. Its proceedings were ordered by the Act to be filed in the offices of the clerks of the peace in the counties of Oxford and Berkshire. I personally examined, but in vain, the contemporary Quarter Sessions Rolls at Oxford. A Bodleian MS. affords the following notes. "Orders and Constitutions made at the Town Hall, Reading, July 1, 1751, under the new Act." They revived all the orders and constitutions made by the commissioners of 1730; and ordered that all of the said Act that was immediately necessary for bargemasters to know was to be printed and displayed in the Riverside marketplaces. All or any three commissioners might go and view all the works upon the River. Their names include a Pleydell, a Pye, a Popham, a Bertie, and a Southby. They might also take evidence upon oath as to former rates and tolls. Signed by W. Brookland, Berkshire Clerk of the Peace.

From Mr. J. T. Morland of Abingdon, whom I thank for much generous help and sympathy, I heard that after search in the Reading sessions papers only the two following short entries had been discovered. Both appear to relate to the same event.

"Extract from Easter Sessions 1753. Ordered that the Clerk of the Peace of this County do give Notice in the publick papers that there will be a meeting of the Commissioners of the Navigation of the River Thames at the George Inn in Wallingford on Tuesday the fifth day of June next in order to go down the said River, and that he then and there attend."

"The Commissioners appointed by an Act of the 24th Year of his present Majesty's reign for regulating the Navigation of the River Thames and Isis, are in pursuance of an Order made at the last Meeting held at Reading on the 2nd Day of November last desired to meet in the Morning of Tuesday the 5th Day of June next at the Town Hall in Wallingford and from thence to proceed to view all the Locks, Weirs, Flood gates, Towing Paths, Engines, Etc. from Wallingford to London and to enquire on Oath what rates have been taken by the Owners thereof. In order to transmitt an Account at the next General Meeting of the Commissioners to be held after making the Survey."

Some of the tolls fixed by this and earlier commissions will be found in my Table. While searching the archives of Oxford University I found some rough

General History 117

pencilled sheets quoting tolls fixed at Reading in 1731, 1754 and 1755, also incorporated in my Table. These are professedly copied from "an old Book containing orders and extracts from Minutes inrolled with the Clerk of the Peace 1751-1771." No county is named. In some correspondence attached to the sheets, dated about the beginning of the nineteenth century, it is hinted that this "old Book" may have been accidentally destroyed in a fire.

Three small glimpses of River life occur about this time in the *Gentleman's Magazine*. The July number in 1757 reports that on the eighth of the month "The Rt Hon. the lord-mayor, returned to the mansion-house from inspecting the fishery of the river *Thames*; he had been three days employed in that service, and had caused the several obstructions to the navigation, and the illegal erections for the fishery to be every where destroyed." The August issue says: "The water bailiff with a number of workmen have by order of the Rt Hon. the lord-mayor, and court of conservancy, pull'd up all the stops from the *London* mark stone above *Staines* bridge down the river *Thames*, which will be a great help to the navigation, as well as add to the beauty of the river, and preserve the fish." These read very like the modern inspired paragraph. Finally, in April, 1763, is presented a drawing and description of a "Machine for rowing of Barges against Stream": a horizontal framework worked with cranks, into which the handles of the oars were fixed. The cranks were to be worked by hand; and it was claimed that therewith four men could do the work of eight. I could not discern any provision for getting the blades inboard in any sudden emergency.

A very interesting quarto was reprinted "for Daniel Prince" in 1767, just before the revival of pound lock building. Its complete title is: *The Present State of Navigation on the Thames Considered & Certain Regulations proposed: By a Commissioner.* It declares that goods were being conveyed by land in preference to water, so high had Thames freights risen and so unendurable the inconveniences and delays. Bargemasters were explaining to shippers that their demand for higher freights was necessitated by the increased tolls charged for passing the flash locks and the preserved towing paths: "and in particular since the passage through the locks was by the Commissioners adjusted to the tonnage of the barge." The flash lock owners, thus accused, explained the increased tolls by their novel and extraordinary expense in raising and supporting the very great extensive works now rendered necessary; they were compelled, they said, to raise and strengthen the weirs in order to pen back a vast body of water to a greater height, because barges of enormous size and so deeply laden could not without

General History

the aid of a very high flash pass over the gulls and shallows below every lock. "While therefore these two Parties acquire any accession of profit, the trader or consumer is the sufferer, for he ultimately must pay for all." The hugely increased size of the barges was considered responsible for much damage and inconvenience. To float them flashes had to be more abundant and forcible, to ensure which the weirs had to be heightened. This caused floods; and the weir dams suffered from so tremendous a rush of water from the greater height. As much as ten feet of fall in some places is indicated. The author mentions barges of 160 to 180 tons making the voyage; and concludes upon a suggestion that only craft of 40 to 70 tons should be admitted upon the River. The great size of the barges "required the [flash] lock to run 2 or 3 hours," which the River could not recruit "in many days." Through this waste of water the miller was prevented from working his mill, and by the height of water accumulated before opening the paddles "the adjacent meadows are often overflowed and converted into morass."

Perhaps the most piquant feature in the book is the author's detail of barges "passing on the River *Thames* from *Lechlade* down to *Caversham Lock*" or Kennet mouth, with their capacities and dimensions. For brevity's sake I have condensed the following figures; they are not to be understood as of one and the same vessel except where marked with an asterisk.

Port	No. of Barges	Maximum Capacity in tons	Maximum measurements
Lechlade	14	65	87'.6" × 11'.9" × 4'.0"
Oxford	12	100	87'.0" × 16'.8" × 4'.0"
Abingdon	13	135	112'.0" × 19'.9" × 4'.1½"
Sutton	1	100*	*97'.6" × 15'.9" × 4'.0"
Day's Lock	1	25*	*61'.0" × 10'.5" × 3'.5½"
Shillingford	3	135	112'.0" × 17'.10" × 4'.0"
Wallingford	6	170*	*128'.0" × 18'.2" × 4'.0"
Goring	4	170*	*127'.0" × 18'.4" × 4'.0"
Pangbourne	1	35*	*66'.6" × 10'.6" × 3'.6"

One point is noticeable: the maximum figure of 65 tons for Lechlade barges in 1767. Hall in 1859 mentions 90 tons as the capacity of the largest craft then (a century later) trading above Oxford. The difference is a proof of two things: the irresistible tendency to load more and more goods into one bottom; and the improved character of the waterway.

The British Museum has only the second edition of this book. The Guildhall library possesses the first edition, published in 1764, three years earlier, which affords the following names of bargeowners:

Lechlade	Hooper, Wyat, Badcock, Crawford.		
Oxford	Grain, Gardener, Twang.		
Abingdon	Collins, Sappin, Leonard, Quaint, Belcher.		
Sutton	Waters.	Wallingford	Jaques, Webb.
Day's	Longford.	Goring	Higgs.
Shillingford	Savory.	Pangbourne	May.

It is remarkable that no single name occurs both in

General History 121

this list and in Bishop's of 1585. It is an evidence of the extent of the trade. Jaques of Wallingford is evidently the man mentioned under Eel Pie Island below as vigorously protesting against the Dysart paygate there.

I will close my notice of this book with some of the author's interesting definitions.

"*Lock*. In the middle of the weir there is an opening, commonly about 20 ft. wide, a strong wooden fabrick, called the *Lock* from its occasional use either of shutting up the Water or opening a passage for the barges. The Machinery for this consists of a number of small floodgates sliding in grooves, and at the bottom connected with the cill. When these are opened the water rushes out with great rapidity, and by its force the deeply loaded barges are carried over the shallows. [It may be observed that twenty feet of opening would barely pass some of the barges of the author's own list.]

Bucks. On the weir, beyond the lock there is another Fabrick, with larger floodgates of a different construction, commonly called the Bucks: their primary use is to carry off the Waste Water, and here the millers lay down their weels for catching fish.

Gull or *Shallow*. At some distance below you perceive a *Gutt* of Water, shallow and rapid; this is commonly called the Gull, a narrow and difficult pass, caused by the violence of the stream."

Chapter VI

THE THAMES COMMISSIONERS

IT IS in the closing third of the eighteenth century that all the old sullen muttering, the sporadic, often inarticulate seething of the previous ages, acquire at length their cumulative effect; and that the modern aspect of Thames navigation, of the River as we know it today, begins definitely to emerge. It was a belated birth, to an existence of very brief prosperity. Stirrings of the huge approaching increase in commerce and industrialism were in all men's hearts: premonitions of the imperious necessity for speedier and ampler communications, not only with foreign countries but between the various centres of their own. The intenser insistence upon a clear Thames highway; the almost innumerable projects for canals, some involving the desertion of long stretches of the River; the pathetic little schemes, one or two of which I particularise, for propelling heavy barges by some primitive mechanism, are evidence of this stirring,

The Thames Commissioners

this foreboding to prepare for a strong if dimly defined necessity. It was but a false birth, doomed to failure within half a century : the various schemes of water traffic, largely realised and temporarily prosperous, were not the line along which intercommunication was ultimately to develope. Their short success was quickly invaded and swallowed up by the new, all conquering power of steam and the railways. But the latter was still latent; and meanwhile the long struggle for an assured and commodious user of the great highway of southern England, the beloved Thames, achieved a brief success. The commission of 1751, strangely debarred from the only effective procedure by way of pound locks, sought powers, after nearly twenty years of patching and mending and ineffectual warning of offenders, to carry out this crucial step; and in 1770 obtained the important Act 11 George III, c. 45.

Their already unwieldy membership was absurdly increased. All the members of Parliament in the seven upper River counties, including those merely residing therein; the Corporation of the City of London; clergy from Westminster, Oxford, St. Paul's, Eton, and all the riparian parishes in these counties; the mayors and recorders of Oxford, Abingdon, Wallingford, Reading, Henley, Maidenhead and Windsor; Kingston officials; the commissioners and proprietors of the Wey navigation; and other officials from Guildford and even Godalming, in addition to the previous £100 estate holders, were entitled to sit and vote; the only ameliorative provision being that the quorum was fixed as low as eleven of their number.

Strengthened thus numerically, and fortunately more effectively otherwise, the new commission entered upon the opening era with new enthusiasm and quickened hopes. They were authorised compulsorily to make and acquire towpaths, to purchase the old flash locks, and above all "to erect and maintain pounds or turnpikes where locks or weirs are now made use of." They divided the River into six districts: (1) from London Bridge to the City Stone, (2) thence to Boulter's, (3) to Mapledurham, (4) to Shillingford, (5) to Oxford, (6) to Cricklade. It will immediately be remarked that an invasion was made, in respect of the first or lowest of these districts, upon the ancient claims of the City of London. These rights were indeed expressly reserved elsewhere in the Act; but the ambiguity caused a great stir amongst the fathers; and I shall shew that the matter was soon regulated. In fact as early as November, 1771, the commissioners themselves passed the self repressing resolution that they had no power to erect any "weir or turnpike" below the "City Stone near Stanes Bridge."

The Act, however, contained, in addition to

The Thames Commissioners 125

some local restrictions particularised in my List, one extraordinary and stultifying general provision. In view of the anticipated building of pound locks, and the consequent disuse of the old flash weirs, it was provided that, wherever craft were diverted from the old to the new passage, there should be paid to the old proprietors by the commissioners "such and the same tolls as such owners would have been entitled to" had the barges passed through the old weirs. It is an egregious example of a vested interest imposing itself upon a new and struggling public betterment. It went even further: the old proprietors were actually relieved of their ancient task of collecting these unearned dues. Another mistake, soon rectified, was the limiting of barges to a draught of only three feet. The 1751 Act had allowed four feet.

The Act fixed the dimensions of the locks to be built. With a view to barges being constructed or reduced within the necessary measurements an extract from the Act was posted at the weirs, and at all the Riverside towns from Windsor to Oxford. In October, 1771, a toll of a halfpenny per ton was placed on all barges between these places. Four oared and pleasure craft were subjected to a charge of 1/- at the new locks; two oars, skiffs and punts sixpence; with free return the same day. For a short time punts accompanying barges passed free; but this concession was repealed at Michaelmas, 1772.

The commission soon set to work obtaining suggestions for improvements. They prescribed two regular flashes weekly: on Tuesdays and Fridays; and fixed the hour at which every miller between Oxford and Staines should pass the accumulated water through his weir, each being required to pen it back to a stated level. In 1770 James Brindley recommended about twelve of what he something atrociously called "cistern locks" as sufficient between Boulter's and Mortlake. The number, it may be remarked, has been ultimately arrived at. An item of his scheme, which it needed a century and a quarter to achieve, in effect if not in letter, was a dam between Mortlake and Kew Bridge, with a lock on each bank, to enable craft to reach Isleworth and Kingston in one tide. This district was then full of shoals which at ebb made it quite unnavigable.

Their earliest large enterprise was the present series of locks between Boulter's and Sonning inclusive; except Cookham, which was not built till much later. The history of all these stations is in my List.

In an article in the *Gentleman's Magazine* for February, 1771, upon a canal from Reading to Monkey Island, it is stated that "the expence of taking a barge of 120 tons burthen" between these points "has been proved to be 50*l*. and the passage cannot be performed in less than 3 days, often 3

The Thames Commissioners

weeks, and sometimes 2 months." This cost is surely absurdly exaggerated; Griffiths, as I have shewn, states £14 for "all the locks" between London and Lechlade. Perhaps the men's wages, for the longest of the times named, are included.

In a Bodleian MS. occur the following "Extracts from the Navigation Rolls with remarks pointing out the proper method of reducing the price of freight, by a Commissioner, printed for C. Bathurst: London 1772."

"A Clause in the late Act directed enquiry into the prices formerly paid at the locks. I have enquired into this, and attribute the advance in freight to the advance in lock tolls. The Spirit of Benevolence to [flash] lock-owners first appeared at Abingdon in 1751, and soon diffused itself down River, and shone at last with distinguished lustre at Reading in the *Orkney Arms*. [Unless my conjecture in Chapter VII be correct, the point of the irony is missing, owing to the lamentable obscurity in which the records of the 1751 Commission repose.] Application for redress to Parliament produced grants of further powers, which the Commissioners are now trying to use; but unfortunately, whereas they were formerly invested with sole right and use of the water in the river, this privilege enjoyed under former Acts seems now lost: in maintenance of such right every bargemaster was formerly able twice a year to require the gates at each mill to be shut down for 2 hours for an upward barge; and at all times whatever water could be spared from the necessities of the barges was allowed for the use of the mills. The new Act seems to alter this, and to lay down that the river must supply a head of water ' sufficient to work the mills whatever becomes of the barges ; and if it should happen that the mills should be obstructed by the improper construction, use or repair of the new turnpike pounds, full and adequate satisfaction shall be made for such inconvenience and damage.' Let the miller compare the state of things before the turnpike pounds were put in, when he was obliged to keep his locks, bucks and gates open 3 hours at every flash, to open for back flashes, and to continue his lock open for 3 or 4 hours or more during the tedious passage of upward barges through the lock : now he will lose nothing but the contents of a turnpike pound. This upward passage may now be performed in less than half an hour through a turnpike pound if it be erected near the lower end of the gull. Barges will never be compelled as they used to be to wait half or a whole day for a flash during a dry season, and so we may reckon the saving of a week between Boulters and Abingdon, if the Commissioners are again vested with the use of the water instead of the millers.

" Well, we applied to Parliament to enable us to effect these improvements. They would of course be expensive. We therefore asked to be allowed to levy an additional penny on every chaldron of coal [36 heaped bushels, = $25\frac{1}{2}$ cwt.] imported at London. It would be quite fair. The Thames counties had been paying for seventy years a sixpenny duty on every chaldron they consumed, and are to pay it for sixty years more, purely for the ornament and convenience of London. The measure however was rejected, although no exclusive advantage was asked for the country : the city must have partaken of it. Opponents had a scheme of their own : a canal in fact. This however was rejected without a division. The public suffered

The Thames Commissioners

from the defeat of both schemes. Now we ought to have a regular erection of turnpike pounds and exchange of hirelings for horses. That would afford some relief, but not enough. Many skilful people say that the navigation cannot be carried on without flashes. [It is not yet.] I am sure that the surveyor's plan of making the river like a canal and restraining the barges to 3 ft. at all seasons is calculated merely for the benefit of the millowners. It is evident from the following records that a large increase of expence has been laid on the barges within these twenty years; that the advance in the tolls at different locks is unequal and partial; and that unless you allow an interested person to sit in Judgment the orders made at Reading August 5, 1754 are wholly void and illegal.

"The fact is that the Commissioners ought to have had powers given them to reduce these [flash lock] tolls; if not what need, on p. 34 of the new Act, of the clause ordering enquiry into the tolls formerly paid? Equity would require such a change. The tolls now are paid for nothing in many cases; the disuse of the antiquated locks, the saving of expence in shutting them, the lowering of the lockshutters' wages, the non-necessity of sustaining a strong breastwork of piles on the upper side of the lock pool to prevent the mounds from being battered down by the upward barges, as well as the disuse of the winches and boats ordered to be provided for the convenience of the bargemen. As to the bucks, weirs, and wastegates, the owners of mills must support these for their own convenience and protection if no barges navigated the river, and therefore those articles ought not to enter into their profit and loss account. Some locks are leased; any reduction of tolls would of course have to begin on expiry of the lease."

I

Lists are subjoined of "Prices formerly and now paid for every barge of 150 tons from Abingdon to Boulters Lock." The former prices I have added to my Table; those "now" paid agree *pro rata* with the 1771 column therein.

Almost every sentence of this vivid and interesting document is illuminating or suggestive. It contains many tantalising allusions to the difficulties and labours of the commission of 1751. An important point is the power, alleged to have been granted in 1751 and withdrawn in 1770, over the use of the water in favour of the navigation as against the millers; and the bargemasters' rights in this connection. There is, too, very much truth in the contention that the new pound locks were making matters much easier for the millers; and that the latter ought to have been deprived of a large proportion of their tolls for the old stations. Instead of which, as I have pointed out, not only was this now unearned income confirmed to them, but they were even relieved of the cost and trouble of collecting it.

The point regarding an allowance out of the coal dues was repeated, perhaps more than once, during the subsequent history of this commission.

In January, 1773, it was ordered that all the "old Locks" from Sonning to Boulter's were to be fastened up as soon as the adjacent pounds were available for traffic; though the "lockshutters" were

The Thames Commissioners 131

permitted to pass any barge, "on request," by the old passage until the following May 1, on payment of the toll fixed for the pound. The toll collectors were instructed to collect their charges before passing vessels into the new locks; and were simultaneously to secure the old lock dues. If any old lock owner chose to employ his own man for the latter purpose he might do so, provided he rendered a monthly account to the commission, and relinquished his claim upon them for such traffic.

A little trait of statutory beneficence was exhibited by the commissioners in October, 1773. Owing to the use of horses for towing many "hirelings" had been thrown out of employment; and a resolution was accordingly passed that to men who for five years previously had made towing their business, and had never been chargeable to their parishes except through sickness, floods, or hard frost, "when the Navigation was stop'd," they would allow half of whatever the respective parishes were allowing, as an additional assistance.

Rates of freight were settled under the Act; and seem, for several years at least, to have been revised quarterly. Below are figures of different dates, being for coal by the chaldron and for other goods by the ton.

From London to	1772	1773	1774	1777	1793
Windsor	8/-				8/-
Maidenhead and Searle's Wharf [near Boulter's]	9/-	7/6	7/-	6/6	8/-
Boulter's and Spade Oak		7/6	7/6	7/6	
Marlow	10/-				8/-
New Lock [Hurley] and Spade Oak		8/-	8/-	8/-	
Mill End and New Lock		8/6	8/6	8/6	
Henley and Mill End	12/-	9/-	9/-	9/-	9/-
Shiplake and Hurley		9/6	9/6	9/6	
Kennet's Mouth and Shiplake	15/-	10/6	10/6	10/6	9/6

Malt by the quarter varied between 7d. and 1s. to these places; flour by the "load" between 5s. and 8s.

In 1774 an amending Act 14 Geo. III, c. 91, was passed. It recites the deadlock that had ensued upon the legislation of 1770 in respect of the two districts between Boulter's and London Bridge: how that the commission had been granted jurisdiction; were, however, concurrently prohibited from encroaching upon the City's rights below Staines and from erecting any new locks below Boulter's; and that meanwhile the City had no authority to instal improvements: the consequence being that these fifty miles of River could receive no effective amendment. It further recited that the City was prepared to spend £10,000 out of its own estates towards the betterment of the River. The first or lowest district, therefore, between London and Staines was removed

DEDHAM LOCK, on the Suffolk Stour. The cross beam in front of the figures illustrates the strides alluded to on

The Thames Commissioners 133

from the survey of the commission and restored to the care of the Navigation Committee of the City of London : to the history of whose subsequent dealings with the Thames below Staines I devote a separate and later chapter.

Under this Act "Morough O'Bryen esquire of Taplow Court" was granted certain privileges in respect of Taplow Mill Stream, the easternmost channel of the River at Boulter's ; which hold good to the present day, and are detailed below under this head.

No towpaths might be driven through gardens, orchards, parks, lawns, or any enclosed ground, without the consent of the owner.

In this same year 1774 a timber stride was ordered across all the new locks, to prevent barges and other vessels entering with their masts up. I do not think a single specimen of these barriers survives upon the Thames ; doubtless the advent of steam vessels, especially with their early high funnels, had much to do with their removal. My illustration is from Dedham lock on the Suffolk Stour.

Special dwellings also for the keepers, adjacent to their work, began to demand attention this year. They took at first the shape of only "small wooden houses," at Temple, Hurley, Hambledon and Sonning ; which, as they cost only £12 each, cannot have been much more substantial, or capacious, than the little cabins or offices still at the lock sides, in addition to the residences. Before long small brick built cottages began to be supplied; but much difficulty occasionally arose in persuading landowners to sell the necessary sites, and valuing juries had to be summoned, as provided in the Act of 1770.

Further in 1774 a regulation was made that no barge should be allowed to enter a lock from below unless there were sufficient water to allow her to clear the cut above; as lying in the lock or the narrow cut was naturally found obstructive of the navigation. The towing also between Windsor and Boulter's received much special attention. This stretch of about $7\frac{1}{2}$ miles was divided for towing purposes into three fairly equal stages: the lowest ascending to "the gate going into Mr. Grover's meadow called Lower Mowsham's," perhaps about opposite Surley Hall. The middle stage went up as far as "the Moat at the Lower End of Farmer Lucas's Garden at Amerden," just below the present Bray lock. The highest ended at Boulter's lock, then on the east side of the natural stream. The lowest stage was to cost, for horse towing, $11\frac{1}{4}$d. per ten tons per mile, the middle 1s. 1d., and the uppermost $11\frac{1}{2}$d.

In 1775 a new Act repealed the mistaken provision of 1770 restricting barges to a whole year draught of only three feet; and permitted them to

The Thames Commissioners 135

navigate between November 1 and May 1, the season of abundant water, loaded to a depth of 3 ft. 8 in.

The details engraved upon Bowen's *Map* of this year are interesting if somewhat obscure. His figures of tolls, which will be found in my Table, differ considerably from contemporary schedules. They appear in a corner of the map, prefaced with a note: "The Thames is navigable for vessels of 140 tons to Wallingford, and of 70 Tons to Lechlade, from whence ye largest pay at ye different Lo^{ks} as mentioned below. The general rule at the Turnpikes or Pounds lately erected is for a Barge going upwards 4^d per Ton at ye 1st pd & 1^d per T at every other." The fourpence at the first pound doubtless refers to Boulter's, then the first above London. At the end of his schedule of tolls he says: "Freight 30/- per ton the whole length of the Navigation; shorter stages in proportion." This is quite irreconcileable with my figures a page or two back. A further uncertainty arises from another statement: "Turnpikes belonging to 8 of the above Locks [Sonning to Boulter's inclusive, except Cookham] for vessels of 70 Tons £3. 12. 10." The sum does not quite agree with the contemporary figures given at these stations in my List. It amounts to one shilling and a halfpenny per ton; whereas the official rates were a penny at the seven higher stations and fourpence at Boulter's: only eleven pence in all.

In this year 1775 a fine of 2s. 6d. was attached to injuring the timbers of the locks through levering against them with barge poles. These first locks were not of solid timber or stone walls, such as are now upon the Thames; their sides were of spaced-out piles between which the water freely penetrated, as may be seen in Owen's view of Shiplake lock in 1810: which I present.

In 1776 the average crew of a 140 ton barge consisted of six men. The usual wage was about 15s., which their keep brought up to about a guinea each, weekly.

From information supplied to the City this autumn I gather the following "Account of Quantity of Tonnage from London to the several places upwards"; I imagine yearly.

	Tons		£	s.	
"To Boulters Lock & Above	69,770				
Maidenhead	5,560				
Windsor	15,880				
Stains	7,460	98,670 at 4d.	1644.	10	
Chertsey	5,470				
Weybridge	1,000				
Guildford	17,026				
Shepperton	5,076	28,572 at 3d.	357.	3	
Sunbury & Walton	1,740				
Moulsey	9,175				
Ditton	8,850				
Kingston	9,550	29,315 at 2d.	244.	5.	10
			2,245.	18.	10"

SHIPLAKE LOCK AND MILL. Drawn by S. Owen about 1810. Illustrates the original locks of the Thames Commissioners. See opposite page. First built 1773; rebuilt 1787.

To face p. 136.

The Thames Commissioners

In April, 1779, James Leonard, bargemaster of Abingdon (you may still discover the name in Riverside places, at Shepperton and elsewhere), was permitted "to go free through all the pound locks for one voyage, on account of the great Misfortune he has received by his Boat being sunk at Benson Lock" (weir that is; the pound was not built till 1788). This is the earliest grant I have noted of this form of compensation. Similar petitions became very common later; but it occurred to the commissioners that overloading might be a frequent cause of the accidents, and overloading being frequently proved it often happened that no compensation was allowed.

In the summer of 1780 it was reported that the first erected pound locks, and the towing gates and bridges, after, be it noted, only nine years' service or less, were "in a General State of Decay and will soon want to be rebuilt." It is proof of what I have already remarked: that they were of very shoddy construction; not like their Jacobean predecessors. The horse towing path was pushed through as far as Pangbourne this year; although of course the old track for human haulage already existed. During this year also one Thomas Hunt submitted a project for towing barges by steam power, forty-five years before the first railway was opened in England.

In 1781 a curious little history emerges, illustrating a perhaps unexpected difficulty the commissioners had to contend with. Several constables, charged with warrants of distress against bargeowners who had illegally overloaded their vessels and failed to pay their fines, had made no return of the warrants; and it was believed they would not act upon them unless compelled. (The commissioners had a sort of unofficial staff of informers in respect of offenders in the matter of overloading.) They determined to make an example by indicting John Ball (ominous name!), supposed constable of the parish of St. Helen's, Abingdon, at the Easter sessions. Ball declared that he was not constable of the said parish, but of the borough of Abingdon; and that he was advised to defend the indictment on the ground that "he had no business with a warrant." The commissioners adhered to their purpose; whereupon Ball climbed down and gave security for the fine with whose collection he had been charged; and the prosecution was stayed upon his undertaking to sign and insert in the Oxford and Reading newspapers an expression of regret for his dereliction of duty. It seems to me very probable that his hesitation in executing the warrant may have been based upon some subconscious memory of the ancient decentralised independence of these provincial boroughs: a subject upon which Mr. F. J. Snell has much interesting matter in his *Customs of Old England*.

The Thames Commissioners 139

Five years later I again find the "Constable of Abingdon" refusing to proceed against John Collins another local overloading bargemaster. It does not appear if this constable was the same John Ball. Doubtless these provincial officers were very loth to offend their neighbours at the bidding of some vague and distant Authority of so few years' standing. A note of Mr. Belloc's in his *Stane Street* may be thought to the point : " The local power of propertied men has been nearly continuously stronger than the general power of the central government."

In 1781 occurs the earliest suggestion of building and rebuilding pound locks in stone or brick. The superior immediate cheapness of fir timber still, however, prevailed.

The final schemes for the Severn Canal, still seven years from its realisation, were being actively discussed in 1782. In a pamphlet published this year upon the subject an *ex parte* description is given of the alleged contemporary condition of the River. " From good information we can aver that the navigation of the river Thames, especially between Oxford and Lechlade, is in the most unfavourable state possible, a circumstance which the common council of the city of London have well considered, by causing surveys to be made of different parts of the river, a canal from Isleworth to Maidenhead seems to be a measure well thought of ; it will appear from an inspection of the map, that a continuation to Reading, and thence to Lechlade, will be a consequence naturally resulting from the difficulties which attend the navigation of those upper parts of the river, obstructed at present by shoals, by private locks, on a principle as barbarous as the times in which they were first made, and totally inadequate to any regular conveyance of merchandise."

In June, 1783, it had become evident to the commissioners that the remoter navigation must be greatly improved if the anticipated growth of traffic from the Severn Canal was to be effectively accommodated. Amongst other difficulties it appeared that in winter, when the water was high enough to pass seventy ton barges drawing four feet, vessels with a load no higher than their sides could hardly pass through the low and narrow arches of St. John's, Radcot, Godstow and Folly Bridges (the old structure in each case). These bridges, therefore, *nefandum dictu*, would have to be enlarged and raised. Many fresh locks were urged, as at Abingdon, Cleeve, Goring and Pangbourne; but were not considered necessary at Day's, Hart's by Basildon, and Moulsford.

During the same year it was suggested to the commissioners that the old ships being broken up at Deptford might yield a supply of sound, cheap

The Thames Commissioners 141

material for building and repairing locks. The experiment was tried; at Marlow, for instance, in 1784; but did not yield very satisfactory results. It is quite possible that some of the older locks, however, contained within living memory sturdy timbers from the old men-o'-war.

Some *Rules & Orders* were made at Marlow in September, 1783. The following are pertinent:

> "*Fourteenth.* No person or persons whom soever shall erect any new bucks, or weirs, or drive or affix any piles or stakes without the permission and consent of seven or more Commissioners.
>
> "*Fifteenth.* That the occupiers of the old flash locks and mills are hereby ordered at all times when possible to keep the water between the high and low water marks set by the Commissioners, and for neglect, the keeper of the pound-lock adjoining is authorised to draw, open, or shut the sluices and floodgates of the bucks, overfalls, and standards of the old flash-locks, and to apply to the occupier of the mills to draw up or shut down the floodgates thereof."

Which opens vistas, day dreams, moving pictures of a thousand scenes of altercation, imprecation, abuse and highly probable personal violence in the heart of these lonely places far from headquarters. Without doubt the old newspapers would disclose many a human document of the sort pertinent to my history; but who, unaided and alone, with a thousand cares of the world, can hope to attack such a search?

The commission in July, 1784, approached the City for financial assistance towards improving the navigation. All the works hitherto completed had been built from public moneys borrowed under authority of the Acts upon the security of the tolls. They were anxious to proceed to the further improvements urged upon them, but investors were hanging back. They therefore appealed that a portion of the coal dues should be set aside by the City in their common interest. The Council agreed that, if Parliament would grant a drawback on the dues, £15,000 thereof should be devoted to improvements between Mapledurham and Oxford: a district not yet attacked by the commission; one third of the balance towards completing the works in progress east of London Stone and buying up private tolls; another third to discharging the debts of the commission, which had now accrued to £28,900, and to improvements between the Stone and Mapledurham; and the residue "to purchase the old Lock Dues, etc., and also the Horse Towing Paths, and all other Paths; so that, finally, the Navigation of the River Thames and Isis, westward of London, may be perfectly free from Tolls of every kind." I have not discovered what came of this amiable and public spirited proposal, so characteristic of the City; nor the reason of its apparent failure.

By 1787 the commission had surmounted their

The Thames Commissioners 143

financial difficulties; and had proceeded to various works in their fourth district. They had succeeded in borrowing another £10,000; the Act of the following year states their liability at £38,900. At this time an amusing attempt at evasion of tolls occurred. In March, 1787, one Thomas Plumbridge, a Reading bargemaster, had worked two barges down to London, of 140 and 71 tons respectively, upon which a charge of fourpence per ton was due at each lock. Failing to secure a return cargo he "floated his small Barge into the large one with a view to save the paying the Toll" on the former, "conceiving he had a Right to do so." He was quickly undeceived; and the craft detained until he paid the dues. It was discovered also that bargemen were endeavouring to pass floats or rafts of timber, towed behind them, toll free through the locks.

The above mentioned Act 28 Geo. III, c. 51, was passed in 1788. It authorised a further borrowing of £25,000; and enabled a toll of fourpence per ton to be levied at any lock; cuts to be made of three miles in length for pound locks (a little draughting ambiguity which led to subsequent difficulty); and negotiations to be completed, as already described, with the Oxford-Burcot Authority. Barges were restricted to a maximum draught of 3 ft. 10 in.

About this time, when Thames navigation appeared at length in a fair way to pass under efficient public control, Robert Mylne emerges as surveyor to the commission : a man of many ideas, not all acceptable ; and of a heart which not all his zeal for improvements nor all his association with stone and iron could rob of its attractive touches of sympathy. One or two of these I shall note in my List ; I will take occasion to allude here to his rescue of Wren's epitaph from the crypt of St. Paul's Cathedral and its erection where we know it. He lies buried at Great Amwell, from whose enchanting hill his ghost may overlook the waters of the New River and the upper Lea : a halting place of my own ancestors.

A little earlier than the date at which I have now arrived he had reported to the commission that the River was in a very unnavigable condition, and full of obstructions ; and it was due perhaps to his persistent recommendations that in 1791 they began, under their statutory powers, to purchase the private weirs. A beginning was to be made with those adjoining the new pound locks. It may be to many a novelty, in these days when, if the matter attract any lay consideration, lock and weir are superficially regarded as two coeval and inseparable parts of one machine, immemorially under one management and of common origin, to remark that the weirs accompanying the well known locks, sometimes close at hand,

The Thames Commissioners 145

sometimes too distant for their thunder to be heard, are, in the very large majority of cases above Bray, many centuries older than the pound locks; and remained, moreover, under separate ownership and control long after most of the latter had been installed. Mylne saw, as indeed no observer could fail to see what a dead weight this dual ownership and management imposed upon the conservancy of the River, rendering the new works, as I have already remarked, scarcely an improvement at all. For it is evident that the weir, and not the lock, is the key of the position; and that its occupier can quickly render the latter valueless by self interested regulation of the water. Mylne, therefore, pressed again and again for the purchase of the weirs, so that the sole control of the stream might be in the commission. "Until that is done," he wrote, "all efforts to improve the navigation will be weak and ineffective. Some of the proprietors are poor, and can't afford to repair them; some of the Weirs are on lease, and it is unreasonable to expect should be amended on a short term of Years. The Working of the Weirs ought to go hand in hand with the Pounding of the water by the New Locks. It was never yet found that two seperate Interests could be so moulded in their Conduct, as to make one general Effort, pointing to the same end. There ought to be a Lockkeeper and receiver of Dues at each Pound Lock."

K

There usually was; but not often a Conservancy official. What Mylne is really attacking is the absurd yet not wholly surprising system of employing the neighbouring miller, or a man in his power, as lockkeeper; whereby the commissioners so long delivered themselves and their works into the hands of their enemies. The man's real interest was the mill; at the navigation he sometimes openly mocked; time after time Mylne gives proof that while taking the commissioners' pay he was neglecting and even thwarting their interests. In 1802, to anticipate a little, he returns to the subject. It was being discovered that not only the mills but the fishery also was a frequent source of the evil; to whose pursuit the lockkeepers were prone to sacrifice their official duties. He declares: "It is absolutely necessary for *some one* to state to you, frankly and firmly, that all the Rights of Fisheries at the Wears corresponding to the Pound-locks should be purchased, leaving the other parts of their manorial rights on the river itself to the present Proprietors."

Charles Truss, the City's clerk of the navigation works, in preferring canals to the natural River in 1791, says: "I have often known many thousand sacks of flour detained by floods upon the river when the city has been extremely distressed for the want of a supply."

In consequence of much urgent persuasion from

The Thames Commissioners 147

the Severn Canal Company the sixth district, above Oxford, underwent in 1793 very minute inspection; and in June "the several owners and occupiers of Buscot, West's, Hart's, Clark's, Tadpole, Tenfoot, Duxford, Shifford's, Langley's, Hart's, Brookin's, Pinkill, and Bold Weirs" were requested to repair the same and fit them for holding up a sufficient head of water. The flashes also were subjected to further regulation. Owing to frequent western flashes at uncertain times and without previous notice very few barges were able to take advantage of them, and the River was drained to no purpose. It was therefore ordered that only two flashes should be run each week, on Saturday night and Wednesday morning: from Hurley downwards. These days vary, it will be noticed, from the settlement under the 1770 Act on page 126. The Saturday flash corresponds with Mylne's graphic description of the scenes at Windsor Bridge, quoted in my List.

Before a parliamentary committee in 1793 interesting evidence was given as to the number of horses required to tow a seventy ton barge against stream over different stretches of the River. The place names are horribly misprinted in the report; the clerk evidently misunderstood them as they were broadly burred off by the Oxford witness. I have corrected most of them. Stadbury, the first, was the meadow on the west side of the lock island at

Shepperton; or perhaps the whole island; if it was then indeed an island, and not merely a peninsula joined to the left bank, across whose narrow neck the floods occasionally broke. It is called Sawbridge Island in one old map.

" From Stadbury to Windsor	10 or 12
Windsor to Amerden Bank	8
To Boulter's	10 or 12
Boulter's to Poulter's Horsing	6
To Hedsor	8
To Spade Oak	8
To Marlow	8
To Henley	5 or 6
Thence to Kennet's Mouth	8
To Geddington [Gatehampton]	10
To Chamberhole [Wallingford]	6
To Benson	7 or 8
To above Abingdon	10 or 11, sometimes 12
From thence we take our own horses	5
Oxford to Lechlade	3 Boats to take up 70 tons, 3 Horses to each Boat.

"A Horse line costs £10 or £11, which if it lasts 3 voyages [a voyage was out and back] is looked upon as a great deal."

At intervals during the last decade of the eighteenth century the River below Boulter's caused the commission much anxiety. They had been at the expense of much local patching and mending, and were reaping no return by way of tolls. Pound

The Thames Commissioners

locks were becoming an urgent necessity in the district, as a source of efficiency and incidentally of revenue. The instant threat of a canal between Boulter's and Isleworth was also goading them into action; and at least two or three locks, with weirs, began to be specified as requisite to set this part of the Thames in order and thwart the canal. It was, however, a vital preliminary to the building of these stations that the prohibition in the 1770 Act should be repealed; but public and expert opinion alike were hostile. Brindley, Whitworth, and Mylne, a formidable trio, all declared in 1794 that these locks "would not be an effectual remedy for the inconveniences of the navigation, and would be attended with serious injury to landowners." Very reluctantly therefore the commission abandoned certain works which had already been initiated.

A noteworthy manifestation of this opposition is afforded by a discoloured two-page folio amongst the Guildhall *London Pamphlets*, dated January 30, 1794, and published by "A Freeholder on the Thames." The author appeals to the "Landowners on the Banks of the Thames, between Boulter's Lock and Isleworth; and especially those of the level Country between Maidenhead and Staines," protesting against the contemplated developments. He writes: "The present alarming Design of a

Junto of the Commissioners of the Thames Navigation, *to Erect Locks and Weirs in the River*, which Nature has formed for the *common Sewer of the Country*, should stimulate all of you to form yourselves into an invincible Phalanx, to oppose the Project." He declares that this Junto, "upon the opinion of an ignorant Carpenter," has not only resolved to make two pound locks in the River, one above and one below Windsor, but has also determined to apply to Parliament for powers to instal others wherever it may choose, notwithstanding that the three engineers just named had stated so adverse an opinion. He objects, in brief, the risk of floods and the statutory prohibition. Who his ignorant carpenter was I do not discover; he reappears almost immediately. The view of the Thames as a "common Sewer" led within a century to a horrible state of things, which large numbers of people now living can well remember, and which needed herculean efforts to remedy.

Vanderstegen, a prominent commissioner of his day, combats this attack in a small octavo of the same year, to which I return. Another contemporary hostile publication is *Reasons for Preferring the London Canal from Boulter's Lock to Isleworth*. The age was one, as I remark elsewhere, of commercial salvation by canal. The Severn Canal and part of the Berks and Wilts were built within it; and

The Thames Commissioners 151

innumerable others, near or distant from the Thames, were projected and sometimes realised. One was discussed to connect Lechlade and Abingdon. The number indeed of proposed artificial watercourses was almost as numerous as we are asked piously to believe exist within the friendly and communicative State of Mars. The particular cutting recommended by this pamphlet was intended, as its title indicates, to leave the River at Taplow mill and run almost due east, across the southward sag of the Thames, through Twickenham to Isleworth. One of the negative advantages anticipated was that the alternative plan of improving the River itself was alleged to necessitate fifteen new locks below Boulter's. The new route was to save eighteen miles out of the River's thirty-seven; £11 per journey in haulage; and to reduce the time expended from three days in the abundant winter season, five days, six, or even a fortnight in summer, to a constant eight or ten hours. Some concluding rhetoric in the over punctuated and highly italicised manner of the age declares that Mylne's report in favour of this canal was rejected for the proposal of a *"Windsor Carpenter"*; and, ironically, that "the Thames must flourish while Mr. Harris, the *Oxford Gaoler*, is employed as an extra official Engineer." The project was never realised; to be cretinised forthwith by the railways.

It was stated during this year that there was "No

Person to take any Care of the Works between the [Severn Canal] Junction and Old Nan's Weir."

Vanderstegen's *State of The Thames*, just alluded to, contains some information upon the time taken by barges in traversing various parts of the River.

> "On account of unloading [at the weirs, or into lighters at the shoals], a boat from Lechlade is three days getting to Oxford; from Oxford to Sunning two days; from Sunning to Boulter's one day; from Boulter's to Brentford one day; & to London, as the tide serves, being eight days. When the river is compleated, above Oxford, it will be gone easier in a day less. A boat is six days returning from London to Oxford. A boat goes from Wallingford to London in four days; return in five days. From Reading to London in three days; return in four."

In February of this year "Mr. Joseph Searle who keeps a Barge trading from Boulters to London delivered in an account of the average Expence of navigating a Barge of 128 Tons and a lighter of 56 Tons from Boulters to London and back amounting per voyage to £65 : 8 : 0."

The frequent flashing still resorted to sometimes drained the locks and cuts almost dry; and it was ordered, therefore, at this time, that flashes should be drawn from not more than two stations above the stranded barges; in no case under low water mark; and never more than once for any one vessel.

The new Act in 1795, 35 Geo. III, c. 106, followed upon Mylne's reports in 1791-3. The

The Thames Commissioners 153

necessity of more locks and of more delicately graduated weirs was forcing recognition; and a horse towing path was becoming urgent. The Act declares that a free and continuous public horse path would be a great benefit, and confers upon the commission powers of compulsory land purchase for the purpose, subject to certain restrictions such as, amongst others, that where a house had been built close to the waterside, or where the required land was in use as a garden or orchard, it might not be taken. Indeed I believe that extremely little was, and perhaps under such conditions could be, effected in this desirable direction: a failure from whose unfortunate results the continuity of the towpath suffers to this very day in many familiar places. It was also ordered that the lock tolls should be made uniform. This also became a dead letter; it was mentioned as long after as 1865 that the rate varied at almost every pound. I fancy this was due to the varying demands of the millers; variations thus caused exist today upon the Lea Navigation. Power was given to build more locks; but not below Boulter's without notice to the Corporation of London, and only then subject to the advice of engineers. Tolls might be farmed: a permission of which advantage was subsequently taken, as I shall relate.

Chiefly in consequence of pressure from the Severn Canal Company tolls were reduced from 4d. per ton per voyage to $2\frac{1}{2}$d., during 1795.

In 1796 the commission decided to build houses at all the locks, and to compel the keepers to live in them. During this year certain bargemasters took leave to publish in the Reading newspapers new, unauthorised rates of freight. The commission thereupon gave public notice that the official figures were :

From Reading to London :	Malt by the quarter	1s.
	Flour by the load	8s.
From London to Reading :	Coal by the chaldron	}11s.
	Other goods by the ton	

an all round advance upon the 1793 figures on page 132. A penalty of £20 was attached to higher demands.

In 1797 a bye-law was considered very desirable "for the more effectual preventing heavy laden barges obstructing the Navigable Channel." It does not appear what regulation was made; it is however a fact that much inconvenience of the sort existed. These vessels were the first to ground upon the shallows, preventing others which could have floated over from doing so. They also necessarily passed the flash locks on the first of the flash, so that when the turn of the lighter craft arrived there was often insufficient water left on the cill; and their excess of burthen was itself illegal.

In the same year it was deemed necessary to raise the toll from $2\frac{1}{2}$d. to 3d. The commissioners were in

The Thames Commissioners

arrear with their interest, and the recent reduction had not proved a success.

For the purpose of letting off an August flood the gates of some of the locks above Abingdon had been "forcibly opened," and thereby damaged. For an interesting reason: that there had formerly been no waterway where the locks now stood, the commission decided that they could not legally permit this forcible relief. It seems a somewhat fine point: the alleged illegality of allowing the water to run freely through; considering that it might pass through by lockfuls in practical continuity, if so desired.

In March, 1798, the half-dozen lockkeepers above Oxford were agitating for increased pay; and it was thought expedient to endeavour to farm these stations, under the powers granted by the 1795 Act. Nothing however was done to this purpose for over thirty years.

I now present a schedule, dated July, 1798, of all the pound locks and official ferries then extant, with the keepers' names and current monthly wages. These particulars are embodied in my List also, under the various stations; but it has its own separate interest as a connected document. An earlier register of 1793, which I discovered later, is the earliest complete schedule in existence; the particulars from it are also attached. The keepers' names are identical in each, unless otherwise noted.

156 The Thames Highway

	1798		1793	Per Ann.
Romney	John Flexman	3 5 0	[not built]	
Boulters	Rd. Ray	3 5 0		33 16s.
Marlow	Geo. Phelps ("pound & stop-lock keeper")	1 19 0		23 8s.
Temple	Geo. Cordery	2 5 6	Cawdrey	27 6s.
Hurley	John Gould (also Hambledon ferryman)	3 5 0		39 -
Hambleden	Caleb Gould	1 14 8		20 16s.
Marsh	Thos. Honey (or Hooney)	1 8 0		13 -
Beggar's Hole Ferry [Bolney]	Joseph Jackson	1 6 0	George Jackson	15 12s.
Lashbrook Ferry		1 5 8	Sanders	13 -
Shiplake	Wm. Small	1 8 0		13 -
Sonning lock & ferry	Thos. Hall	2 0 0	Jas. Pither at ferry	14 19s.
			Lock Wage	15 12s.
Caversham	Wm. Leech	1 4 0		13 -
Purley ferries	A. M. Storer, Esq.	1 12 0		
,, lock (Mapledurham)	Alex. Geddes	1 4 0		14 6s.
Whitchurch	Widow Walters	1 4 0		14 6s.
Goring	Thos. Child	1 4 0		14 6s.
Cleeve	John Pitman	1 4 0	Charles P.	14 6s.
Benson	Joseph Ashby	1 6 0	with ferry	15 12s.
KeaneHedge ferry	Wm. Lafford	15 0		7 4s.
Day's	James Batting	1 4 0	with ferry	14 8s.
Cullum ferry	Danl Gibbons	1 4 0	Widow Hewit	7 4s.
Sutton bridges (the small weir bridges; main bridge not yet built)	Thos. Keep	12 0		7 4s.
Abingdon	Rd. Bradfield	1 4 0	with ferry	14 8s.
Sandford	Wm. Beckley	17 0		
Ifley	John Danby	1 2 0	} "Let"	
Osney	—	17 0	Mrs. Hill	9 2s.
Godstow	James Bishop	17 0		9 2s.
Pinkill	Thos. Brocks "on Accot of the distance of the residence."	1 0 0		8 8s.
Rushey	Joseph Winter	17 0	Rudge	8 8s.
Buscot	Eliz. Gearing	17 0	Richard G.	8 8s.
St. John's	Wm. Wells	17 0		8 8s.

The Thames Commissioners

While the later register was being drawn up there was "much dissatisfaction prevailing in the upper parts of the River on account of the lowness of the salaries."

In the autumn of 1799 the commission were aggrieved by the "Navigation shallop of the Committee of Navigation of the City of London" passing up to Reading and back with the committee on board and refusing to pay toll at the locks. A demand for the dues was forwarded; and in reply the town clerk requested a note of the amount claimed. The incident is mentioned in the City records also; but in neither account is the settlement defined.

Next summer the establishment of two flashes weekly was again found desirable; and the farming of the upper stations again discussed. In December, 1800, much complaint was prevalent of the excessive raising of the water above head "by the owners and occupiers of the locks and weirs," above and below Oxford, "to the great annoyance of the Inhabitants of the Neighbouring Country and the Injury of the Lands bordering on the River." Offenders were ordered to be prosecuted; and whenever needful all flash locks and floodgates were to remain open.

Chapter VII

THE THAMES COMMISSIONERS (*continued*)

THE nineteenth century opens with an animadversion on the part of the commissioners upon the district below their control. In September, 1801, they were informed "that there is not sufficient Water in the River to admit the Barges to pass in the lower part of the Navigation laden more than 3 ft. in depth and that several Barges have lately been stopp'd in the Shallows about Laleham, Kingston, Hampton and Walton." The only order they felt competent to make was "that no barge should be allowed through Marlow lock drawing more than 3 ft of water, for a month." Lockkeepers were "strictly enjoined not to leave their Pounds full of water nor to permit the sluices at any time to remain open but for the purpose of filling or emptying the Pound." It should be explained that the City had not yet begun to build the series of locks which they ultimately installed up to Penton Hook.

The canal enthusiasts were still very active in

The Thames Commissioners

1802. Two short cuts connecting points above Oxford were much debated: one from Tadpole to Shifford; the other from Langley weir to Botley Mill. Both schemes failed; ostensibly for lack of means, actually through counsel's opinion that the "three miles" allowed for cuts in the Act of 1788 was intended to be cumulative, and not the maximum length of any one cut. The artificial channels made since this date aggregated about a mile and a quarter; and either of the new schemes would raise the total above this supposed statutory limit. I have already commented on the ambiguity. The commissioners decided not to oppose any private enterprise for the purposes named; and would forego the tolls at Pinkhill, Godstow and Osney on such traffic as passed along the new cuts and so avoided their locks; herein displaying much less of the wisdom of the serpent than the old lockowners. In opposition to another proposed canal it was declared, about this time, that

> "from Reading downwards, as far as the Commissioners' jurisdiction extends, there has not in the course of this year (notwithstanding the great length of dry weather) been any Obstruction to the Navigation of Barges laden to the depth of 3 feet except for a short time after the flashes and during the time that Boulters was repairing. About Laleham and Sunbury the Obstruction has been greater, but even there the Navigation has always been open on the flash days with one or two exceptions, and

even then the Vessels might have passed had they not been laden more than 3 feet in depth."

Robert Mylne was insisting in 1802, as already mentioned, that a keeper and cottage ought to be established at every lock, with authority and duty over his own adjacent reaches of the River. "At almost every mill at and below Oxford," he wrote, "and at every fishing weir above Godstow (there being no Mills further up) either the miller or fisherman was generally the lock-shutter; whereas the lock-shutter, as the Commissioners' servant, ought to be the check on the conduct of the millers, and entirely independent of them." In view of this state of things it is interesting to observe the City, a little later, refusing to let land and waste water adjoining their locks for milling purposes. Mylne adds the warning that the weirs were originally so poorly constructed that they could not and must not be strained with the great head of water the new locks provided for. He anticipated that if the official head of water were insisted upon the weirs would blow up, one after another.

The expression "running a wane" occurs in the records for the first time in August, 1803; it means running the water low, usually in order to facilitate repairs to underwater works at the locks and mills.

In January, 1805, the Government appears to have asserted a right to free navigation. The bargemen

The Thames Commissioners

conveying stone and ammunition for his Majesty's service gave verbal notice at Blake's lock at Reading that the Ordnance office would not pay any tolls, and intended to apply for a refund of those already paid. The commission petitioned for reconsideration; with what result does not appear. (I have not included this lock in my List; it lies upon the Kennet, and not on the Thames. It was, however, built about 1802 by the 1770 commission; and has always remained under the Thames Authorities.)

In 1810 Z. Allnutt, secretary to the commission, reported that a total sum of £66,800 had been borrowed; and had been expended, with the annual surplus of the tolls, in building twenty-seven locks, mostly with cuts, "in places where the Water has been anciently penned up for the purpose of working Mills or fishing." This remark about the sites is noticeable; none of the stations on virgin sites, such as Northmoor, Clifton and Old Windsor, had yet been erected.

Two Reports, printed at Oxford in 1811, state that "prior to the making of the Severn Canal, boats of 8 or 10 tons did navigate to Cricklade": prior, that is, to 1789. It is added that "no money was ever expended between that place and Lechlade by the Commissioners," so far as the writer had heard. A statement follows of the proportion observed in distributing the revenue from tolls between the old proprietors and the Authority.

L

"The tolls paid for penning the water, and that paid for the pond locks and horse towing paths, is divided into two parts. The first of these payments to the old lock-owners from Abingdon to Stanes, amounts to 2s. 2d. per ton ; and from Reading to Stanes, 1s. 5d. per ton. The second of these payments, which is applied only to the necessary expences of management and repairs, and to satisfy the interest at 5% of the money borrowed to make the pond locks, towing paths, &c. amounts to *three-pence* per ton only, at each pond lock ; which, as there are 17 pond locks between Abingdon and Stanes, amounts to 4s. 3d. per ton ; and as there are ten pond locks between Reading and Abingdon, amounts to 2s. 6d. per ton."

On payment of this downward toll "a vessel is allowed to return up the stream, *fully laden*, without any other charge being made ; and if it returned empty, the Commissioners return half the tolls already paid."

During this same autumn the Thames above Lechlade pathetically emits one of its rare articulate pleas for consideration. Mr. Ward, of Marlborough, expressed to the commission the "intention of the Land Owners near the River between Lechlade and Cricklade to apply to Parliament for Powers to cleanse and open the River and Watercourses leading thereto in order to drain their respective Lands which they complain are flooded and damaged from that Part of the River since it has been disused as a navigation being grown up"; and desired "the Commissioners' assent to such intended Application."

The Thames Commissioners

The commission replied that they would not oppose the measure; though they pointed out in December, 1812, that during the previous ten years their expenditure on the sixth district, between Oxford and Cricklade, had been £7,764, and their receipts only £5,093. It is observable that they did not claim to have spent any money specifically above Lechlade; so that the neglect above that point alleged by the author of the *Two Reports*, just mentioned, may actually have existed. To complete this little history immediately I will add that the Petitions for Commissions of Sewers in the Record Office contain two documents of 1813 and 1823 pleading for some consideration of this far off, untended district of the River, with which the warring interests had so little troubled themselves. The earlier paper, condensed, reads:

"The Petition of the Rt. Hon. John Lord Eliot and the Humble Petition [you will note the entertaining discrimination in the matter of humility] of the several Persons whose names are annexed Sheweth: That great injury hath been for some time past and still is sustained in the parishes of Lechlade, Inglesham, Lower Inglesham, Upper Inglesham, Kempsford, Hannington, Hannington Wick, Marston Maisey, Castle Eaton, Lushill, Eisey, Water Eaton, Cricklade St. Sampson's, Chelworth, Cricklade St. Mary's, Down Ampney & Latton [if you know the country you will not desire any abbreviation of the catalogue] by the increase and accumulation of Sandbanks, Islets, and Flams and by Weirs, Trees and other

> obstructions lying in the bed of the River and preventing the due and speedy discharge of the flood Waters, and it would be of great advantage to have the said obstructions removed."

The interest of the navigation would naturally notced in plea; the mirific new canal had taken it all a quarter of a century earlier. A commission was desired for all these places " except so much of Lechlade as lies east of the junction of the Severn Canal." The 1823 document is merely a renewal of the petition; much had been done, but more was necessary.

To return to 1811: in July the City committee and the commissioners went on joint survey from Lechlade to London; and the former subsequently reported to the Common Council:

> "We cannot but admire the general nature and state of the Navigation of this Noble River. The Navigation from Lechlade to Oxford, though much improved by the erection of Pound locks, is in very great want of a substantial and uninterrupted Horse Towing Path.
>
> "Oxford to Marlow: your Committee has only to recommend the repairs of such Locks as need it; and above all a Horse Towing Path uninterrupted as much as possible by Aits and Fences which your Committee cannot but consider the greatest defect in this otherwise Excellent Navigation.
>
> "The difference between a River navigation improved by pound locks and one not so improved cannot be more strikingly exemplified than in the 2^d district vizt from

The Thames Commissioners 165

Boulters Lock to Staines where for want of Locks (there being only Windsor which although it has a very beneficial has only a partial and local effect) nearly double the number of Horses and strength of Towing line is necessary. The Navigation is more uncertain, the mischiefs done by floods is much greater & the banks & Towing paths in worse repair altho' a greater expence is bestowed upon them than in all the three districts above it united."

The City had just begun their series of locks, on the strength of which they were adopting a critical tone towards the upper Authority. The allusion to interruption of the towing by aits, in the second paragraph, refers to the fact that islands, large and small, often intervened between the path and the barge channel, so that they were swept by the lines of passing vessels; and the commissioners were often compelled by the owners to put up guard rails along the ait banks to save the osiers and other growth from destruction. The third paragraph is a brief but excellent epitome of the advantages of a locked over an unlocked navigation; though the City, forty years behind the commission in the matter of improvements, were scarcely justified in moralising too forcibly on the subject. It had been, moreover, largely in deference to their susceptibilities that no locks had yet been built in the district criticised.

Early in 1813 the tolls were raised throughout the jurisdiction from 3d. to 4d. per ton.

In April, 1816, the City, flushed with the roseate

and militant self approbation just hinted at, founded upon the locks they had quite recently installed below Staines after many years of repeated petitions and persuasions from the commission and the public, descended upon the much labouring Authority with the peremptory threat that, "in consequence of the great delay in carrying out improvements in the upper districts, the Corporation, if these are not done, will apply to Parliament to extend the Corporation's jurisdiction to Reading." There had indeed been much of this sort of thing recently: of independent surveying of the upper River by the City, and of acrimonious reporting to the commission, threats of application to Parliament for transference of powers, suggestions, counter reports, and deadly parallels. It was in the midst of this state of things that Mr. Loveden's admirable and diplomatic letter, quoted under Buscot lock in my List, came to be written.

During the following summer a deputation from the City made the grand tour, not unknown in even these degenerate days, by the Thames, the Kennet and Avon Canal, the Avon, the Severn, and the Stroudwater and Severn Canals, into the River again at Inglesham. There is nothing very piquant or pertinent in their report until the passage about the last named canal which will be found under this head in my List. One or two of their remarks about the Thames itself are interesting:

The Thames Commissioners 167

their hostility to the ferries is particularly noticeable. To condense:

> "Fifth District: Locks out of repair and the attendance of the Lock keepers thereat is necessary, particularly at Abingdon. Much inconvenience also arises from the frequency of Ferries in this District.
>
> "Fourth: Too frequent ferries; locks out of repair and absent keepers.
>
> "Third: Ferry at Caversham and some others are kept locked and it is frequently necessary to go two miles to get the key while the Boat and Horses are waiting.
>
> "Your Committee terminated at Strand on the Green on Saturday the 20th of July last, after having travelled about 60 miles by land, 275 by water, and passed through 166 Pound Locks in nine days."

The commission retorted that the ferryboat at Caversham was only a quarter of a mile from the ferryman's house, and many others less. The craft, they alleged, were necessarily kept locked up to prevent fishermen borrowing them and leaving them on the wrong side of the water.

In September, 1818, Messrs. Parsons of Newbury applied for permission to navigate free of toll a boat with a steam engine on board, probably a tug, "for the purpose of Towing their Loaded Boats." This is the earliest note I discover of the actual introduction of steam upon these waters; though I noted on page 137 a kindred suggestion as far back as 1780. Permission was granted "by way of experiment."

This firm is perhaps the same as that similarly mentioned at this date in the City history below.

The commission and the City co-operated during 1820 in ballasting and removing impediments in the second district between Boulter's and Staines.

A formal specification of the duties of the various servants of the commission was drawn up in June, 1821. The lockkeepers are thus alluded to:

> "The Poundkeeper's duty is to reside and be constantly present at the Pound—to open and shut the Locks, to collect the Tolls—and to see that the orders of the Commissioners respecting the lading of the Barges etc are not violated. For these duties he is remunerated by a monthly salary varying at the several Locks from £5. downwards. The Committee cannot but observe upon the insufficient check which so far as their information enables them to discover there exists upon these last named officers, upon those whose situation in life renders them peculiarly unfit subjects for such temptation. The Committee are not at the instant of making this observation in possession of sufficient materials for enabling them to determine upon the means for securing this check, but they strongly recommend some course for effecting this desirable object and for removing from these officers a temptation to which the Committee feels that it is neither prudent nor justifiable to expose them."

And I, transcribing in the midst of the snappy modern journalism, "cannot but observe upon" this excellent piece of English, written not for the public eye but as a purely domestic report from a sub-

The Thames Commissioners 169

committee to the general body of the commission. Even upon so private an occasion they could still employ the grand style of a Dryden or a Johnson.

In August of this year I find a notice of a matter that somewhat exercised the commissioners' minds for some time. It was being recommended that the flash days should be altered back from Wednesday and Saturday, as fixed in 1793, to the original Tuesday and Friday. Among other advantages it was urged that "the alleged necessity for the disgraceful practice of navigating on Sunday" would thereby be obviated. A contemporary and not unamusing paragraph occurs in the *Times* of December 11, 1822, announcing a meeting of "The society for promoting religion and morality amongst watermen, bargemen, and *rivermen in general.*" (I originate the italic.) The meeting was held at the *City of London* tavern, and was numerously attended, "principally by ladies." "Amongst the speakers were two watermen, whose addresses were received with great good humour." The objection to Sunday navigation is by no means so recent as this period. It was specially, though not even then originally, militant in Commonwealth days. An Act of 1641 prohibited bargemen from working on Sundays. Another of 1650, c. 9, enacts "that no person shall use, imploy, or travel upon the Lords-Day, or the said days of Humiliation or Thanksgiving, with any Boat, Wherry, Lighter,

Barge either in the City of London or elsewhere (except it be to or from some place for the service of God, or upon other extraordinary occasion, to be allowed by the next Justice of Peace) upon pain that every person that shall use such Boat etc. shall for every such offence forfeit the sum of Ten Shillings, and that every Boatman etc. shall forfeit Five Shillings." And again in 1656, c. 15: "Any one coming by water to his Lodging on the Lords Day" is to be guilty of "prophanation." Justices of the peace and constables on both sides of the River had authority to apprehend and punish offenders irrespective of the county or parish wherein the offending craft happened to be upon detection. Miss G. M. Godden states that soldiers were posted on the River banks to prevent infringement of this order. Similar legislation was renewed in 1677; and Humpherus mentions two precepts of a like nature issued to watermen by the Lord Mayor in 1693 and 1698. One or two local prohibitions, at Iffley and elsewhere, will be found in my List; and the general debate revived, as will be described, in 1841. The statutory inhibition against Sunday travelling was expressly repealed in a Watermen's Act of 1827.

To return to 1821; I find in the summer of this year the following list of the old flash weirs then still existing, with notes of their tolls and of other incidental matters.

Name	Proprietor	Toll as in 1771	Toll in 1821	Proposed new rate	Remarks
St. John's Bridge	Mrs. Wells	3d. per 5 tons per voyage	6d.	3d.	In 1751 it was agreed that if proprietor raised the arch of the bridge a foot he should be allowed to take 6d. He raised the toll; but not the arch.
Buscot West and East	Mr. Loveden Mrs. Hart	1/- per 5t. per passage 5d. per 5t. per voyage	same 75t. barge 9d. 60t. and under 8d.	same 4d. West 3d. East per 5 tons	Each voyage is always intended unless otherwise expressed (i.e., through and back again inclusive.
Clarke's	Mr. Clarke	1751 3d. 1762 1d. 1764 1d. —— per 5t. 5d. ══	75t. barge 7d. 60 do. 6d. 40 do. 4d.	5d. per 5t	
Old Nan's	C. Loder, Esq.	Exceeding 50t. 2/6 Under 50t. 2/-	50t. and up 3/-	3d. per 5t.	
Rudge and Winney Wegg's otherwise called Rushey	Mr. Perfect Southby	Order of 1764 Per 5t. 4d. For Thames Weir 1d. —— 5d. ══	5½d. per 5t.	5d. per 5t.	
Ten Foot	Sir C. Throgmorton	Order of 1762 50t. and up 3/- Under 50t. 2/6	60t. and up 4/- Smaller boats in proportion	3½d. per 5t.	
Duxford	Rev. Rt. Symonds	Order of 1761 50t. and up 4/- Under 50t. 2/6	same	4d. per 5t.	
Shifford	do.	50t. and up 3/- Under 50t. 2/-	same	3½d. per 5t.	Shifford is not named in any order, but it is supposed to have been called "Newditch" in an order of 1762.

Name	Proprietor	Toll as in 1771	Toll in 1821	Proposed new rate	Remarks
Langleys or Limbery's weir above Newbridge	Mr. Langham	Order of 1751 1½d. every 5t.	5d. every 5t.	4d. every 5t.	This was one of the cases in which the Committee considered the legal claim to be too small.
Granny Cock's, or Rudge's, below Newbridge	St. John's College	As foregoing	4½d. every 5t.	As foregoing	The like.
Langley's and Pinkle's	Mr. Spenlove Lord Harcourt	Order of 1751 3d every 5t.	6/- for 70t, and for smaller boats in proportion	Langley's 4d. p. 5t., Pinkle's 1½d. per 5t.	The like as to Langley's only.
Bold's	Earl Abingdon	—	3d. per boat.	3d. every 5t.	Not mentioned in any order prior to 1771.
Iffley old lock and Swiftin's weir	Miss Danby	5d. each, per 5t.	5d. per 5t. at each	the same	No order prior to Mar. 28, 1781. Supposed to relate to former orders.
Sandford old lock	Mr. Swann	10d. every 5t.	the same	the same	The like
Abbey lock at Abingdon	Mr. Phillips	Order of 1752 Barges navigating between Lechlade and Sutton and passing thro' Culham bridge 1/- every 5t. and the like for every other barge passing by or thro' Culham bridge. Barges navigating from Lechlade to Abingdon, and no further, for every fare 2/6.	In conformity to the order	the same	

Lock	Owner			
Sutton old lock	Mr. King	Order 1751 : 1/8 p.5t.	the same	the same
Day's	Dowager Lady Holland	Order of 1752 : 6d. per 5t.	the same	the same
Benson	Mr. Ashby	8d. every 5t.	2d. per ton and 3d. per horse for a private ferry	8d. every 5t.
Cleeve old lock	Mr. Pitman	Order of 1754 : 8d. per 5t.	For a large barge of 140t. £1 0s. 10d.	8d. every 5t.
Goring old lock	do.	As foregoing	The like excess	As foregoing
Whitchurch old lock	Mr. Turner	As foregoing	As foregoing	As foregoing
Mapledurham	Mr. Blount	As foregoing	As foregoing	As foregoing
Caversham	Mr. Deane	As foregoing	As foregoing	As foregoing
Blake's	Kennet & Avon Co.	Order of 1752 : 4½d.	140t. 19/-	4½d. every 5t.
Sonning	Mr. May	Order of 1754 : 3½d. including winch and bucks	140t. 10s. 0½d.	As 1771
Shiplake	Mr. Newell	As foregoing	As foregoing	As foregoing
Marsh	Mr. Elsee	Order of 1754 : 3½d.	Up to 60t. per 5t. 6d.; 60t. to 140t. 3½d.	3½d. per 5t.
Hambledon	Sir W. Clayton or Mr. Baker	Order of 1764 : 3d. per 5t.	140t. 9s. 0½d.	3d. every 5t.
New and Temple	Mr. Williams	Order of 1754 : 3d. per 5t. at each including winch.	140t. 15/- inclusive and for winch 2/-	As foregoing at each, including winch.
Marlow	Mr. Wright	Order 1762 : 3d. p. 5t.	the same	the same
Boulters	Mr. Fuller	Order 1754 : 3d. p. 5t.	140t. 10/-	3d. per 5t.

The various orders of and subsequent to 1751, mentioned in this list, may be taken as small items of the missing transactions of the commission of that year. It is noticeable that Buscot is the only instance of the toll being levied on every passage; everywhere else it covered through and back. The long note under Abingdon contains incidental evidence of the contemporary navigation along Swift Ditch; and it appears very probable that the permission to Mr. Phillips to collect dues in respect of his flash lock at Abingdon (part of the present weir), in spite of the fact that the barges were no longer passing thereby, may be the key to the sarcasm in Bathurst's *Extracts* of 1772, quoted on page 127, that "the Spirit of Benevolence to lockowners first appeared at Abingdon in 1751."

In August, 1825, the City busied itself with another survey of the upper River. The deputation originally intended starting down from Oxford, "when an Advertisement, in a Country Newspaper, was accidentally seen, announcing, that the Navigation would be stopped for repairs at Hambleton Lock." They therefore started from Henley; it does not appear why they could not have done so from Oxford, Henley being equally above the obstruction, unless perhaps they had just time to reach there from Henley before the repairs began. They embraced the opportunity of subacidly remark-

The Thames Commissioners 175

ing that such advertisements would be more useful in London papers; and, perhaps more justly and certainly more usefully, that such stoppages should be confined to large and heavy laden barges, "allowing the passage of small craft by the old locks, for the maintenance of which, Tolls to a great amount are constantly paid to the proprietors." This course had certainly been adopted in the case of previous stoppages of the pound locks; but seems to have died out owing perhaps, at first, to the old tackle becoming choked with weeds and drift through disuse; and later doubtless to the more rigid construction of the newer weirs. In this instance the City acted upon its own suggestion: their shallop, nearly ten feet wide and drawing two feet of water, shot the old flash lock at Hambledon "with tolerable facility." From which I gather that they might, after all, have started from Oxford; as they would scarcely have passed in the fearless old fashion had the pound been available.

Perhaps unusually interesting is a time table of flashes as ordered to be let free from the various locks on and after November 10, 1826. It will be remarked that the flash took 70 hours, practically three days, to travel downstream from Lechlade to Sonning: a distance of about 75-80 miles reckoning along the old natural channel with all its bends, and a rate of just over a mile an hour including the delay at each weir.

	"First flash to be drawn.			Second flash to be drawn.		
St. John's	Sunday	2	p.m.	Wednesday	5	p.m.
Buscot		3	,,		6	,,
Hart's Upper		4.30	,,		7.30	,,
,, Lower		6	,,		9	,,
Clarke's		8	,,		11	,,
Old Nan's		9.30	,,	Thursday	12.30	a.m.
Rushey		10.30	,,		1.30	,,
Tadpole		12	,,		3	,,
Ten Foot	Monday	1.30	a.m.		4.30	,,
Duxford		4	,,		7	,,
Shifford		5.30	,,		8.30	,,
Langley's		8	,,		11	,,
Rudge's		10	,,		1	p.m.
Skinner's		2	p.m.		5	,,
Pinkhill		3	,,		6	,,
Ensham		5	,,		8	,,
King's		7	,,		10	,,
Godstow		8	,,		11	,,
Medley	Tuesday	4	a.m.	Friday	7	a.m.
Folly Bridge		6	,,		9	,,
Iffley		8	,,		11	,,
Sandford		10	,,		1	p.m.
Abingdon		2	p.m.		5	,,
Sutton		3.30	,,		6.30	,,
Day's		7	,,		10	,,
Benson		10	,,	Saturday	1	a.m.
Cleeve	Wednesday	2	a.m.		5	,,
Goring		3.30	,,		6.30	,,
Whitchurch		5.30	,,		8.30	,,
Mapledurham		7.30	,,		10.30	,,
Caversham		10.30	,,		1.30	p.m.
Sonning		12	,,		3	,,

It would be interesting to discover why eight hours were allowed for the flash from Godstow to accumulate at Medley. It was possibly because of the great width of the stream along Port Meadow.

The Thames Commissioners

In Wm. Westall's *Thames* of 1828 the following retrospective note occurs: "This navigation was formerly carried on in very large barges of 200 tons' burthen, drawing four feet water, passing downward by the force of the stream through old flash locks or pens of four or five feet, which produced a rapid and dangerous torrent, causing shoals and obstructions; and being haled in the upward passage against the stream in some places by gangs of from 50 to 80 men." I do not know of any other authority for this huge number of hauliers. Westall describes them, as I have said, as a terror to the Riverside. He adds that barges in his time went 25-35 miles a day downstream, and about five miles less upstream; and that the toll to the old weir owners amounted to about 2s. per barge throughout the River, at each weir.

In December, 1828, "Messrs. King & Davis" were cautioned "to remove their House Boat out of the way of the Navigation." The exact locality does not appear; but it is the first notice I have of these contrivances within the commissioners' jurisdiction. Under the City history, however, I print an allusion to them at Richmond as early as 1780. Also in 1828 I find further

RULES FOR POUNDKEEPERS AND BARGEMEN.

1. The poundkeepers are expected to keep a look

out for the approach of Barges, and to prepare the Pound for their reception.

2. All the sluices are to be down whilst the boat is entering, and until the gates are shut, and a proper hold made from the barge to the fast pile, and that such hold be sufficiently short to prevent the boat from swinging.

3. The poundkeeper is to take the opportunity whilst the barge is so made fast, and before she is permitted to move, to make his gauge and settle his account with the costbearer.

4. No person other than the poundkeeper to be permitted under any pretence to use the handle of the sluices.

5. In the event of its being at any time necessary to run the upper sluices, for the purpose of facilitating the downward passage, the poundkeeper is to draw the sluices himself, first properly securing the lower gates.

6. After the passage of a barge, all the gates and all the sluices are to be shut and kept shut, unless and until the water shall have become too high for barges to work, from which time the lower gates at the two new pounds are to be opened and made fast, and the sluices of the upper gates shut and kept shut down, excepting only under particular instructions to be given by the Surveyor. [The "two new pounds" were perhaps Clifton, built in 1822, and Culham, *circ.* 1810.]

7. No Pole is to be put overboard from any barge whilst within the Pound, nor any Pole placed at any time against any of the Banks, Bridges or Towing paths."

In a letter of 1830 it is stated that, under the Act of 1770, "at many locks upon the Thames a sum of sixpence is still paid for" disused winches.

The Thames Commissioners 179

The commissioners, flushed with prosperous revenues from the barge traffic, appear up to this time to have neglected the small income derivable from pleasure craft, leaving it as a perquisite to the lockkeepers to compensate them for the extra labour it involved. In May, 1829, however, the latter were for the first time instructed to bring these takings into their accounts. In November, 1830, the whole was returned to them. I give details under Iffley in my List of the special arrangement made with the keeper there. It was stated that, at this date, "the tolls, at least in the upper district of the River, are very imperfectly collected." In March, 1831, it was piously resolved to be inexpedient that females should, at any time or under any circumstances, hold the situation of poundkeeper. Officially or otherwise, however, females long continued so to do.

In the latter year the commissioners could no longer close their eyes to the fact, hinted at on page 168, that they were being seriously defrauded by the lockkeepers. In June their committee reported: "It has been established beyond the shadow of a question that Barges, in considerable numbers, which were entered and duly accounted for as passing through Poundlocks A and C, are altogether unnoticed at the intermediate Poundlock B, and thus the tonnage at the last mentioned pound is wholly lost to the Commissioners." These practices they found fairly general; but Romney lock was specially signalised, "where instances of omission approaching 200 in number and £30 or £40 in amount, are wholly unaccounted for." The committee easily argued that if on a random enquiry they had discovered so many cases of negligence or fraud spread over a few months, "it is quite manifest that the extent to which the revenue has suffered in the course of years must be frightful." They had no very clear notion of a remedy; but it was agreed that the sixth district should be farmed, as its distance beyond Oxford made the general receiver's visits very infrequent and irregular.

This step was actually and immediately taken. An auction was held in November, 1831, at which bids were made by apparently only two competitors, named Hicks and Brown, rising from £250 to £285. This offer was at first considered unacceptable; but at a second auction the district was knocked down to John Strange of Amney Crucis at only the maximum figure previously bid: £285 annually for three years, as from March 1, 1832. Strange entered upon his contract; and at the end of 1832 it was found he was not providing proper keepers. He was warned to do so; but a year later the same complaint was raised against him, "whereby great damage is constantly accruing to the locks and gates." He was again threatened with the contract penalty. In December, 1834, he renewed at the increased rental of £335; but at the end of 1835 gave notice to vacate his undertaking. In February, 1836, Berkeley Hicks, presumably one of the original bidders, acquired the district at £287, and apparently kept it three years. In February, 1839, Thomas Keen succeeded at an annual rental of £362; and was in the following December allowed £50 on account of the failure of the navigation through floods. In February, 1842, Charles Hodges secured the contract at £310; and in May, 1845, John Bossom is noted at £398. After a year's experience he desired to be relieved; and William Bossom of Osney lock succeeded him. The last holder was John Bossom, at only £250 rental: a symptom, doubtless, of the fierce new competition of the railways. In 1852 the commission contemplated letting all the locks between Abingdon and Caversham inclusive in two lots: Abingdon-Benson and Chalmore Hole-Caversham. Other counsels, however, prevailed; it being noted that "there are circumstances which prevent for the present an advantageous letting of the locks between Abingdon and Benson." And the end of all things for the commission being then at hand, the farming question dropped into oblivion; except at Iffley and Sandford, as described under the former head in my List.

Incorporated into the City records of 1834 is a list dated January 1, 1831, of the tolls payable at this date at the old flash locks within the upper jurisdiction, per twenty tons. It will be remarked on reference to the Table, where they are detailed, that they shew a considerable increase upon the next earlier schedule of 1821.

It was ordered in the summer of 1832 in a new bye-law that no barge should be towed except from its mast. In August, 1833, the City "observed most of the Locks that were constructed with wood to be out of order," below Reading. And in the following October sounded the first note of the doom of Thames commercial traffic. The Great Western Railway Bill was before Parliament; and the commission were straining all their resources in resisting it. Their traffic receipts for 1832 constitute, I believe, their highest record: £13,169. In August, 1834, the Bill was thrown out by a large majority, and the Authority was jubilant over its "victory over the Railers," which had cost them £1,500.

The "Railers," however, could not be denied. In the early part of 1835 a correspondence took place between the commission and the City concerning the re-introduction of the "Grand Western Railway Bill." Further opposition was expected to cost £1,500; and the City promised £100 to the cause, not being themselves in any apparent immediate

The Thames Commissioners

jeopardy. It was not "intended that the Subscription List should now or ever be made public." In June of the same year the two Authorities held a conference, and "entirely concurred in their conviction of the expediency and necessity for the earliest practicable abolition of the system of flashing and the consequent restriction of lading, by penning the water where necessary, so that barges may pass at all times laden to the maximum legal depth of 3 ft. 10 in." A further immediate conference being demurred to by the commission, the City persisted, in order that they might not be "driven to apply to Parliament during the present session for an enquiry into the subject, and providing some remedy for the continued decrease of the tolls." Some sort of consultation was thereupon held at Marlow; at which it was mentioned that the upper Authority's debt was £91,000, shortly to be raised to £95,000.

It was mentioned at this time, as a special feat of despatch, that a loaded barge went from the Pool of London to Mapledurham, 86 miles against stream and through 20 locks, in 36 hours. This seems to require very cautious acceptance.

In November, 1839, I find the City commending the commission for certain works just completed; but commenting adversely upon the suspension of traffic in the upper districts during recent floods, the navigation below London Stone having meanwhile successfully continued. It was suggested that raised towpaths were requisite in the upper River.

An Act was passed in 1840, not specially for the benefit of the Thames but including it in its purview: "To provide for keeping the peace on Canals and Navigable Rivers." Private companies were empowered to appoint their own constables "for the Security of Persons and Property against Felonies." Such constable might apprehend "every Person whom he shall find, between Sunset and the Hour of Eight in the Morning, lying or loitering upon any Towing Path and not giving a satisfactory account of himself." *Cavete, quantumst hominum venustiorum in ripa prandentium!*

In August, 1841, the City expressed to the commission a polite "surprise that a charge is made for the passing of the Corporation shallop" through their locks. The City would not have dreamed of taking toll from the commission. It was promised that no further charge should be levied.

Sunday traffic once more attracted unfavourable attention during this year. I find a recommendation that no "Pound, Lock, Weir, or Shutting Tackle for the purpose of passing Boats on a Sunday between the hours of 10 in the Morning and five in the Afternoon" be allowed to be worked. In 1842 a bye-law gave effect to this recommendation between "six o'clock on Sunday morning and twelve o'clock on Sunday night." In February, 1849, Charles Clark, captain of the barge *Susanna*, forced her through Marlow, Cookham and Boulter's locks in defiance of the regulation; and was called to account therefor. The point was raised, which seems to be a strong one, whether the common law would uphold the commission's bye-law in bar of traffic upon a highway, Sunday or weekday. In 1841 indeed the City had challenged the commission's right to make the regulation; and the reply had been that in framing it they had been conscious of its legal dubiety, but that Dr. Arnold of Wallingford had insisted upon it.

A General Union of the Canal Interest was proposed in May, 1844, to promote a campaign against the railways. It was recalled that at their inception the latter had advertised valuable prizes for useful inventions and suggestions, and that "many splendid" results had accrued; but "no similar improvements have cheered the Canal interest. Is there," it was plaintively demanded, "anything in these useful and important Works that renders them unsusceptible of improvement?" It was acutely pointed out that the very novelty of railways had worked to their advantage; all the ingenuity of human skill had been focussed upon a virgin field of activity; while upon the older canals only trifling improvements upon ancient methods could be suggested. "A series of very handsome premiums" was proposed; it was remembered that "the locomotive in its present state owes its birth to a premium of £500." Two or three thousand pounds were to be raised for the purpose. The Union held a few more fruitless meetings; and seems to have dispersed about July, 1845.

At a meeting of the commission in November, 1844, tolls were reduced twenty *per cent.* throughout the jurisdiction as an aid to the barge traffic in respect of the railway competition. The step did not meet with unanimous approbation, even from the parties most intimately concerned. In March, 1845, "two very considerable Traders who are Commissioners voted against" the reduction, "saying that they would prefer improvements upon the River, which the commissioners with crippled means would be unable to carry out." In July of the same year a proposal was discussed, of which something has again been heard in these last days, "to drain several of the Canals of this Kingdom and to convert them into lines of Railway." A few short lengths have actually been so transformed. In this connection a Mr. A. J. Foster mentioned his invention of a "submerged propeller, which will enable canals to be navigated at far greater speed and less cost than ever yet accomplished."

In a MS. report of the Lord Mayor's view in

1846 in the Guildhall Record Office the following list appears of the old flash locks, their owners, and their tolls per five tons. It indicates a general reduction upon the previous schedule of 1831.

"Boulter's	Lord Orkney	3d.	Whitchurch	J. Pearman	8d.
Marlow	Wright	,,	Goring	J. Stone	,,
Temple	T. P. Williams	,,	Cleeve	J. Pitman	,,
Hambledon	C. S. Murray	,,	Benson	Green &	
Marsh	C. Elsee	3½d.		Brown	,,
Shiplake	Dr. Phillimore	,,	Day's	leased to Crs.	
Sonning	D. May	,,	Abingdon	J. S. Phillips	1s.
Caversham	J. W. Grave	8d.	Sandford	J. Swann	8d.
Mapledurham	M. Blount	3d.	Iffley	Danby 8d. or 10d."	

In July, 1848, it was accorded that thenceforth all barge and other horses and all persons employed in the navigation might pass toll free over the commission's ferries. This was probably intended in aid of the horse towing against the new steam haulage. Tugs needed the use of neither towpath, bridge, nor ferry; and so contributed nothing toward their maintenance. It was probably deemed equitable, therefore, to relieve the older method of this expense.

A resolution was passed in October, 1850: "that Steam having been introduced as an improved and cheaper means of Haulage it is incumbent upon the Commissioners to consider so important a change in the conduct of their business." In view of the deplorable habits of the modern launch it is amusing to read a bye-law framed in the following December:

"That no steam vessel shall be worked at any greater speed than 4 miles an hour with the stream or 3 miles against," under a £10 penalty. In February, 1851, an acknowledgement of £150 was voted to "Messrs. Allen & Skinner as some remuneration for their trouble and expense incurred in their introduction of steam upon the River as a means of haulage, which the Commissioners believed would greatly improve the Navigation." In this same year, being Exhibition year, this enterprising firm was proposing to run a passenger service "from Yantlett to Oxford," anticipating the custom of "vast numbers who will perhaps have no other opportunity of visiting England."

During November, 1850, a further omen of doom had appeared to the Thames barge traffic. "The Commissioners, in the hope of increasing the traffic upon the Navigation by a reduction of the charges upon it, and to enable the traders to meet as far as practicable the present competition of the Railways, recommend that from January 1 to December 31, 1851, no tolls be taken at Old Windsor and Abingdon locks." As I mention under these stations in my List, no reason appears why these two locks were selected for the experiment. In December, 1850, it was further compulsorily announced that "in consequence of the Railway competition the tolls of the navigation had greatly fallen

The Thames Commissioners

off for some time past and were now so reduced that the funds of the Commissioners will be insufficient to pay the creditors five *per cent.* interest"; and the rate was accordingly reduced to four *per cent.*

Another dark symptom of decreasing traffic and dwindling revenues appears in the reduction of lock-keepers' wages in March, 1853. The four locks from Cleeve to Mapledurham were reduced by one-half, the keepers, however, being permitted to retain the pleasure tolls for their own benefit. Other stations also were reduced, as noted in my List. At the four locks above-named tolls were suspended for a year from the same date; and at Shiplake for a similar period a twelvemonth later.

In July, 1854, it was announced that the bond-holders could be paid only two *per cent.* interest for the Midsummer half year.

The excellent resolution was again passed in December, 1855, that the system of running flashes on the River ought to be abolished. It was objected that

> "however desirable it may appear, and doubtless is, to abstain from this primitive and wasteful plan of passing Boats, yet *above* Oxford there exists hardly any other mode. The only plan for retaining the Water to a certain level being by *private* Weirs, of most rude and inefficient construction, the whole of which have to be removed for the passage of every Boat, great or small, thereby draining off the Water till then retained or

penned up by these inefficient Expedients. To obviate this and to abolish Flashes it would be necessary to construct 5 or 6 Pound Locks and Weirs at a cost of many thousand pounds, an Expenditure which is not warranted, either by the State of the trade in that District, or the finances of the Commissioners."

In June, 1856, the Authority reimposed the tolls everywhere except at Hurley and Sutton Courtenay. At these two stations they had purchased, at an inclusive cost of about £4,000, the old flash locks and their private rights : the only such interests they ever acquired, in spite of many recommendations. I suppose, therefore, that, not having the old owners to satisfy, they could more easily continue the exemption in these two cases.

In 1857 the first Thames Conservancy Act was passed, with which I deal later. It affected only the City and its jurisdiction eastward of London Stone at Staines. Meanwhile the upper Authority pursued their hopeless task as courageously as possible. At Christmas in this year it was decided that only one *per cent.* could be paid to the bondholders. A new blow threatened in May, 1859, when a Mr. Pyecroft wrote to the new Conservancy urging them to seek powers to extend their jurisdiction, "and amalgamate with the Trustees of the Navigation between Staines and Oxford."

Complaints were becoming frequent of damage

The Thames Commissioners 191

caused by undermanned barges going adrift, and in October, 1860, a bye-law was passed that every vessel of ten tons and over should, unless under steam, be towed by horses.

As from Christmas, 1861, the general clerk to the commission volunteered to accept a salary of £200 only, being I believe one half of what he had been receiving. His name was Wm. Graham; he died about June, 1862, after about twenty-two years' service.

It is an illumination of the dreary decline of the barge traffic that in 1862 only nine vessels had passed from the Severn Canal into the Thames up to the month of May. In the *Times* of the following June 4 is a note of a deputation to the Home Secretary, including the Duke of Marlborough, the mayor and many gentlemen of Oxford and others, urging that "no systematic provision has yet been made for deterring towns from casting their sewage" into the River, and that many towns were so offending: "Richmond, Staines, Windsor, Maidenhead, Henley, Reading, Oxford." A commission of enquiry was asked for: the view of the River as "the common sewer of the country" was producing its nauseous harvest.

In March, 1863, it was decided to pay only one half *per cent.* interest at the ensuing Midsummer. In July, 1864, driven by circumstances to what must have seemed a miserable parsimony, the commission began to awaken to the possibilities of the pleasure tolls, which, as I have said, they had hitherto abandoned to the lockkeepers. They accordingly instituted an enquiry as to what the annual returns might be under this head; for which purpose the keepers were instructed to keep daily accounts.

In this same month the Board of Trade requested that Mr. Leach, the Conservancy engineer, might examine and report to them upon the River westward of Staines.

In December, 1864, it was decided that as soon as practicable all the commission's liabilities for towpath and other rents, and for salaries, wages, materials and other kindred matters, should be discharged; and that no further expenditure should be undertaken until these were fully met. Also that no orders for new works or maintenance should issue unless funds were in hand to meet them. This practical, and inevitable, abandonment of the navigation to its fate naturally led to two resolutions in April, 1865: (1) that there appeared urgent necessity for the immediate outlay of a considerable sum upon repairs to the locks and weirs; and (2) that a loan should be obtained upon the security of the tolls. So hopeless, however, was the situation that it was further resolved that if any millowner or other person or corporation cared to undertake the upkeep of the works, or any of them, authority should be deputed to them for the purpose.

Some twelve years later a Mr. Darvill of Windsor claimed that he had been the prime mover in this abandonment:

> "The various locks were out of repair, and we had no money. We were about to enter into contracts to restore and reconstruct various works; and I objected to it, inasmuch as we were not a corporate body and acting under a common seal. I, as a lawyer, believed that we should be personally liable, and I would not therefore incur personal liability without we took counsel's opinion; counsel's opinion was taken, and counsel said that we should be personally liable. We then agreed to stop the works."

The imminence of the final *débâcle* appears in the commission's resolution of December, 1865: to watch the parliamentary progress of the new Conservancy Bill. In April, 1866, the £100 shares of the Authority were valued at two shillings. Their total debt was about £90,000; and their annual income from tolls had fallen in 1864 from a previous maximum of over £13,000 to £3,000.

There is interesting evidence of the contemporary state of the navigation, and some intimate retrospective glimpses, in an enquiry held in the summer of 1865 preparatory for the above Bill. All the works and tackle along the whole River above

Staines were fallen into a deplorable condition bordering in many cases upon actual ruin. "The gates and weirs are all so leaky that they do not sufficiently store the water, and the gates of many of them are in such a bad condition that they can hardly be opened," and were unsafe for the passage of boats. "The part between Lechlade and Cricklade is now almost grown up; and a part above Oxford, which 20 or 30 years ago was navigable, is now so grown up that two persons in a flat-bottomed pleasure boat could not go up it in the summer time." This "part" is not more definitely named; probably the Duxford neighbourhood is meant. The commissioners' staff had been reduced, for want of funds, to the general surveyor, the secretary, and the lockkeepers. The complete breakdown of any lock was a matter of hourly expectation. Bargeowners were said, perhaps somewhat euphemistically, to be relinquishing their businesses; owing partly to the danger to, and frequent actual loss of, life and property, and partly to the intolerable delays and inconveniences of the navigation.

"The consequence of giving up the navigation," and of leaving the works utterly to collapse, "would be that the River would then become a broad ditch. There would be no reservoirs for the supply of water or irrigation of lands; the mills and their interests would entirely cease; and in many cases

The Thames Commissioners 195

where the country is flat the land would become swampy and a marsh."

An intimate description occurs of navigation by flashes. A bargeowner explained:

> "If we have boats lying at Oxford to wait and go down the River, every Tuesday and Friday the mill-owners are obliged to draw for so many hours and let it run through the [flash] locks: we go five miles beyond Oxford, and there the water is purchased. A man is sent forward to the next lock to wait there so many hours; the man goes on again, and so the water goes down with the boats. The water would accumulate to a certain height; when it got to that height I should draw that lock, and start off with the boats; I should send a man on to the next lock, and the miller who has the care of that lock is obliged to keep it closed for such a time. It has the effect of flooding the country frequently, from Lechlade to Oxford frequently. The man stands at the lock till the water comes down, and then, when the boats come down to that lock it is drawn, and the boats go down to the next pound. That state of things could be remedied by the institution of a low, as well as of a high, water mark."

It is quite clear that not even the large number of locks now existing availed to obviate the necessity of flashes; the millers still insisted upon their secular control of the flow of the River. Through these flashes the River often became almost exhausted; and the bargeowners had frequently "to precede their boats 20 miles and to return the same distance, to solicit and pay dear for water to bring them over the shoals and bars." And after all this drudgery and expense "the millers stand and laugh at our men when they cannot go on, after they have paid for getting the water. We had a case last summer where it cost 18s. (I think there were six boats to share it) to get the water; and at Sandford Lock the miller's man stood and laughed at our man and said: 'Thank you for bringing the water'; and he had to lie there till the next flash."

As I have said, the old flash lockowners, millers chiefly, were guilty of rendering the locks ineffective. "They are the very men who cause the difficulty; they will not pen for the flash," but gleefully turned it under their millwheels and ground away the faster; mocking at the helpless barges meanwhile. It is little wonder that the bargemen became celebrated for philippic: "It is said in the Act that the millers are to pen for a flash; and instead of penning they grind!" It is small wonder, too, that under such conditions barges are spoken of at this time as taking on occasion "about a fortnight coming from the docks at London" to Eton "on account of the insufficiency of the water and the locks being so leaky and dilapidated."

Some other points in this 1865 evidence are worth reprinting. One highly debateable statement was made: that there had never been mills between

Wytham and Lechlade. This is not only inherently improbable; there are actually notes of three at least: at Skinner's, at Rushey, and at Monk mill. Another point is the statement that there were about twenty flash locks still under private ownership, in respect of which the proprietors still drew tolls although not these but the adjacent pounds were used. If the three pounds above Oxford: Rushey, Buscot and St. John's (I think there was no private toll at Pinkhill, the fourth and only other then existing) be added to the seventeen of the 1846 list on page 187, the conjecture of twenty will be found exact. No public service of any description, not I believe even maintenance of the tackle, was rendered in return for these tolls. A third point is the complaint that landowners or their tenants had erected embankments along the Riverside to preserve their lands, which restricted the waterway in flood time to the great prejudice of the navigation, as the consequent increased velocity of the stream rendered it impossible for craft to head up against it. And a final and unpleasant detail emerges, already hinted at more than once: the discharge of sewage had become a serious impediment to the navigation. The accumulation in the locks was at times so great that it had to be removed at considerable expense, before the gates could be opened.

Such is the gloom of failure and insolvency in

which the history of the Thames Commissioners determines, after the bright expectations of a century earlier. They had done good work, intimate details of which will be found in my volume on the Locks and Weirs. They had originated the whole of the locks we possess today from Bell Weir upwards, except one or two above Oxford; and they had done it on surprisingly little money, perhaps too little. It was more than their bondholders desired to lose; but on the other hand the total was less than the City of London spent on their short series from Penton Hook to Teddington. As I have said, their hopes were foredoomed to failure upon the advent of the railways; and their last twenty years of existence must have been a period of heartbreaking disappointment. The details of their surrender to the Thames Conservancy will be found in a later chapter.

Chapter VIII

THE CITY OF LONDON JURISDICTION BELOW STAINES

FROM the time of the charter of Richard I in 1197 the City exercised at least a theoretical and general supervision over the whole navigable Thames, crystallising below Staines into a sole and jealously guarded jurisdiction. I indicate elsewhere with what irresistible authority they launched this charter against encroachers, notably at Kingston. And as after the tussle between 1770 and 1774, when this right had been in jeopardy of being transferred to the Thames Commissioners, they succeeded in retaining their jurisdiction below Staines; as, moreover, they frequently and at times a little amusingly affected still to exercise a supervision westward of Staines also, and paternally to advise and criticize their young and nurseling successors; I have thought well to devote a separate chapter to the history of their dealings with their unchallenged district of the River between 1774 and 1866, when the whole Thames from Cricklade to Yantlet Creek was for the first time vested in one reconstructed Conservancy.

Stimulated doubtless by the enthusiastic procedure of the new commission, the Navigation Committee of the Corporation of the City of London, first appointed in 1770, decided in the spring of 1774 to set in order the district of the River westward of London Bridge. Charles Truss, Clerk of the Navigation Works, reported that the obstructions were numerous, "and much increased by the last extraordinary Flood: the Banks of the River has been washed away in many places and new Shoals raised by that Flood so that the Barges are laid aground in Places where they used to meet with no Obstruction. The Towing Paths in various Places are become intolerable and in several parts quite taken away." This flood lived long in the memories of men; I note under Shepperton and Isleworth two stones bearing its record; there is another in the wall of the churchyard at Twickenham; and yet another, it is said, against the wharf at Richmond.

As a first step a large western barge, 132 ft. long, was acquired for use in connection with the proposed works. In August, 1775, the Corporation proposed to levy a navigation toll to form a revenue for the purposes of their improvements. In the following year, with their immemorial public spirit, they set about buying up all the towpath tollgates below Staines "at a fair valuation": thirty years' purchase. The scheme was expected to cost nearly £10,000.

City of London Jurisdiction 201

The enabling Act, 17 Geo. III, c. 18, took effect as from May 1, 1777. It empowered them to purchase all the tolls and dues usually being paid by barges to the private riparian owners, and to levy a small toll on the navigation in lieu thereof; which the traffic protested itself prepared very cheerfully to disburse, in view of the promised improvements. The rates fixed were from London to Brentford one halfpenny per ton, rising by the same amount per ton at each of the following stages: Richmond, Teddington, Kingston, Hampton, Shepperton or Weybridge, Chertsey, and finally Staines at fourpence per ton. There was to be no toll on vessels below three tons' burthen, and on pleasure craft; which accounts for Ravenstein's silence about sixpences at and below Penton Hook in 1861. The privilege was repealed only in 1870. Horses might not be used for towing between the king's bargehouse at Kew and "the scite of his Majesty's ancient palace of Richmond"; nor between Isleworth and the upper end of the Earl of Buckingham's land in Twickenham. But a new horsepath might be made between Kew and Richmond outside the existing public walk.

There died at Kingston in 1776, at the age of 72, "an eccentric humourist" named Dr. Wm. Battie, who acquired the character of being "the promoter of Barges being towed by Horses, which had before been haled up the River by gangs of men." His jest seems to have been taken too seriously by the class affected, and became so unpopular that "he narrowly escaped being tossed over Kingston Bridge by the incensed bargemen." He is said to have spent £1,500 upon this little joke.

The earliest notice I am aware of respecting houseboats occurs in a letter of one Baynes in 1780 to John Hewett of Shire Oaks:

> "August 12. I was all yesterday on the most cheerful water party up the river, as high as Sunbury. At Richmond we were fortunate in overtaking Mr. Sharp's barge (or his country house, which has every accommodation of beds, &c.), and also the Navigation barge with my Lord and Lady Mayoress, etc., going the boundaries of the river, which drew people of all ranks down to the water-side. As I believe they call it the Swan-hopping season, all the gardens next the river are lined with ladies and gentlemen to see the show and hear the music, which brings down all the belles to shew off."

The navigation barge, for its original purpose of collecting tolls and other dry business, was at first stationed at "Fulham" Bridge; but was very soon removed to the tail of Oliver's or Strand Ait. A little local inn still possesses the reminiscent title of the *City Barge*.

In 1792 it was complained that "there are very many places in the Cities Jurisdiction in which the Towing path lies very wide from the Channel; and

City of London Jurisdiction

where the Horse towing path goes through the water."

The barge traffic was now relieved of the private tolls, the Corporation charging itself with the responsibility, and recouping itself from the statutory toll. Out of this arose a curious little quarrel. The City levied its toll on the tonnage of the barges, but settled with the riparian owners on the old basis of the number of horses passing the private paygates. The bargemasters took a perhaps ungrateful advantage of this circumstance, and began employing many more horses than before. This the Corporation naturally resented; and in January, 1795, they instituted an enquiry into the matter. The following table discloses the state of affairs at Lord Dysart's paygate opposite Twickenham; and the proposed amendment thereof.

Tons Burthen	Horses Used	Sufficient Number
148	12	8
130	10	7
115	9	6
90	8	5
70	7	4
45	6	3
20	4	2

A lighter in tow necessitated two extra horses. At Kingston (Stevens') Ait the same conditions prevailed, also at "Parrott's": the lower paygate at Laleham; though here it was acknowledged, perhaps on account of the difficult shallows, that the larger number was not excessive. Lord Lonsdale's, the Laleham upper gate, shewed similar results.

In the *Annual Register* for July 1, 1801, a pregnant incident is recorded:

> "An experiment took place on the river Thames, for the purpose of working a barge or any other heavy craft, against tide, by means of a steam-engine, on a very simple construction. The moment the engine was set to work, the barge was brought about, answering her helm quickly, and she made way against a strong current, at the rate of $2\frac{1}{2}$ miles an hour."

From the mention of the tide it is evident that the experiment was made in tidal waters, somewhere below Kingston. In the same issue mention is made of the first Thames steamboat.

At the birth of the nineteenth century increasing pressure was brought to bear upon the City of London to improve the River below Staines. Actuated perhaps by little more than curiosity as to what might turn up, and having yet no power to build locks, they advertised for suggestions. One or two were submitted. In November, 1802, a Colonel Tatham wrote that he was "desirous to engage to make a good and complete Navigation from London upwards to the highest practicable Source, at a small comparative Expense, by simple and easy means, all which I have Models &c[a] to demonstrate, without subverting the Natural Current." A deputation proceeded to the colonel's "Apartments in Staples Inn Buildings," and reported the scheme worth attention. I discover no details; except that it relied upon "equilibrium gates." He was invited to select a trial site, and named £500 as the cost. Nothing further resulted, owing partly to the colonel quarrelling with his partner.

Exactly a twelvemonth later Robert Edington made a proposal, consisting chiefly in a method of dredging which was discovered not to be new. Two large lighters were to be moored against each shallow in turn, one under either bank; and to and fro between them a strong harrow and scoop were to be dragged across the River bed by means of a sort of turbine driven by the stream. When not wanted on this work the lighters were to be stationed temporarily at the head of strong currents and by means of the same motive power drag up the barges with a long "towling." Rennie pronounced against the idea; it had been already tried unsatisfactorily upon the Clyde; and the lighters moreover would seriously obstruct the traffic.

During this year, 1803, the bargemasters of the Riverside between Reading and Hampton petitioned the Corporation to expedite their improvements. And in 1805 Zachary Allnutt, secretary to the Thames Commissioners, published some *Considerations* concerning needful improvements below Staines. In the opening of his slender octavo he prints a petition dated December 6, 1804, from bargemasters below Staines. They had, they declared, for many years navigated as high as Lechlade, and had paid very considerable tolls for the betterment of the waterway; but notwithstanding this there still remained at "Laleham Gulls, Oxley [Chertsey Abbey] Mills, Chertsey Bridge Hill [a sandbank seventy or eighty yards below the bridge on the left bank], Ballinger's Weir [three quarters of a mile below Walton Bridge on the left bank], Sunbury Flatts, Kingston Overfalls, and other places below Staines, many Shallows and rapid Currents rendering that part of the Navigation Difficult, Dangerous, Tedious and very Expensive; and in short Water Times impassable for barges laden to the usual Depth of 3 ft. 10 in." They anticipated a compulsory advance in freights if conditions were not quickly improved. They had observed that attempts had been made to remedy defects "by Jetties and Weir Hedges only"; but these merely created "very rapid and dangerous Currents." They had formerly experienced similar troubles westward of Staines, but these had been largely remedied by locks and ballasting; and they prayed that similar improvements might be effected below that limit. The upper waters, they declared, were run off and wasted by the frequent and lavish

City of London Jurisdiction

flashes requisite to float them over the lower reaches: flashes, it is remarked, "run from Sonning Lock, and at all the Locks from thence downward, twice (and sometimes oftener) in every Week, during the Summer Months." Allnutt proceeds to suggest three new locks: one immediately below Laleham Gulls, realised at Chertsey; another realised at Sunbury; and a third at Kingston Overfalls, below the bridge, for which perhaps Teddington may stand. He even contemplates others: as, for example, at Fisherhouse Point below Staines, represented by Penton Hook. These unfavourable reports upon the City's management are an entertaining comment upon the criticisms the City itself shortly began to shower upon the upper Authority.

Stirred by these and similar appeals the Corporation arrived at the conclusion that they could proceed no further with their improvements without pound locks; and they proposed to petition Parliament for authority to build them in the parishes of Laleham, Littleton, Shepperton and Sunbury in Middlesex; and of Chertsey, Thorpe, the Moleseys and Kingston in Surrey. The suggestion was, however, received with such fierce hostility in these places that for the moment it was abandoned. In 1810 the City were more successful; and obtained their first lock-building Act, which received royal assent on June 20th of this year. It authorised the construction of Chertsey Lock (to the north of the infall of the Abbey River; not where we know it), and others at Shepperton, Sunbury, and Teddington. None was to be less than 150 feet long and 20 feet wide; each was to contain three pairs of gates; and the weirs were to be open. Instruments for working them were to be affixed to the locks, so that barges might pass if necessary "without the Assistance of the Lock keeper." Barges might be laden to a depth of 3 feet 3 inches between May 1 and October 31; and to 3 feet 10 inches during the remainder of the year. The tolls fixed in 1777 were increased: from London Bridge to Brentford one penny per ton, to Richmond $1\frac{1}{2}$d., Teddington $2\frac{1}{2}$d., Kingston 3d., Hampton 4d., Shepperton or Weybridge $4\frac{1}{2}$d., Laleham $5\frac{1}{2}$d., Staines 6d. These were in addition to the lock tolls.

In 1812 a new Act was found necessary. The site of Chertsey lock, owing to the opposition of Lord Lucan described in my List, had to be statutorily removed to the position we know, and a lock was imperative at Molesey. The lock gates were now limited to two pair; I believe that only Teddington and Sunbury possessed the three of the 1810 Act. Bargemen were forbidden to use ironshod poles in the locks. The navigation tolls were increased at the four lower stages: at Richmond by a penny and at the others by a halfpenny. "And

City of London Jurisdiction 209

for going thro' the several Locks 3d. per ton should be collected at each Lock."

Penton Hook lock evoked a further Act in 1814. It was stipulated therein that the ancient course of the River should be maintained, so that the Abbey river should continue to be fed with Thames water. The Corporation were empowered to let on lease heads of water for mills: a right which was never used; in this very year they refused the use of Teddington weir for this purpose.

Like the upper Authority, the City drew up rules for their lockkeepers in February, 1815.

> "To reside constantly in the house provided and be ready to pass all vessels at all times thro' the lock, giving no undue preference and suffering none to remain in the lock or cut longer than absolutely necessary.
>
> To take the Tolls agreeably to the authorized Table: To keep a correct account of all vessels passing up, and of all going down and not returning; and to keep a strict account of tolls in the proper book.
>
> To preserve the City's property from injury: Not to allow the weir paddles to be moved at any time unless themselves be present.
>
> To keep the lower gates and the sluices of the upper gates constantly open in times of Frost and break and remove the Ice from the Lock and Cut as much as possible. And
>
> To Consult the Several Acts of Parliament with which he is provided for his Guidance in the faithful and correct discharge of his duties."

o

Intelligent obedience to the last clause might prove an admirable soporific in perhaps highly improbable cases of insomnia amongst the lockkeepers. The City committee men, however, who drew up these rules a century ago, afford in themselves an admirable model of energy. In early days they would be up and afloat in the summer time at four or five o'clock in the morning, to "take the views" above bridge or below. And they were often men of considerable affluence and position.

One of the recollections of my very early boyhood is seeing, from the deck of a Kew steamboat, the *Maria Wood* lying moored to the bank at Strand-on-the-Green, as I fancy. She was built in 1816 at a cost of nearly £5,300, and went her maiden voyage in August of that year, being so named "in compliment to the Rt. Hon. the Lord Mayor and the Lady Mayoress." She was the last of three. Her predecessor, called *The Crosby*, was built about 1794; and the first of the line was the West Country barge already mentioned. The latter was about 1777 fitted up "for the occasional pleasurable summer excursions" of the Lord Mayor, the Corporation and their guests; upon one of which trips one Baynes, as just noted, saw her at Richmond three summers later. She formed a permanent residence for the engineer, and for some time of clerk Truss. For the summer berth of the *Maria*

City of London Jurisdiction

Wood a dock and bargehouse were built at Strand-on-the-Green : still to be seen ; her winter quarters were at the Old Barge House at Lambeth. Some casual notes of her expense, both of navigation and of maintenance, may be interesting. The hotel and other expenditure upon the mayoral view in 1826, from Oxford to London, was £684, of which nearly £100 was for "towing, locks, provisions for men and hire of boats." Her average annual cost of upkeep for the years 1831 to 1835 was about £650, with an additional £175 for the shallop. In 1836 it was proposed to sell her ; but as she was in excellent repair, and would fetch it was thought only £500, it was decided to retain her. Eight horses were required to tow her upstream ; two or three down. A single day's excursion, from Kew to Twickenham and back, cost £13 ; the two days' trip to Hampton Court and return cost £23. By strict economy her annual cost for the seven years 1837 to 1843 was reduced to an average of £350. At a Lord Mayor's view in 1839 the bellringers at Henley and Staines received a £2 gratuity at each town ; and at Marlow and Cookham £1. The man who fired the salute at Staines had 5s. For the Lord Mayor of London was a great man then ; the populace crowding the banks at Windsor stand bareheaded in a print of 1812 as the "City of London State Barge" passes by, with her flags interestingly floating towards her prow: perhaps there was a high wind aft! This would have been the *Crosby*; the print shews her being rowed by ten oarsmen; she must have been much smaller than her successor.

Early in 1851 the *Maria Wood* was reported to be in an "extremely dangerous" state under water. In October, 1857, the navigation committee, now supplanted by the first Conservancy, discussed the future of the old vessel of pleasant memories. Perhaps the result was the *Maria Wood* Company I read of in November, 1859; she was certainly sold at auction close to this date. The Conservancy charged her new owners £5 for housing her in her old berth at Kew; and in the summer of 1860 demanded toll for passing her through the locks, and a navigating toll of 10s. every time she passed the Kew tollhouse. During the 'sixties and indeed into the 'eighties I find complaints of her undesired presence at various places: Twickenham and Kingston amongst the rest. She was finally turned out of the Kew bargehouse in 1881, and was then moored withinside Isleworth ait. In 1897 *Punch* noticed the fact that she was up for sale there, with some facetiousness: "*Maria* .... is enjoying the *osiers cum dignitate*." I believe her poor old lower timbers still haunt this very spot, in use as a raft for repairing those barges which once, at her approach .... !

City of London Jurisdiction 213

The *Globe* of August 10, 1819, notes that "one of the Richmond steamboats has been seized for not having a regular licence on board. She was obliged to be towed up and down her usual Journeys till the irregularity was adjusted." An earlier note is of the bursting of a boiler in one of these vessels in June, 1817.

In January, 1821, the commissioners of customs approached the Lord Mayor upon the fact that the revenue had derived little or no benefit through their Staines collector of coal dues, and desired to be informed if there were any canal into the Thames above Staines by which coal could arrive at that place and below. They enquired also if the City would co-operate, through the lockkeepers or otherwise, in preventing evasion of the customs. It was apparently suspected that Oxford Canal cargoes, which should have passed thence down the River to Staines and London, were being diverted, and the 10s. per ton duty evaded. The Corporation instructed the Penton Hook keeper to report coal barges to both the Inland Revenue and themselves; and allowed Stephen Leach, their new clerk of the navigation works, who had been assistant to Charles Truss, now dead, to be appointed revenue officer.

In June the management of the City jurisdiction was reported to be very inefficient. Under Leach two inspectors were employed: one between Staines and Hampton Court and the other between there and Putney; and it was complained that they were very seldom in their respective districts. The upper official had his home in Westminster, "besides having a Lodging at Moulsey and another at Weybridge; and we are therefore not surprised at his frequent absence from his work." The lower officer was to be found usually at Kew, but seemed equally lax. A further complaint was that no proper check existed upon the lockkeepers' accounts. The inspectors visited them about once a week, usually on Fridays; "but seldom or never receive the precise amount collected." There was "not the most distant idea that any fraud is committed or that the whole amount of the Tolls is not ultimately received"; the system, however, was inefficient and should be "most materially altered."

I fancy there was something more in the complaint of the upper inspector's three addresses than was actually expressed; for the poor man devoted most of his defence to the point, bringing five or six written testimonials to his good character. Leach also pointed out that the circumstance possessed a favourable aspect: it enabled him to be more promptly and regularly at any necessary point of his work. Leach's report as regards the collection of tolls is interesting:

"An account of all barges passing upwards liable to

toll is taken at Strand-on-green being about 6 miles below the first lock. They have then to pass Lord Dysart's Bargeway at Ham, about 4 miles higher up [beginning at the end of Petersham Lane], where an Account is kept by his Agent. After which an account is taken at Teddington. The bargeowners have the option of paying all or any part of the Tolls at any of the Locks below Shepperton; but at this place those which go so high are compelled to pay all that is there due, to prevent eluding the Toll by passing the two Upper Locks undiscovered. Those barges which only go to Weybridge into the Wey are compelled to settle all at Sunbury if not before done."

The system, if properly executed, seems effective enough at Shepperton and above; but below that point there certainly seems an opportunity of fraud. Doubtless, however, the lockkeepers came to know precisely enough where barges hailed from.

In April, 1822, one John Gordon laid before the Corporation a proposal for a line of "light Steam Packets" between London and Staines; enquiring if he might be granted an exclusive privilege of passing his vessels through the locks "at a moderate rent for a term of years." The suggestion was for the moment declined.

During a flood in January, 1825, Leach interestingly pointed out "the new circumstances in which most rivers, but particularly the Thames, are placed from the general enclosure and draining of lands."

An Act of 1825 was purely financial, authorising

the raising of further funds. Inclusive of this increase the gross amount now raised by the City for their River works was £168,700, not much short of double the sum raised altogether by the upper Authority.

In September, 1826, it was ordered that "at each Lock the name of the Lock and of the Keeper thereof be painted in legible characters in front of the Lock keeper's house." I do not discover whether this was yet done westward of Staines.

During 1827 evidence appears that the third clause in the schedule of the City lockkeepers' duties on page 209 was not unnecessary. In a complaint against a bargeowner of overloading it was stated that "her people shut in [Shepperton] weir to produce an extraordinary height of water." She was drawing 4 feet 4 inches, six inches above the legal maximum.

Under Osney in my List I refer to the disallowance by the Thames Commissioners in 1800 of a claim by the freemen of Oxford to pass the locks free of toll. The claim was revived in 1829. A firm of solicitors of this city addressed the Corporation of London on behalf of a Mr. Richard Parker, freeman, claiming right of free navigation. Mr. Parker was a corndealer of Witney, and claimed in respect of his barges trading between Oxford and London, under an Oxford charter. His vessels were being detained until certain tolls were paid.

City of London Jurisdiction 217

His solicitors, in short, demanded to know the Corporation's intentions in the matter; and enclosed a copy of the charter, an extract or two from which may be interesting.

> "To all Christian People.... among other Liberties Privileges.... granted by the illustrious Lord King Henry II and by the serene King James I .... it is declared that the Citizens of Oxford.... shall be free throughout all England and Normandy as well by land as by water by land and by strand from all Customs Tolls Murrage Pannage Pantage Pontage Passage Stallage Lastage Riage Picage Carriage Rivage Anchorage Strandage Chiminage Terrage...." and the rest.

And the mayor of Oxford desired that Parker might henceforth pass and repass free of toll; threatening legal proceedings against any who should detain his barges. The claim was disallowed by the Corporation, just as the more general demand had been by the commissioners. They pointed out that the tolls had been created by Parliament for the benefit of the navigation; and expressed the opinion that neither Oxford nor any other freemen had any right of exemption.

Several owners of steam tugs petitioned the Corporation in June, 1829, for free passage through the locks; one desiring that his vessel might occasionally carry goods and passengers. General leave was granted for three months, but nothing was to be carried on board beyond fuel for the engine. It was pleaded by the petitioners that pleasure boats, including steamers and small passage or market boats, were at this time exempt.

The City in September, 1830, discussed the expediency of farming the tolls, in imitation of the upper Authority's action at this time. It was decided that they had no right to do so under their Acts; and that power should be sought in subsequent legislation.

A little domestic incident illuminates October, 1833, when the City lockkeepers sent up a united petition for a regular allowance of coals and candles. They took the opportunity anxiously to deny the "impression that is abroad, as equally unfounded in fact and distressing to their feelings, that they receive presents of coals from the Bargemen navigating the River." They pleaded the damp situation of their homes, but their request was refused; not, I think, for the first time.

I have already mentioned the alarm that fell upon the upper Authority this year in consequence of the progress of the Great Western Railway Bill. Similarly in March, 1834, the City began to express anxiety upon the same account; the "London and Southampton Railway" adding a further omen of the evil at hand. It was most laudably and naturally resolved by the Corporation, without success in the result, to endeavour to procure the insertion of a clause in each Bill providing compensation for loss of tolls. I shall return again to this subject; I will observe here that there appears to me a foundation of just reason in the attempt. Parliament had authorised both the City and the commissioners time after time to raise subsidies to a total sum of practically a quarter of a million sterling upon the credit of the tolls, in respect of which the Authorities were paying four and five *per cent.* interest respectively. Parliament was now establishing far wealthier and more extensive enterprises which were bound in a very short time to destroy the old River traffic and rob it of these tolls; and the River Authorities very rightly pleaded that Parliament should safeguard their bondholders. The City's average income for the five years 1829-1833 had been £14,375, of which about two-thirds accrued from their locks, Teddington heading the list, and one-third from the navigating toll. They failed, as I say, in their just attempt; and had to content themselves with a resolution that their revenue was expected to be "materially affected." Two or three months later the commissioners enquired of the Corporation "what steps have been taken towards opposing that most useless and mischievous project the Great Western Railway." I have already noted the temporary defeat of the "Railers."

What inference was drawn does not appear, but in May, 1834, the increasing practice of barges working by night over the City jurisdiction was pointedly noticed.

The official attitude of contempt formerly maintained towards pleasure traffic receives a further illumination from two incidents of this date. One occurred at Molesey. A party of two ladies, each with her baby and her maid, had been sculled by a waterman through the lock and down to Kingston. Here the ladies landed, leaving the others to return by water. After re-entering the lock the waterman, expecting according to custom no assistance from the keeper, tied the craft to the lock wall, closed the gates and opened the sluices. The boat caught under a projecting timber; and only after a most desperate struggle were the maids able to throw the children on to the sloping grassy bank and scramble out themselves. Peart the lockkeeper pleaded, with success, that he was not responsible for pleasure traffic nor anything else under three tons, neither class paying any toll and being evidently expected to lock themselves through.

Teddington was the scene of the second incident. A gentleman had sculled his wife down from Windsor, and arrived there about ten o'clock at night. He woke Savory the assistant keeper to let him through, who, however, only abused him from his

City of London Jurisdiction

open window. The poor man tried in vain to open the upper gates, and seems ultimately to have had to dragg his skiff across the island in the dark and float her again in the weir stream. For all which young Savory was severely reprimanded.

I gather in 1838 that a great deal of stone from old London Bridge was used upon the towpaths and other works in the City's jurisdiction, especially in the Shepperton and Walton districts, and on the right bank below Richmond.

I now arrive at a matter of history which, while not as to its immediate purport pertinent to my subject, acquired ultimately a very important and far reaching effect upon the conservancy of the River Thames. Just prior to 1840 the engineering of the Victoria Embankment was projected; and thereupon arose a seventeen years' dispute between the Crown and the Corporation of the City of London as to the ownership of the bed and soil of the River Thames within the ebb and flow of the tides. In April of this year the solicitor of H. M. Woods and Forests communicated with the Lord Mayor, advancing a claim that "the Thames being a navigable river and an arm of the sea *prima facie* belongs to the Crown, by virtue of its prerogative, as far as the water ebbs and flows. The office of Conservator is merely a ministerial office, the grant of it vesting no right of property in the holder." It was therefore demanded that the title of the Crown to the bed and banks of the tidal River should be fully recognised and admitted. In May the Corporation rebutted the claim; and expressed its desire that the cause should be submitted to proper legal authority as soon as possible. Following this thunderbolt the Corporation learned as soon as the following July that a petition, possibly inspired, "had been presented to the House of Commons from residents in the Metropolis praying that the Conservancy of the River may be taken from the Corporation of London." In February, 1841, the City's legal advisers recommended caution in abating encroachments, as they were "not prepared to say that the Lord Mayor or Corporation are in a condition to justify any abatement which could not be equally justified by any other subjects of the Realm." "Mouldy heaps of documents" were now eagerly dug out from the recesses of Guildhall, and appeared to justify the City's claim. During 1843 very eminent counsels' opinions upheld this view. The Woods and Forests, however, exhibited no little incuriousness about the "mouldy heaps of documents"; and applied for certain other papers and information. In June certain shoals in the neighbourhood of the Houses of Parliament were being publicly complained of, and the Crown agents proposed themselves to remedy the matter. The City lawyer urged his Authority to forestall the proposal by immediate and thorough action, lest "such a measure might be used as a pretext to acquire a claim to interfere with the bed and soil of the River, which are in the Corporation."

It soon became very evident that the Crown, justly or unjustly, intended to have its own way. I have a very long standing impression, gathered I know not whence, that the Queen herself was very determined on the subject. In November, 1843, the Common Council agreed to the Embankment plans, expressly as "owners of the bed and soil of the River." Nothing salient happened for some considerable time. In June, 1845, the Corporation solicitor took occasion to recapitulate the whole history, in view of the somewhat bitter pursuit of the Woods and Forests; who, it was complained, were proceeding by way of an information in Chancery by the Attorney-General against the Lord Mayor and Corporation. Amongst a great deal else he said: "The [Navigation] Committee will perhaps be surprised that I do not speak of our Charters as evidences of the City's right to the soil of the River: the truth is that Charters tell better at a distance than a close examination will warrant; vague and indeterminate as they are." He was convinced that the City's case was so strong from immemorial user that the Crown, "from a similar conviction, instead of resorting to a court of common law, have adopted this most unusual and unconstitutional proceeding to gain by sinister and indirect means an advantage they could not otherwise obtain." This is strong language, but I imagine it must have been justified by the facts ; it was certainly natural to the old Adam even of a lawyer under the domineering attitude of the Woods and Forests. In August a stay of proceedings was obtained upon a legal point, the Corporation having to agree to the damaging condition of advising the Crown beforehand of any intended grants of wharfing, quays, and the like. It is not surprising that, upon the very first information so given, the Crown entered a vehement objection and endeavoured to forbid the grant altogether.

In June, 1847, I find the first mention of a Thames Conservancy Bill before Parliament : promoted it appears by the Corporation itself. About a twelvemonth earlier an array of counsel had advised them to agree with their adversary quickly ; and this Bill had consequently been drawn up in October, 1846. The preamble recited the dispute, and indicated the necessity of immediate legislation in respect, among other matters, of the multitudinous landing stages, many of them unauthorised, that were being set up for the accommodation of steamboat passengers. The suggested new Authority was

City of London Jurisdiction

to comprise the Lord Mayor, the First Lord of the Treasury, the First Lord of the Admiralty, the First Commissioner of Woods and Forests, the last Lord Mayor, the chairman of the Trinity Board, two aldermen, the Admiralty hydrographer, and eight common councilmen; and was to continue the functions, generally, of the navigation committee.

The dispute now entered upon a period of several years' simmering. The Bill made no progress, in spite of being presented every year; and nothing occurred but a series of pin pricks from both sides. Meanwhile the navigation revenue was suffering increasingly from the railway competition; falling £8,000, to less than half its highest level. The works were consequently decaying; and the locks needed rebuilding. And here I will return to the general occurrences of the intervening period.

On November 30, 1842, died Stephen Leach, clerk of the works to the City Authority, after more than forty years' service as assistant and chief. His son Stephen W. Leach obtained the succession in January, 1843. In the following March the City endeavoured to arrange a conference with the upper commission, with the object of a general reduction of tolls in view of railway competition.

Even at the risk of irrelevancy it is irresistible briefly to note that in April, 1843, one Purvis, a

Scot o' Dunbar, importuned the City to grant him a lease of the whole of the Victoria Embankment to establish there an exclusive salmon fishery, which delicacy he imagined might still be abundantly taken in the Thames. He desired a seven years' lease, the first year gratis and thereafter at £50 annual rental, subject to an option of surrender if unprofitable; asking also to enter free of rent between the current date and the beginning of his term. After a long siege, nothing diminished by fruitless requests for his exact proposals, and the intimation that he must first become free of the Thames fishery, the City stated that they could not "comply with his request to have an exclusive right to fish in the River Thames." Even this did not immediately extinguish him.

In May, 1843, arose the interesting incident of the passenger steamer *Locomotive*. In passing between Teddington and Hampton Court she had damaged the towpaths and other works to the value of about £300. (No steamboat, it is stated, appeared westward of London Bridge before 1810; and even then none ventured for a long time above Richmond.) The evidence seems to imply that this vessel was the first of its kind to pass through the locks. The City decided that she must be stopped; although their solicitor advised them that he thought the step illegal, and that the proper remedy was to regulate her

City of London Jurisdiction 227

speed. The owners also protested, alleging that the Thames highway was free to every species of craft, and instancing other steam vessels, probably traders, that had made the voyage, "particularly a Barge called the *Shoal*, which for a length of time navigated to Oxford." The City contented themselves with limiting her speed to two miles per hour, and levying a toll of eightpence per ton upon her at Teddington lock on forty-five tons, being about three-fourths of her builders' measurements of capacity. Her owners declared these tolls to be prohibitive, and offered without prejudice (no toll being statutorily chargeable on pleasure boats) to pay fourpence per ton, or stand the risk of a friendly action. The reduction was accepted. In January, 1844, Lord de Ros, General Bligh, and other residents of Thames Ditton wrote the Corporation raising the subject of the violent wash of this steamer, which undermined their lawns and meadows. "Another annoyance," they wrote, "caused by this vessel is the danger to which it exposes the numerous small pleasure Boats in this part of the Thames, where neither the experience of the watermen, nor the habit of watching and avoiding the steamers, as in London, secure the craft against accident in this narrower part of the River." Two months later an opinion was secured that tolls were legally chargeable on steamers above three tons' burthen, being comprised in "all barges and other vessels whatever" of the first two City Acts of Geo. III. In April the owner of the *Locomotive* was declared bankrupt; and his assigns claimed unsuccessfully upon the Corporation for the refund of over £100 of toll paid under protest. They also announced that her new season was about to begin, notably upon a Sunday. The damage she caused the towpaths soon reappeared; and in July the City framed a new byelaw: that no steamer should work between Teddington lock and Staines at a greater speed than five miles an hour with, or four against, the stream, subject to a £5 penalty for each offence. No further complaint arose for a little, except in 1845 on the owners' part against a toll of 30s. per voyage. In July, 1848, they were fined £5 for exceeding the regulation speed. In May, 1852, they complained of having to pay £1 daily for passing Teddington lock, especially in view of the fact that a new railway to Hampton Court was depriving them of their passengers.

The tonnage of goods passing from London on to the Kennet Canal shewed a diminution between 1840 and 1843 of nearly thirty *per cent.*, decreasing from over 54,000 tons in the former year to about 38,500 in the latter.

In March, 1844, traders within the City jurisdiction were saying "that the Establishment of a Steam Tug to take vessels out of the Tideway would be a greater boon than even a considerable reduction in Tolls. Such a thing is, however, almost impossible, from the great risk which would be encountered by barges in tow passing" Chelsea and Putney Bridges, "occasioned by their narrow openings and bad position with reference to the set of the current." These two bridges remained for much longer an enormous nuisance to the navigation. They were both of the sort represented today by Streatley Bridge; and were not at all ancient.

A suggestion by the City of a twenty *per cent.* reduction in tolls had been thwarted through the disinclination of the upper Authority. They now recommended a reduction by no less than one-half, if the commission would co-operate. Various diminutions in the lockkeepers' wages were effected, as detailed in my List; and Leach was "to arrange as far as possible that the average of the work people's Wages should not exceed £16 per week." No word was breathed of the higher officials being abated; the poor fellows at it night and day, in all manner of weathers, were to endure all the economy.

A scheme of steam haulage was laid before the Corporation in October of this year. It would save, among other things, notably "10s. per week per boat" for barge lines. The promoters desired free passage at the locks; to receive for fourteen years all the savings effected under the scheme by the

Corporation, and £1,000 after it had worked efficiently for three months. Perhaps it was too grasping to be entertained.

Depleted revenues and persistent appeals from the bargeowners for aid against the railways now began seriously to depress the navigation committee. In March, 1849, a canal and water supply for London was threatened, originating at Henley. In connection therewith the City sturdily declared "that so long as the Navigation of the Thames shall be open to the public, even though a large proportion of the traffic be diverted or destroyed, yet the works must be maintained as heretofore; and officers and lock-keepers employed." The income from tolls was now barely sufficient to maintain the works and pay the interest recently reduced to three and a half *per cent.*; and quite incapable of paying off principal to the amount required under the Acts. It had fallen from nearly £16,000 in 1839 to less than £8,000 in 1849, as already hinted; and as the permanent charges for 1850 were estimated at nearly £7,000, exclusive of maintenance and repairs, the outlook was indeed gloomy. Coal was the only appreciable freight now obtainable; and the railways were making strenuous efforts to secure this also.

In 1850 Messrs. Allen and Skinner, one of the most energetic firms of Thames steam hauliers of their day, and already alluded to, suggested that the

Corporation should assist them in securing an Act "for the shutting up all parts of the Towing Path used simply as such"; of course with an eye to the total abolition of horse towing. They declared that they had the countenance, not only of the upper commission, but, more ominously, of the Woods and Forests; the latter being very desirous of bringing "the Park at Windsor down to the River": an ambition unfortunately achieved.

We owe a small but valuable convenience to a Mr. Shebbeare, who, in June, 1855, wrote complaining that there were no chains upon the lock walls by which small craft might be steadied. They were promised; it was explained, however, that chains previously supplied had been stolen by barges that passed in the night.

This summer began the thirty years' outcry against the foul state of the River. "Almost numberless" sewers debouched into the stream; "and the filthy refuse from gas works was invariably though secretly" disposed of in the same way. One suggested remedy is interesting. "The mouths of the Danube were maintained in a navigable state under Turkish authority, by large rakes attached to vessels passing down; and sand has blocked up the Channels considerably, since this simple precaution has been neglected by the Russians."

It now remains, in order to complete the survey

of the City's management of the River below Staines, only to pursue, from the point at which I left it, the history of their defeat and supersession. In 1854 the Corporation was refusing, influenced doubtless by the quarrel forced upon them by the Crown, to advance any further funds from their general estate for the benefit of the navigation; and so critical had the business of the Thames become that in September they sought a conference with the Government. They had vainly brought forward every year the Bill which I have described; doubtless it was not intended that they should have the privilege of reforming themselves. In December it was influentially suggested, in order to arrive at the settlement which had become imperative, that the Corporation should admit the title of the Crown by the acceptance of a charter regranting the bed and soil to themselves, subject to payment to the Crown of one-third of the River rents and fines. This suggestion would doubtless have been accepted without demur, as many rents and fines were being withheld, and encroachments made in their despite; it being now common knowledge that the Authority was being overborne by the Crown. It was, however, discovered that the Woods and Forests, now in this connection the Board of Works, were recommending that the conservacy should be placed in the hands of a newly created commission; "which would

City of London Jurisdiction 233

deprive the Corporation of the conservancy of the River Thames."

Meanwhile £30,000 was urgently needed for repairs and rebuilding. The common council declined to lend it; and the navigation committee turned in despair to the Government. In February, 1855, they were coldly informed that it was their own duty to find the money, with or without any guarantee that it would be repaid if the conservacy were transferred. In July all towing horses were sold. In February, 1856, the Board of Works was taking the extreme step of warning applicants against embanking below high water mark on the sole foundation of the City's permission. And on January 15, 1857, arrived the beginning of the end. On that day, six hundred and sixty years after the Crusader's grant: "The Committee considered relative to the alteration in their powers under the recent agreement with the Crown with respect to the right to the Bed and Soil of the River Thames." Under these articles of agreement, dated December 18, 1856, between the Queen, the Hon. Charles Alexander Gore, commissioner of H. M. Woods and Forests, and the Mayor, Commonalty and Citizens of the City of London, the City withdrew all claim to the ownership of the bed and soil of the River so far as the tide flows and reflows, and admitted the claim of the Crown. They were adjudged to pay £5,000 in respect of the rents and fines already received. Litigation was discontinued; and by March 1, 1857, the Crown right was to be reconveyed to a new Board of Conservancy, except in places immediately adjacent to royal property. One-third of future rents and fines was, as already stated, to be paid to her Majesty's credit; the remainder to be devoted to the benefit of the navigation. The approval of the Board of Works and of the Lord High Admiral was to be obtained in respect of new concessions of embankment. And the new Board was to consist of eleven persons: the Lord Mayor, two aldermen, four nominees of the common council, the deputy master of the Trinity House, and three nominees of the Crown.

These conditions were embodied the same year in the Act 20 and 21 Vict., c. 147. This Act recited that extensive dredging was necessary, that many unauthorised encroachments must be removed, that the steam traffic needed regulation, and that the whole River up to Staines ought to be placed under one Authority possessing the powers formerly enjoyed by the City. This body was forthwith constituted, with a few differences from the original suggestions. Instead of the three Crown nominations two were to be exercised by the Lord High Admiral, one by the Privy Council, and a fourth by the Trinity House of Deptford Strond: forming a Board of twelve in all. As a matter of detail the rights of the Abbey Mill stream were again reserved: "The present course of the River from the west end of the Lock to the head of the Abbey Mill River shall always be continued and preserved so that the said River may be fed with water as before the Lock was made."

In October of the same year the waterbailiff and his assistants, and all the gay watermen of the Lord Mayor, were pensioned off. And thus, by *peine forte et dure*, the City of London was at length and finally expelled from the ancient office it had enjoyed and exercised during the larger part of seven hundred years.

Chapter IX

THE THAMES CONSERVANCY (1857)

IN October, 1857, the Corporation of London handed to this new Authority an inventory of all its machinery and stores. The first meeting of the conservators was held on the seventh of the month at the Mansion House; and others were also held there till the offices in Trinity Square, Minories, were ready. It was decided at the outset that reporters should not be admitted "for the present." Mr. Leach retained his position as engineer; and in November Captain Burstal was elected first secretary.

In the same month the ex-waterbailiff drew the conservators' attention to the "improper practice of letting boats for hire to inexperienced persons": a caution that might still be usefully heeded. In July, 1858, it was ordered that every steam vessel should pay 15s. toll on passing Teddington lock, and that the speed above that point should not exceed five miles an hour: varied in January, 1860, to five

The Thames Conservancy (1857)

miles with the stream, and four against. Netting, except for bait, was this month prohibited between Richmond and London Stone for ever.

Early in the following October the conservators went a survey from Reading downwards. It is not expressly stated; but the step was very probably taken in view of a possible speedy extension of their jurisdiction westward.

It is pleasant to discover the new Authority emulating the proper spirit of their predecessors. In July, 1862, a Mr. Grissell of Hampton Wick complained that Lord St. Leonards had interfered with his fishing at Thames Ditton. "The River," wrote the conservators, "is not the property of Lord St. Leonards"; suggesting at the same time that the complainant should not moor too close to private houses. In October a Mr. Boucher submitted a scheme for "Boat Railways to pass the Locks without opening the Gates"; in all probability some sort of forecast of the modern boat slides or rollers. The scheme was at the moment judged inexpedient.

In July, 1863, it was "observed that the Wood work of the Locks was in a dirty and slimy state"; and scrubbing was ordered. This may be collated with my note on page 197 regarding the upper locks.

The conservators in the summer of 1865 had a little controversy with the Woods and Forests quite on the lines of the struggle between the latter and the Corporation. The new Authority was widening the side channel on the left bank above Hampton Court Bridge, in consequence of complaints about its foulness. Whereupon the Crown agents enquired about the right to perform this cleansing, and were referred to the 1857 Act. For once they were checked; but craftily praising the action of the conservators as beneficial to the Crown property they announced their intention of erecting a boom across each end of the channel to protect the Crown tenants. The Conservancy immediately replied that the watercourse was part of the River Thames, and as such was under their sole control for the benefit and use of the public.

In July of this year the Corporation of London handed over to the conservators "the documents relating to the conservancy." And I find no further specific incidents of interest in connection with the nine years' history of this body, in its restricted form.

Chapter X

THE THAMES CONSERVANCY (1866)

THIS Authority, in essence though not in extent of control the one we know today, is the only body that ever held sole jurisdiction under statute over the whole navigable River from Cricklade to Yantlet Creek. It was constituted under the Act of August 6, 1866. The preamble recites that the preservation and improvement of the upper River was an object of great local and public importance; that the Thames Commissioners were inconveniently numerous and not a body corporate; that the locks and works were in a very bad and dangerous condition and the income for long insufficient for the expense of the works, most of the staff having also been dismissed; that if the upper River were placed and maintained in good order under moderate tolls the traffic would increase; that the Conservancy of 1857 already controlled part of the non-tidal waters and that it was expedient to place the whole navigation under one management. It was therefore enacted that five new members should be added to the now eighteen existing conservators: one nominated by the Board of Trade and four by the moribund commissioners; that all the locks, canals and other works should be transferred to the Conservancy; that the commission should surrender its authority; that its debt to its bondholders should be postponed to the liabilities of the Conservancy; and that the property in all the works should be absolutely conveyed to the Conservancy, who were to maintain them, the former owners of weirs being freed from all liability in respect thereof. The latter might, however, object to the transference within six months from the date of the Act; whereupon either the Conservancy might disclaim by deed such reserved weir, or the dispute might be referred to arbitration. Compensation was of course to be paid for all privately owned works so taken over.

The trees on Temple Lock island were protected under the Act; Buscot and Eaton weirs were expressly reserved to Mr. R. Campbell of Buscot Park, although he, in common with all the old lockowners, was compelled to relinquish his private tolls; and certain rights were saved to Mr. Danbe, the Weirs miller near Iffley. The Conservancy might not regulate the water without regard to the millhead requirements. New revenue was to be secured by a £1,000 annual contribution from each of five

The Thames Conservancy

Metropolitan Water Companies. No new flow of sewage into the River was to be allowed; and existing sewage works were to cease using it after due notice.

Under the Act the numerous bondholders to whom the Thames Commissioners were in debt, to an amount "not exceeding £88,400," were guaranteed in their holdings on the security of the new Conservancy tolls, with three and a half *per cent.* interest. Their claim to arrears of interest was, however, extinguished. I have felt much sympathy with these unfortunate investors; but the subject is obscure. I fancy they obtained but little solid satisfaction. In the *Times* of September 7, 1874, there is a letter signed "Interested Enquirer." It states: "My grandfather who died in 1851 held some £10,000 worth of Thames Bonds. They were not sold at his death; and the trustees some very few years afterwards were told that the bonds were worth nothing." In 1895, under the Act of the previous year, the bonds were being exchanged for Thames Conservancy Stock at only five *per cent.* of their face value. Some of the original 1771 bonds were so transferred this year. The whole affair appears to me an obscure State scandal.

With regard to the mills, whose immemorial veto upon the River's flow was recognised by an Act so modern, it was stated in 1866 that there were then twenty-eight of them between Oxford and Staines, fifteen of which were named in *Domesday*, the others being nearly as ancient; proving their long prescriptive title to their position and their control of the water. Parliament recognised this right; but transferred their weirs, under compensation, to the conservators, "so that private interests should no longer interfere with the navigation of one of the most important highways of the kingdom." The number of mills might require some ingenuity to complete. It seems to demand the inclusion of one at both Oxford and Staines, of the Weirs mill at Iffley, and of others now vanished, such as Iffley, New, Hurley, Cookham, Ray, Clewer and Tangier. The number may only thus be made up; unless, as may justly have been done, Sutton Courtenay was counted as two and Marlow as three.

It is a curious circumstance that when the record of the lockkeepers is revived under the new Conservancy, after the break caused by the defection of the commissioners, higher wages than the old schedule are named in many cases; in spite of the reductions that had taken place and the almost entire exhaustion of funds.

In August, 1866, the Conservancy inspected the works between Oxford and Windsor; and impressed upon the lockkeepers that the old-lock tolls had ceased.

The Thames Conservancy

In September a table of through tolls was settled, to come into force on October 1.

	Per ton		Per ton
London to Staines	9d.	Oxford to Abingdon	6d.
Windsor	1/-	Wallingford	1/-
Maidenhead	1/3	Pangbourne	1/6
Marlow	1/6	Reading	1/9
Henley	2/-	Henley	2/-
Reading	2/6	Marlow	2/6
Pangbourne	2/9	Maidenhead	2/9
Wallingford	3/3	Windsor	3/-
Abingdon	3/9	Staines	3/6
Oxford	4/3	London	4/3

Intermediate distances at twopence per ton per lock. These were evidently inclusive charges for all the locks between the different points named. Rates were fixed for pleasure craft also: one pair oars 6d. per lock per day, two pair 1s., steamers 2s., houseboats 2s. 6d. Steam tugs were free, unless with passengers or cargo on board.

A contemporary order reads "that notices for the sale of refreshments be not exhibited at the premises of the lockkeepers." It was also now decided to divide the River above Oxford into four districts: Cricklade to Radcot, Radcot to New Bridge, hence to King's weir, and hence to Botley Bridge. Lockkeepers were strictly forbidden to demand or receive gratuities, under an order of this date. In December, 1866, lock tickets for pleasure craft were resolved upon; I believe for the first time.

A fresh code of rules for keepers issued in

February, 1867. It mentioned that the old terms "pounds or pound locks, old locks or pens," were to be discontinued in favour of "locks" and "weirs" respectively. Locks were to be kept clear of dirt, weeds, and "dead animals"; and the turf was to be neatly mown. Floods were not to be relieved by the opening of the sluices at both ends of the locks. Laden vessels were to take precedence of empties and pleasure craft; and downstream of upstream traffic, where both were laden.

A curious series of incidents began in April of this year, and lasted some considerable time. A certain gentleman hit on the idea of lifting his craft, a light canoe, out of the water, and carrying it along the towpath past the locks, thereby desiring to evade the tolls. Three others did the same thing at Temple. In July the trick was performed at Boulter's and Old Windsor. I get no more instances till April, 1872, when the evasion occurred at Molesey: tolls had been payable at the "City" locks since 1870. There was evidently some legal difficulty about preventing the offence, as the Conservancy pleaded very gently with this latest offender that "he must surely be aware that the head of water was maintained at great expense as much for small boats such as his as for others not so portable." The keepers were piously cautioned not to allow craft to pass without payment of toll. In July, 1873, several

The Thames Conservancy   245

gentlemen were varying the evasion by pulling their craft over the weirs; and one actually addressed a complaint to the Conservancy that the Shepperton lockkeeper had detained him and demanded toll. Indeed, the right to exact toll under such circumstances was being seriously and publicly questioned; and some great difficulty evidently existed, a the keepers were instructed not to detain the adventurers, but to obtain their names and addresses whenever possible. Several further instances occurred in 1875; at Odney, Shepperton, and other places. The Conservancy declined a suggestion to erect prohibitory notices at the weirs. Evasion recurred as late as April, 1878, at Sunbury; but under the Act of this year toll was made payable for passing "through, *by*, or over" the locks; and the incidents ceased. Certainly, in the absence of the word "by" there seems a clear loophole for the somewhat poor sport of toll-dodging; though it should be remembered that the contemporary toll was sixpence at each lock, in place of the threepence we know.

In September, 1867, a small tax upon pleasure boats was discussed. A litle later this year a proposal was made to issue batches of lock tickets at a cheaper rate; for ordinary small craft 10 for 4s., 25 for 8s., 50 for 12s. I do not know if any effect was given to the suggestion.

It was publicly advertised on January 1, 1868, that the navigation from Oxford to London, from Duke's Cut to New Bridge, and from Inglesham to Radcot, was open; also that the old-lock tolls were abolished, and that the barge toll at the locks was twopence per ton at each and every lock. It does not appear what bearing the last announcement has upon the schedule of October, 1866. In February it was ordered that no tolls were to be paid at the weirs above Oxford; only at the three locks St. John's, Buscot and Pinkhill. Rushey, curiously, is omitted; possibly it was in too disgraceful a state of decay.

In March, 1868, the British Museum was permitted to retain a bronze helmet and two swords that had been dredged up, "until the Conservators form a museum of their own."

In July complaints of the weeds in the River were arriving from all quarters; the Conservancy screw launch was stopped by them, and the Inspector asked for a paddle launch meanwhile.

In August, 1868, a question reached the Authority with regard to the public right of ascending the weir streams, with special reference to Sonning. The conservators would express no opinion, but suggested that it was desirable that voyagers should confine themselves to the navigable waterway. The suggestion was unfortunate; the weir streams are still, at least in theory, the immemorial Thames.

The Thames Conservancy

In September "an increase was reported in the number of barges leaving Oxford." During the following month the landowners between Cricklade and New Bridge called attention to the deplorable state of the River in that district. The Authority was sympathetic, but declared their funds did not allow them to undertake immediate works in the neighbourhood. During November, 1869, however, they announced an intention of seeking powers to cleanse the River between Cricklade and Abingdon. They contemplated also the erection and maintenance of landing-places at various points of the Thames; and the establishment of ferries above Teddington lock. I do not think much was done with reference to the landing-places. The distances from London and from Oxford were ordered to be painted up at each lock, about this time.

The only matter of general interest in the 1870 Act was the imposition of a toll on pleasure traffic at the locks from Penton Hook downward. Quite early in this year a Landowners' Committee seems, somewhat contradictorily, practically to have compelled the Conservancy to abandon their scheme for the improvement of the River between Cricklade and Abingdon. Amongst various bye-laws made in August, 1871, was one reducing the pleasure toll to threepence. On the 23rd of the same month "Pair of Sculls" wrote to the *Times* complaining of being still charged "the old preposterous lock-toll": apparently at Boulter's. He acidly suggests that the greatest improvement would be to put the new regulations into operation. In October the lockkeepers were forbidden to take lodgers; an exception being made at Day's as the house there was not Conservancy property.

After much public pressure, particularly from the Severn Canal Company, the conservators in February, 1872, promised to re-open the navigation between Radcot and New Bridge by repairing Rushey lock and weir and dredging at Clark's Garden and Sansom's ford. A complaint of the firing of guns on the River and towpaths occurs in the following September.

Funds were evidently still very scarce, as in January, 1874, the Authority were compelled to refuse performance of their promise of two years before to improve matters above Oxford, "for the benefit of Faringdon coal barges." The greater frequency of changes amongst the lockkeepers, compared with old times, is apparent in my List. Almost all the upper locks and weirs during this period became subjects for public complaint. A great deal of somewhat impatient criticism appeared in the newspapers, especially towards the end of the summer of 1874. The new Authority had been eight years in existence; and it was hastily concluded that they ought to have done far more to retrieve the ruin left by the old commission. It was not generally understood that the handsome revenues of the tidal River were by statute barred from supplying in the least degree the deficiencies in the upper districts; and much misplaced indignation arose from the oversight. The campaign of 1874 opened with a letter in the *Times* of August 20. "What does the Conservancy do? The upper parts of the River are almost impassable on account of the weeds. The Conservancy never cuts them. The owners of the gardens sloping to the water annually drag the portions bordering on their property, the result of which is that there are acres of cut vegetation round the approaches to many of the locks. The upper locks are simply falling to pieces." In reply to this letter the Rev. F. T. Wethered of Marlow wrote to "testify to the great and substantial improvements effected by the Board since they replaced that effete body the Thames Commissioners"; and pleaded in other letters for time to restore the ruins. He was called "Eyes and No Eyes"; and one assailant wrote: "Temple Lock appeared to me last Sunday a conglomeration of rotten piles feebly maintained by sound ones driven in behind them."

Robertson in 1875 wrote: "When the water is low the river is flushed twice a week by the weir-keepers, each waiting till the water from the weir next above has reached him." In 1876 a notice issued prohibiting shooting upon or near the River.

The Thames at this time must have presented a sickening appearance through sewage; and the *Times* leading articles and correspondence exhibit a very strong public resentment on the subject. The Conservancy's powers had been greatly increased in respect of this matter, but the powerful corporations they had to coerce were very dilatory; and it can have been, moreover, no easy matter entirely to divert the sewage of a large town from its ancient depository. It must be remembered that not only the towns and villages actually on or close to the banks of the River, but those also on tributaries situated as much as ten miles from the junction with the Thames, and hundreds of isolated houses and farms, had to be dealt with : an enormous labour, and one the people coerced could scarcely be expected to sympathise with : as indeed they emphatically did not. A swiftly running brook : surely a heaven-sent opportunity for one's own cleansing; and to be forbidden ever again to use it because of people ten or a hundred miles away ! But it is not pertinent to pursue the subject.

In an Enquiry into Flood Prevention in 1877 the interesting point was mentioned of railway embankments at right angles to the River causing and aggravating floods. It was declared that there had

RADCOT WEIR. Drawn by S. Owen about 1811. Illustrates the obstructions alluded to on the opposite page.

To face p. 25]

The Thames Conservancy

been no navigation above Lechlade "for many years past; in fact, scarcely within the memory of man." The appointment of women lockkeepers was animadverted upon. There were only two cases, however, at Hambledon and Penton Hook; under which heads I remark upon the matter. The contemporary state of the River was thus described.

"I got up [in a small launch] as far as I could, 17 miles above Oxford, where I found only 2 feet of water, and I had to stop. [This would be just below Shifford lock.] It took me all day to do 17 miles, because the weirs are taken to pieces to let you through. There are very few locks above Oxford, but a great many weirs, and the weir is taken to pieces to let you through; they actually unbuild it, whether you are in a steamer, a barge, or a boat; and when the water of the upper part gets nearly on a level with the lower part, you get through in the best way you can. You have to warp yourself through, and then the weir is built up behind you, and you have to wait till the water rises again, which is a most barbarous condition of things; it wastes the whole of the water between the two weirs. I was told that it takes a barge five days to go 32 miles from Oxford to Lechlade." Six of these old weirs are said to have existed at this date; there had been fourteen 10 years earlier: "miserable stumps and sticks, a great obstruction."

During 1881 electric alarm bells were fitted to "all locks where there are mills," to indicate fluctuation in the water level.

In November of this year Mr. S. W. Leach the

engineer died, and was succeeded by Mr. C. J. More. Father and son had between them given eighty years to the River service.

Under the Thames Preservation Act, 1885, shooting on the River was happily prohibited between Teddington and Cricklade. This was the first Act specifically directed towards "the preservation of the River above Teddington lock for purposes of public recreation, and for regulating the pleasure traffic therein." The preamble recites that "the Thames is a navigable highway, and has come to be largely used as a place of public recreation and resort; and that it is expedient that provision should be made that it should be preserved as a place of regulated public recreation." It enacts that it is lawful for all persons, for pleasure or profit, to travel or to loiter upon any and every part of the River through which Thames water flows, excepting private artificial cuts and any other channels which, by lawful title, had been considered private for twenty years previous to the Act.

The *Daily News* noted in June, 1886, that "a dangerous practice recently introduced is that of towing small boats with a pony at a trot." I have seen this done quite recently up at Kelmscott, though the pony only crawled. The writer proceeds: "Surely the time has come for the slow and creepy old country lockkeeper to be superseded at

The Thames Conservancy

the busy stations by a smart, active, and organised staff more after the style of a busy railway station." This shall remain without comment.

In May, 1887, the Conservancy laudably declined a request to advertise at the locks. Next month one of the River keepers was "actively engaged in removing dead animals from the River." It says a great deal for the vigilant cleansing of this nature constantly proceeding that the only unpleasantnesses of this sort I have seen in over twenty years, beside rare dead fish and a dead kingfisher, were some blind kittens hurled to their doom at Hedsor.

In 1894 a long, complicated and important Act was passed, gathering up and perpetuating in a detailed and decisive fashion all the older enactments from 1770 downwards, and considerably adding to them. The various capital sums borrowed by the successive Authorities are recited:

> £88,400 by the Thames Commissioners
> £94,700 by the Corporation of London up to 1857
> £79,906 by the Conservancy.

As already indicated, the commissioners' bonds were now redeemable for Conservancy stock in the ratio of £100 to £5 respectively. The heirs of the old bondholders naturally lost no time in realising what lay open to them of their fathers' investments. The number of Conservators was increased to thirty-eight as from January 1, 1895. The long list of reservations under the Act includes:

Taplow Mill Stream: "between the lock in the said stream and a meadow called Clemash [sic] Mead."

Abbey Mill Stream: to be constantly fed with Thames water.

Buscot and Eaton Weirs to the Buscot Park estate, subject to the rights being exercised only to the extent of working the waterwheel at each place; and generally to the Conservancy bye-laws.

The Hedsor Water privilege to Lord Boston.

In 1897 a resolution was passed which might make the old bargemasters turn in their graves. It ran to the effect that "at Richmond and Teddington locks passenger steamers plying to Molesey be given precedence over the barge traffic; at the other locks the passenger and barge traffic be passed by alternate lockages; and at Teddington on Saturdays, Sundays, and all public holidays priority be given generally to all pleasure traffic over the barges." It was the revenue from this traffic that used to be presented as a negligible perquisite to the lockkeepers for their extra trouble in passing it.

The first prizes for attractive lock gardens were offered in January, 1898. It was anticipated that by the end of the same year "works will be completed which will enable a vessel drawing four feet of water to be navigated to Lechlade and thence through the Thames and Severn Canal to the west of England."

Chapter XI

CONCLUSION

SO far as it is anywhere derived from the archives of the various chief Authorities, the general history of my subject is now complete. It remains only to mention the Act of December 21, 1908, under which the Thames eastward of a point about three hundred and fifty yards below Teddington lock, being the parish boundary of Teddington and Twickenham, was transferred to the reconstituted Port of London Authority. Under this Act the jurisdiction over the non-tidal waters became for the first time, it may perhaps be said, truly democratic; and the extent of the Conservancy jurisdiction submitted to its most recent modification. The number of conservators was reduced to twenty-eight. Four were deputed by the Board of Trade, to represent, expressly, the barge and the pleasure traffic. One came from the Port Authority, two from the Metropolitan Water Board, three from the London County Council, two (it is a pleasure to note) from the Corporation of London, and the remainder from the seven upper riparian county councils, and various Riverside borough and urban councils.

The Conservancy have at various dates been approached to allow floating restaurants to ply for custom on the River, but have always laudably set their faces against the innovation, "objecting to the Thames becoming a highway for hawkers from one end to the other." The exorbitant sums charged at the riparian hotels and inns might seem a point in its favour, were there any guarantee that these enterprises would prove more reasonable. The Authority has also hitherto always declined to display advertisements at the locks.

This notion of floating restaurants is by no means new. I am enabled to present, from the MSS. at Longleat, the following successful petition, nearly three centuries old, for permission to place such vessels upon the River.

To the King's most Excellent Matie.
The humble Petition of John Rookes, Gent.

Sheweth—

That y^r Pet^r (at his greate charge, after many experiments tryed) hath discovered a new and plausible invencion (to builde upon one Boate or Boates, Bottome or Bottomes) wch shall be passable upon the River Thames in all seasonable tymes in the yeare, for the entertainement and honest Recreacon of such persons that may have

Conclusion 257

liking to the said Invencon as therein to take such provisions and necessaries as are vendible in Tavernes and Victuallinge houses especially in the sumer season. W^{ch} Invencon wth yor Maties aprobacon the pet^r will put in practise and shortly bring it to perfeccon.

May it please yor Matie to graunt unto the pet^r his servantes and assignes, yor Maties gratious Lres Patents for 21 yeares to put in practise and make benefitt of the said Invencon to be builded and putt in execucon 4 nobles yearely, during the contyneuance of yor Maties graunt, and as in duty bound the pet^r will pray for yor Matie etc.

[Written in another hand]

Att the Court att St James 5th Maij 1636.

His Matie is pleased to graunt the Pet^{rs} Request and Mr Attorny or Sollicitor Generall is to prepare a bill of the same fitt for his Royall signature as in such case is usuall.

[Signed] Edw: Powell.

The description of the invention as being built upon one boat or bottom looks as if something very like our modern houseboats was intended; and that it was not to be a mere drinking bar, like some of the more recent propositions, is evident from the mention of "provisions and necessaries." I do not think there is any appreciable public demand for these floating shops. I believe that within recent years some few houseboats have been licensed to provide teas, but I do not think they proved remunerative. One was moored on the left bank

R

just below the Albert Bridge at Datchet in the years about 1900; but I think it is no longer there.

Here then is the history of eight and a half centuries of the inland navigation of the River of Thames. It antedates the Norman Conquest, when the user was regulated by the king in council, and the popular appeal against the encroachments of the lords still lay direct to the Crown. For over seven and a half of these centuries the traffic relied for motive power wholly upon strength of body, of wind and stream. No mere scene of pleasure, of holiday and idleness, the River was the everyday commercial highway of southern England, where she lies broadest, between London and the sea in the east and the great and notable port of Bristol and the sea in the west: as vitally a highway to those elder men as any railway or trunk road is to us. A man undertaking the conduct of a barge to its remoter parts in some dry summer might easily be absent from his home as long as a modern captain who navigates a liner to the Cape; and ran perhaps greater risks of life and limb. Queens and kings and nobles, as well as squires and lesser men, used it as a matter of course. At two o'clock of a July morning Elizabeth will leave a masque at Richmond and step into her barge for home and rest; and a few miles of River formed a well understood stage in

Conclusion 259

journeys to places far from its banks. And for none was there any shirking of the weirs and other obstructions in their way. All, whether in well-found private barge or public wherry, must run the gauntlet; and found no safety in pound lock or lazy boatslide.

It was, as I have shewn, nearly six centuries from the opening of my history before any vestige of popular control of the Thames can be traced. Acts of Parliament there were, it is true; but the executive was always vested in individuals appointed by the Crown, or later in small local and quite unrepresentative bodies. And more than two other centuries had to pass before, within living memory, representatives of actual users of the Thames could obtain any share in its regulation.

Finally, and ideally considered, there resides something very noble and epical in the watching and shepherding of this great living water streaming down perpetually and spontaneously from its springs to its rest in the sea. It is a conjecture for the vigils of the night: where will the great water break its banks in some quickening flood, what poor framework of iron and timber will it crush and sweep away, over what meadows will it exult, what peasant will it wash out of his home and rob of his little all? It is a dream of dreams to picture Thames streaming over his green carpets of swaying weed, thundering over his loftier weirs, "whispering over

Bablock Hithe," summoning out many a man in the depth of night to allow him a little more way here, or there to pen him back when his violence abates. His waters descend without our thought; they are alive and fierce and cunning; and must by lively and cunning forethought be eased or confined lest they turn and rend you. "I cannot get away from it," says Mr. Belloc, "that the Thames may be alive." For all I can ever see, watching him by night at Strand-on-the-Green, in the grey dawn at Dorchester or Buscot, huddling in flood through the old strong bridges, or sucking and whispering, green and deep, past the haunted aits at Moulsford: for all, I say, that I myself can discern, here or anywhere, Thames is one living spirit, whole and indivisible, from the loneliness at Trewsbury Mead to his final loneliness seaward of the Nore.

Appendix I

TABLE OF PRIVATE TOLLS AT THE FLASH WEIRS

I KNOW of no general schedule earlier than Overton in column 2, whose *Map of Thirty Miles round London*, from which I derive the figures, is undated, but may I think be placed about 1720. He and Griffiths both precede the 1751 Commission; and based perhaps upon regulations made by the Commission of 1695. Bowles's figures, incorporated in the same column, are dated 1774; but are probably an out-of-date copy with a few trifling variations. Bathurst's notes of various dates, in column 4, are interesting. The figures from Bowen's *Map of the Thames*, published in 1775, make column 6 a complete puzzle; they disagree with everything else; I can offer no comment upon them.

The only figures I know of an earlier date than column 1 are those noted *passim* in the Oxford-Burcot chapter, pp. 62-89.

With regard to the bridges included in the Table, a systematic search in the Patent Rolls and elsewhere for grants of pontage would probably reveal the fact that the barges were mulcted in an almost perpetual tax for the sole benefit of the road traffic.

NAME	(1) House of Lords MSS No. 927 prae 1681 — No tonnage named	(2) Overton, ? 1720 Griffiths, 1746 C. Bowles, 1774 — Probably per 60 tons	(3) 1751 Scattered Notes — Probably per 60 tons	(4) Bathurst 1772 — Per 150 tons
1 St. John's		1/6	3/- or 6/-	
Buscot		2/6	12/-	
3 Farmer's		1/-		
4 Hart's, Eaton or West		1/-	} 5/-	
5 Day's or East		1/-		
6 Monk Mill			9/-	
7 Clarke's or Beck's		Free	3/-	
8 Old Man's		1/-		
9 Old Nan's		1/- B	2/6	
10 Rushey		1/-	2/-	
11 Winney Weg's			2/-	
12 Lower Rudge's			4/-	
13 Tadpole, Rudge's or Kent's		1/- B "Free"		
14 Thames		1/-	1/-	
15 Ten Foot				
16 Duxford			4/-	
17 Shifford		1/-		
18 Limbre's		1/-	1/6	
19 Ridge's or Cock's, &c.		1/-	1/6	
20 Ark or Hart's		1/-		
21 Skinner's or Langley		1/-	} 3/-	
22 Pinkhill				
23 Eynsham or Bolde's		1/6		
24 King's	Never any	charge ;	owned by	the Duke of Marlborough

Table of Private Tolls

(5) 1771 60 ton barges	(6) Bowen, 1775 70 tons ab. Wallingford 140 t. bel.	(7) Mylne 1791 per 60 tons	(8) 1821 per 60 tons	(9) City Records 1831 p. 20 tons	(10) Guildhall Record Office 1846 p. 5 tons
1 3/-	9/9	3/-	6/-		
2 12/-	16/-	12/-	6/-		
3 } 5/- 4 5	5/- 5/-	} 5/-	} 8/-		
6	"Old Eye" 9/9	9/-			
7 5/-	7/6	5/-	6/-		
8	2/6				
9 2/6		2/6	3/-		
10 } 5/- 11	5/-	2/- 2/-	} 5/6		
12		4/-			
13	5/-				
14 1/-					
15 3/-	"Newnton" 3/-		4/-		
16 4/-	4/6	4/-	4/-		
17 3/-			4/-		
18 1/6	4/-	} 1/6	5/-		
19 1/6	4/-		4/6		
20					
21 } 3/- 22	8/6	} 3/-	} 6/-		
23	3/-		"3d.p. boat"		
24					

	(1)	(2)	(3)	(4)
[25] Godstow Bridge				
[26] Osney				
[27] Castle Mills				
[28] Rewley				
[29] Folly Bridge				
[30] Iffley		2/6	5/-	
[31] Sandford		22/-	10/-	
[32] Nuneham		2/6		
[33] Swift Ditch Poundlock				
[34] Swift Ditch flash lock		20/6	12/- [Probably inclusive]	1734 15/-
[35] Abingdon				
[36] Sutton Courtenay		35/-	20/-	1732 30/-
[37] Day's	1/- "Little Witnam"	1/-	6/-	1734 5/-
[38] Benson	10d.	15/-		1734 15/-
[39] Wallingford Bridge		2/6		
[40] Moulsford		O 2/6 : G & B 1/-		
[41] Cleeve	3/-	25/-	8/-	1753 15/-
[42] Goring	3/4	25/-	8/-	1753 15/-
[43] Hart's		Free		
[44] Whitchurch	2/- " Locks & Turnp'ks"	15/-	8/-	
[45] Mapledurham	1/8	12/6	8/-	1753 15/-
[46] Caversham	2/-	"& Bridge" 12/6	8/-	1753 16/-
[47] Sonning	1/8	do. 10/-	3/6	1731 8/-
[48] Shiplake		7/6	3/6	no date 6/-

Table of Private Tolls

	(5)	(6)	(7)	(8)	(9)	(10)
25		10/- [prob. error]	"For winding up," 1/-			
26			} 1/6			
27		6/-				
28			1/6			
29		6d.				
30	5/-	4/8	15/-	10/- Should p'rh'ps be reversed	3/10	8d. or 10d.
31	10/-	Old Lock 4/8 Turnpike 11/8	17/6	5/-	4/2	8d.
32		5/6	1/6			
33	} 12/-	} 13/8		} 12/- [Probably inclusive]	} 8/4	
34						
35	Perhaps inc. with Swift Ditch	13/-	12/- [Perh. includes Swift Ditch]		5/6	1/-
36	20/-	25/8	20/-	20/-		
37	6/-	8/6	3/6	6/-	3/8	
38	8/-	10/10	8/-	10/-	4/3	8d.
39		1/-	1/			
40			"10/- half-yearly"			
41	8/-	10/-	8/-	"140t" 20/10	} 6/4	8d.
42	8/-	10/-	8/-	do.		8d.
43						
44	8/-	10/-	8/-	do.	2/8	8d.
45	8/-	10/-	8/-	do.	3/8	3d.
46	8/-	10/-	8/-	do.	3/2	8d.
47	3/6	4/6	3/6	"140t." 10/0½	1/9½	3½d.
48	3/6	4/6	3/6	do.	1/3½	3½d.

	(1)	(2)	(3)	(4)
⁴⁹ Marsh	6d. "NewMill"	7/6	3/6	no date 5/-
⁵⁰ Hambledon*	1/-	9/-	3/-	,, 6/-
⁵¹ Hurley, or New	8d.	7/6	3/-	,, 4/-
⁵² Temple		3/-	3/-	,, 4/-
⁵³ Marlow	8d.	4/-	3/-	,, 4/-
⁵⁴ Boulter's*	1/-	7/6	3/-	,, 6/-
⁵⁵ Windsor Bridge				
⁵⁶ Staines Bridge				
⁵⁷ Kingston Bridge		10/-		

* The rough notes in the Oxford University Archives alluded to on pages 116-117, and seemingly related to col. 4, afford the following particulars. *Hambledon Lock*, 1731 : Barges of 100 tons and upwards 6/-, between 70 tons and 100 tons, 4/-, between 45 and 70 tons, 3/-. In 1753 : 190 to 120 tons, 7/- ; 120 to 80 tons, 5/- ; 80 to 50 tons, 4/-. In August 1754 an over-all rate was made of 2½d. per 5 ton ; increased the following month to 3d. "At the Winch 1/- for the largest Barges and 6d. for all others." *Boulter's Lock*, 1731 : the same as Hambledon ; also 1753. August, 1754 a universal rate of 2d. per ton ; increased in September to 3d.

Table of Private Tolls

	(5)	(6)	(7)	(8)	(9)	(10)
49	3/6	7/6	3/6	6d. p. 5t. up to 60t. 3½d. do. 60-140t.	2/9½	3½d.
50	3/-	7/-	3/-	"140t." 9s. 0½d.	1/6	3d.
51	3/-	8/-	3/-	do. 15/- & winch 2/-	1/-	.
52	3/-	4/6	3/-		6/-	3d.
53	3/-	4/6	3/-	do.	2/6	3d.
54	3/-	4/6	3/-	140t. 10/-	2/6	3d.
55		6d.	1/6			
56		8d.				
57						

Appendix II

TOWARDS the end of my work I came upon Thorold Rogers's interesting and stimulating remarks, in the fifth volume of his *History of Prices*, upon ancient water carriage. I refer the curious to his large collection of concrete payments for freight ; and content myself with a short reference to his general remarks. I experience no slight diffidence in venturing to disagree with so distinguished an authority ; but some of his statements appear to myself so incompatible with the information I have presented that I feel bound to suggest a demurrer.

The professor asserts : " In the fourteenth century Henley appears to have been the furthest point to which [the Thames] was ordinarily navigable, and apparently this was the limit as late as 1541." It might seem incredible, *a priori*, that up to the middle of the sixteenth century there was no continuous passage for merchandise along the River between London and such important places as Reading, Wallingford, Abingdon, and Oxford, and all the smaller communities that gradually became dependent upon these centres. No history of either the River or of Henley affords the slightest hint in support of the professor's theory. Not only so : there is surely abundant positive evidence to the contrary. The *A.S.C.* declares that in 894 the Danish host "fared up along the Thames till they reached the Severn." The way in which the pre-Conquest Oxford-Abingdon traffic is

Henley as Head of Navigation

alluded to, in the very outset of my history, appears to imply a lengthy voyage for the barges: "up and down" past Abingdon Abbey. The toll of *allecia* must surely have come from London. In 1205 there is "William son of Andrew" his "one ship going and returning upon the Thames between Oxford and London"; and the earlier ship of the said Andrew himself, "from Abingdon to London," with which the officials of various riparian towns were forbidden to interfere. In 1227 Henry III commanded that Henricus de Appelworth should be allowed to take his vessel back to Wallingford from Windsor, whither he had brought the king by water, toll free through the flashlocks for this turn. Seven years later the same king ordered that the riparian landowners should not obstruct the passage of timber along the River from Reading to Oxford, for a hospital he was building there. In 1254 two shiploads of corn were not to be obstructed passing down from Goring to London. In 1267 the passage of corn is facilitated from Wallingford right down to Rayleigh. In 1274 the River was "to be so widened that ships and great barges might ascend from London to Oxford, and descend." The petition of 1294 and the other of near date were presented by traders actually in the habit of passing by water between London and Oxford. Obstructions to general traffic are complained of at Abingdon in 1316. In 1320 a complaint originated in Oxford that vessels "passing between London and Oxford" were obstructed. In 1351 the River was twice ordered to be cleared, between London and Oxford and between London and Radcot: the latter point immemorially an important terminus for River traffic; in 1352 between London and "Henlee" Bridge, and in 1364 between Oxford and London. In 1403 there is the Drayton indictment for absence of a proper winch at Marsh to accommodate the traffic between London and Oxford; also the allusion the same year to the prioress of Goring her "lock" at Shiplake, which, it was certified, all men could pass without danger as of old time. Similar evidence might be multiplied abundantly.

I have discovered only three references to Henley as a terminal point: in 1352; in 1358 when a petition of Parliament directed attention to the obstructed state of the River downwards to London; and in 1369, when the district upwards to Radcot was criticised. Only the last supports the professor's theory; and unless he possessed some unpresented evidence the mere absence of quoted rates is a slender foundation for his sweeping generalisation. True, very few barges made the through voyage: that must be conceded; but they were sufficient, or more would have been provided; and it would not be an ordinary use of language to assert that the railways to the extreme north are not in this year of grace ordinarily travelled upon, simply because so small a proportion of trains need to perform the complete journey. The *Lansdowne MS.* of 1472, containing the oracular statement that there was then "no common passage for barges so far as Marlow and Bisham," should be allowed to the professor for what it is worth.

The professor continues: "But in course of time the bargemen got as far as Burcot": at some time, the suggestion is, subsequent to 1541. "The owner of Burcot constructed a pier, from the bank over the stream, and probably to an eyot in the middle of the River which is here deep." This eyot I assume to be the one still *in situ* about a mile below Clifton Hampden Bridge. It is scarcely, I fancy, in midstream; its distance from the Burcot bank is, as I recollect it, at least double that from the other. To have built a sort of bridge-pier or jetty across to it from the left bank, leaving only the narrow righthand passage open, would have

Burcot as Head of Navigation

been so egregious an obstruction that I must believe that the dead silence of the whole body of Thames history upon its existence is conclusive against the professor.

There is perhaps not much else to advance against his vivid and intensely interesting remarks; though I do not think the period during which Burcot was "the head of the Thames navigation" was so extended, or the impassability of the spot so absolute, as he imagines. The only independent evidence in his favour occurs, curiously, in 1635: at the very moment when the improvements in this district were on the verge of completion. Long after the James I works were carried out, down even to this very day, the rocky bed at Clifton has given trouble, only to a degree less than formerly; and I have no doubt whatever that a certain regular traffic has at all times penetrated to Oxford. From Burcot, he writes, "freight was hauled through the grounds near the house to the Abingdon road, from which a short cut was constructed to the main Oxford road. I visited Burcot in 1887, and could easily discover where the pier must have been placed, from the ruts, four or five in number, cut deeply through the ground between the water and the high road, and all converging to a point on the river. The depth to which these ruts were cut into the soil was clear evidence of the great amount of traffic from this farthest point of Thames navigation to and from Oxford and the district, especially as there is good reason to believe that the period between the extension of the waterway from Henley to Burcot with the establishment of the pier, and the subsequent extension from Burcot to Oxford, was not longer than seventy or eighty years." The interpolation may be pardoned: surely only seventy or eighty weeks of so huge a traffic would leave marks as indelible as the longer period. "The present appearance of these deeply cut ways proves beyond question that, during the time the pier and cross road were in use, no part of the River was more busy than Burcot pier. It seems to me that the owner of the pier exacted progressively heavy dues for the use of his wharf; and that these dues, light at first, were considerably reduced when the Government began to pass Acts for extending the navigation." What Acts were these, so loosely referred to? There was no legislation, except upon the City of London's district, between the professor's date of 1541 and the Act of 1603. The Act of 1623 followed; but neither seems in the slightest to affect any wharfage rates at Burcot. "I could not, when I examined this spot, but picture to myself, in contrast with the sleepy quiet which now reigns over the deserted landing place and forgotten pier, what a scene of activity Burcot must have been when it was the head of the Thames navigation, and was thronged all the year through with River traffic; how it swarmed with bargemen and carriers, how the heavily laden waggons were dragged up those roads or carried their freight down to the water's edge; and how the numerous barges, ready to unship or receive their cargoes, were waiting at the pier."

All very eloquent, very fascinating; but in the whole history of the River there is for Burcot, as for Henley, no tradition of any such thing, or of any pier blocking the stream. How came Bishop to miss it in his manifesto of 1580? Nor of any such accumulation of traffic. Wharves upon wharves on both sides of the River, and a substantial bridge thrown across, now vanished without the smallest trace, would scarcely have coped with such traffic at such a Pool of Burcot. The navy yard complaint of 1633, beginning "Every barge coming from Burcot," should not be forgotten, so far as it is in the professor's favour; though it is later than the period he discusses. Indeed, timber for the

Burcot as Head of Navigation 273

navy, constituting a tolerably regular downward traffic, seems to have been the staple cargo dealt with at Burcot. It is nearly always in connection with timber that the place is mentioned in the S. P. Dom. But until I discover some more extensive independent evidence I must look upon the professor's picture as an entertaining extravaganza. I believe that whatever temporary importance became attached to Burcot as a River port accrued not from any traditional impassability of the district thence to Oxford, such as we are asked in his book to believe, difficult though it always inherently was; but from the very simple, accidental reason of the gradual increase in the sizes of the barges and the unusual local cost and trouble of periodically increasing the floating depth for their accommodation.

It is quite conceivable that the constant dredging up of relics along the whole River bed might be elaborated into a very strong argument in favour of the ancient continuity of the Thames highway.

S

Appendix III

Landing Places

THE question of public landing places on the River Thames is one, perhaps, of more theoretical than practical interest today. More than once it has been publicly asserted, usually by riparian owners, that except by courtesy no landing places whatever exist upon the River banks, or so few as to be negligible, westward of Staines. The claim might be granted without much loss, eastward of Oxford at least; so frequently is the courtesy accommodation provided. Barges have always found wharves, at town or mill, for the purposes of their business; where their crews could leave them and go ashore at will. The pleasure traffic has always found, in proportion with its growing volume, an increasing sufficiency of rafts and boatyards by means of which the general public has been able to leave the waterside.

But I do not think the claim, at least in its absolute form, can be successfully maintained; unless indeed with the right to land be coupled a right to moor; and for a traveller by water the one is of little use without the other. Setting aside for the moment, however, the mooring of one's vessel; every observant user of the Thames knows here and there some short strip of timber campsheathing, some flight of perilous stone steps, some little alley way between high walls, where he can land independently of boatyard or stage, and where

Landing Places 275

the matter of mooring will be guilelessly quitclaimed by the attendant *gamin* for mere pence. The instance that always presents itself to me most vividly in this connection is one I have very often used at Wargrave, a very little above the *George and Dragon*. Almost unnoticeably a tiny, primitive stage projects a few feet into the water, landing upon which you find yourself at the foot of an ascending way between lofty walls that winds up past beautiful houses and old cottages into Wargrave against the *Bull*. No-one is officially in charge of the stage; like the sun, it is just there; and you think no more of it than of breathing. Many a man will recall some similar accommodation in other districts.

Westward of Oxford, in those solitudes of which I have written in my *Stripling Thames*, opportunities of landing, whether of courtesy or right, are very infrequent. The thirty two miles, however, between the Severn Canal and Oxford were, for the barge traffic, rather to be hurried through with all possible speed than to be stayed in; business had very few appointments there in its palmiest days, and has almost none now. And as for the pleasure traffic, men who enter that Far Off Country learn to chance it.

The following list of places which, or at which, are officially reputed to be public landing places was given me in 1910. The comments after colons are my own.

" Lechlade Bridge: probably at the wharf.
St. John's Bridge.
Tadpole Bridge, at the *Trout* wharf.
New Bridge, at the *Maybush* wharf.
Eynsham Bridge: probably at the wharf.
Oxford, at Grandpont.
Abingdon, above the Berks and Wilts Canal entrance: probably at the steps against St. Helen's.
Sutton Courtenay, in the mill stream: probably at the roadway against the mill.

Clifton Hampden, in the weir stream opposite the lock.
Shillingford, at the hotel wharf.
Wallingford, at the Oxford Canal wharf.
Little Stoke Ferry, on the Berks side : probably at the roadway against the railway bridge.
Moulsford, at the *Beetle and Wedge*.
Streatley, by the mill.
Basildon, in Mr. Morrison's meadow, near "The Grotto."
Pangbourne, above Whitchurch mill, and by the *Swan*.
Norcot Scours.
Caversham Lock : probably at the steps just below.
Sonning Bridge : probably at the roadway just below.
Henley, above the bridge.
Aston Ferry.
Marlow : probably at the foot of St. Peter's Street, where the old bridge was.
Maidenhead.
Windsor, at the coal wharf.
Queen's Ait, just below at the roadway on the Berks side.
Bells of Ouseley : the towpath here is a public road.
Egham, below the gasworks.

And numerous lower places: not detailed; but the difficulty never arose, I believe, in the old City jurisdiction. There are therefore, with my Wargrave instance which is curiously omitted, twenty-eight places in these 108 miles of River at which there is a reputed public right to land; one in about every three and three-quarter miles of River: a number fully sufficient to rebut the denial of the right. To what extent, however, any mooring right obtains I do not know.

Index of Places

Abbey River (Chertsey), 208, 209, 235, 254
Abingdon, 16, 50, 62, 67, 69, 71, 79, 84, 85, 87, 93, 103, 112, 116, 120, 123, 127, 128, 130, 137-139, 148, 162, 172, 174, 243, 247, 268, 269, 275
— abbey, 13, 22, 39, 56, 269
— constable of, 138, 139
— flashlock and weir, 51, 56, 93, 172, 174, 176, 187, 264
— lock, 140, 156, 167, 181, 188
— mayor of, 71
— mill, 45, 81, 82
— road, 271
— St. Helen's church, 275
— wharf, 67, 71
Albert bridge, 258
Aldworth, 25
Amerden, 134, 148
Amney Crucis, 181
Amwell, Gt., 144
Ankerwyke, 98
Appleford, 51
Ark weir, 262
Aston ferry, 276
Avon, River (Bath), 102, 166

Bablock Hithe, 260
Ballinger's weir, 206
Barking, 32
Barton (Abingdon), 13
Basildon, 55
— landing place at, 276
Beck's weir (Radcot), 262

Beggar's Hole ferry, 156
Bells of Ouseley, 276
Bell weir, 98
— — lock, 198
Bensington, Benson, 148
— flashlock, 51, 56, 94, 99, 104, 137, 173, 176, 187, 264
— lock, 156, 181
— mill, 45
Bisham, 36, 44, 54, 270
— church, 96
Black Potts, 97
Blake's lock, 161, 173
Boatman's Way, 81
Bodleian Library, 65, 115, 127
Bold's weir, 147, 172, 262 (See also *Eynsham*)
Bolney weir, 50, 54
— backwaters, 54
Botley bridge, 243
Boulter's flashlock and weir (See also *Ray*), 97, 99, 104, 124, 173, 187, 266
— lock, 97, 126, 128, 130, 132-136, 148, 149, 151-153, 156, 159, 165, 168, 185, 244, 248
— locks prohibited below, 97
Bourne End mill, 45
Boveney church, 97
Bray church, 97
— lock, 134, 145
— mill, 97
Breach's weir, 55, 95
Brentford, 152, 201, 208
Bristol, 258
British Museum, 120, 246

Broken wharf, 100
Brookin's (Skinner's) weir, 147
Brooks's wharf, 112
Buck ait, 95, 96
Bull inn (Queenhithe), 112
— — (Wargrave), 275
Bull wharf, 99
Burcot, 63, 64, 66, 69, 72, 73, 82, 84-86, 98-101, 103, 105
— ait at, 270
— as traffic terminus, 62, 72, 83, 270-273
— pier at, 270-273
Buscot, 260
— lock, 156, 166, 197, 246
— park, 240, 254
— weir, 147, 171, 174, 176, 240, 254, 262

Canals: Abingdon-Lechlade, 87, 151
— Berks and Wilts, 150, 275
— Henley-London, 230
— Isleworth-Maidenhead, 139, 140, 149-151
— Kennet and Avon, 166, 228
— Langley-Botley, 159
— Oxford-Coventry, 59, 213
— Stroudwater, 166
— Tadpole-Shifford, 159
— Thames and Severn, 139, 140, 147, 150, 153, 161, 164, 166, 191, 248, 254, 275
— — Junction, 152, 164
Carpenter's weir, 94
Castle Eaton, 163
Castle mills weir, 264
Caversham, 55
— bridge, 55, 95, 264
— ferry, 167
— flashlock, 51, 55, 104, 119, 173, 176, 187, 264
— lock, 156, 181, 276
— mill, 45
Chalmore Hole, 148
— lock, 181
Chawsey weir, 51, 55

Checkenden flashlock, 55
Chelsea bridge, 229
Chelworth, 163
Chertsey, 99, 102, 112, 136, 201, 2
— bridge, 98
— — hill, 206
— lock, 207, 208
— mill, 206
Cherwell, River, 83, 102
Childsworth farm, 58
Chilswell Pool, 58
Chiswick, 92
Cholsey, 55
— mill brook, 55
— railway bridge, 55
Churn, River, 34
Cirencester, 34, 111
City Barge inn, 202
City of London Tavern, 169
Clark's garden, 248
— (Radcot) weir, 147, 171, 17 262
Cleeve ferry, 156
— flashlock, 51, 55, 94, 104, 17 176, 187, 264
— lock, 140, 156, 189
— mill, 45
Clemarsh mead, 254
Clewer mill, 242
— stream, 97
Clifton Hampden, 62, 94, 271, 2
— bridge, 270
— ferry, 64, 85
— lock, 161, 178, 276
Clyde, River, 205
Cock's weir, 262 (See also Gran Cock's)
Colnbrook, 99
Colne River, 15
Cookham, 54, 97, 211
— lock, 126, 135, 185
— mill, 45, 242
Cottrell's flashlock (Shiplake),
— weir (Cookham), 97
Cricklade, 25, 64, 124, 161-16 194, 199, 239, 243, 247, 252
Crockley-in-the-Edge, 63
Cubberley, 111

Index of Places

Culham, 56, 75, 80-82
— bridge (*old*), 67, 73-75, 172
— ferry, 156
— lock, 178
— weir (*Swift Ditch*), 51, 56
— wharf, 85

Danube, River, cleansing of, 231
Datchet, 258
— ferry 97
Day's flashlock (Dorchester), 56, 85, 94, 99, 108, 120, 173, 176, 187, 264
— lock, 140, 156, 248
— weir (Grafton), 60, 176, 262
Dedham lock, 133
Deptford, 99, 140
Dorchester (Oxon), 56, 260
Down Amney, 163
Down mead, 85
Duke's Cut, 246
Duxford, 194
— weir, 147, 171, 176, 262

East Anglian Navigations, 25
East weir (Grafton), 60, 171, 262
Eaton weir (Hart's), 3, 7, 240, 254, 262
Ebro, River, 46
Eel Pie island, 121
Egham, 276
Eisey, 163
Enclosure of lands affects rivers, 215
Eton, 123, 196
— college, 97
Exe, River, 38
Exeter canal, 68
Eynsham bridge wharf, 275
— monastery, 39
— weir (*See also Bold's*), 3, 7, 39, 176, 262

Faringdon, coal barges, 248
Farmer's weir, 262

Fisherhouse Point, 207
Fleet River, 101
Folly bridge, 140
— — flashlock, 176, 264
Frogg's mill, 45, 96
Fulham, 101
— bridge, 202
Fyfield, Berks, 24

Gardyn, le, 32
Gatehampton, 148
George & Dragon inn, 275
Gill's bucks, 97
Godalming, 124
Godstow, 160
— bridge, 58, 140, 264
— lock, 156, 159
— nunnery, 38
— weir, 176
Goring, 120, 269
— flashlock, 51, 55, 94, 104, 108, 173, 176, 187, 264
— lock, 140, 156
— mill, 7, 45
— prioress of, 270
Grafton lock, 60
Granny Cock's weir, 172 (*See also Cock's*)
Great Western Rly, 182, 218, 219
Guildford, 112, 124, 136
Guildhall library, 120, 149, 187
— record office, 222, 263

Hallsmead eyot, 96
Ham, 215
Hambledon ferryman, 156
— flashlock or weir, 28, 50, 54, 96, 104, 173, 175, 187, 266
— lock, 133, 156, 174, 251
— mill, 45
— winch, 266
Hampton, 35, 49, 112, 158, 201, 205, 208
— Court, 211, 214, 226, 228
— — bridge, 238

Hampton Wick, 35, 237
— — weir at, 49
Hannington, 163
Hardwick, 95
Hart's flashlock (Basildon), 51, 55, 94, 140, 264
— (Ark) weir 262
— (Eaton) weir, 3, 7, 176, 262
— (Grafton) weir, 147, 167
— (Rudge's) weir, 147
Haules weir, 95
Hedgworth weir (Cookham), 54
Hedsor, 253
— Water, 254
— weir, 54, 148
Henley, 17, 26, 27, 100, 123, 132, 148, 174, 191, 211, 243, 276
— as head of navigation, 268-70
— bridge, 269, 276
Hennerton backwater, 54
— — mill in, 54
Hinksey, South, 58
Hokehawes, 32
Holderness's weir, 97
Holgyllys weir, 32, 33
Hungerford stairs, 112
Hurley, 132, 147
— (New) flashlock, 54, 96, 104, 173
— mill, 45, 242
— (New) lock, 133, 156, 190, 266
— winch, 8

Iffley, 240, 242
— flashlock, 56, 172, 176, 187, 264,
— lock, 67, 72, 73, 75, 77, 86-88, 93, 156, 170, 179, 181
— mill, 45, 242
Inglesham, 163, 166, 246
"Isis," River, 69, 111, 116
Isleworth, 35, 49, 91, 126, 149, 151, 200, 201
— ait, 212
— weir at, 49

Keen Edge ferry, 156
Kelmscot, 252
Kemble, 111
Kempsford, 163
Kennet, River, 83, 102, 115, 161, 166
— Mouth, 119, 132, 148
Kennington (Oxon), 56
Kent's weir, (Tadpole) 262
Kew, 34, 210-212, 214
— bargehouse, 211, 212
— bridge, 126
— the king's bargehouse at, 201
— tollhouse, 212
Kingston, 10, 34, 58, 99, 123, 126, 136, 158, 199, 201, 204, 207, 208, 212, 220
— bridge, 202, 207, 266
— bridgewardens, 49
— overfalls, 206, 207
— weirs at, 49
King's weir, 3, 7, 176, 243, 262

Laleham, 158, 159, 203, 207, 208
— gulls, 98, 204, 206, 207
— paygates, 203, 204
Lambeth, 211
Langley weir (Limbery's), 147, 172, 176
— — (Ridge's), 159
— — (Skinner's), 172, 262
Lashbrook ferry, 156
Latton, 163
Lea, River, 144, 153
Lechlade, 4, 59, 74, 85, 106, 113, 119, 120, 127, 135, 139, 140, 148, 152, 162-164, 172, 175, 194, 195, 197, 206, 251, 254
— town bridge, 275
— wharf, 275
Limbery's weir, 172, 262 (*See also* Langley)
Little Stoke ferry, 276
Littleton, 207
Loddon, River, 83
Lombardy, 67
London, 15-17, 19, 21, 22, 26, 27, 32, 63, 65, 66, 72, 83, 98, 99-103, 105, 111, 113, 116, 127,

Index of Places

128, 132, 135, 143, 152, 154, 164, 170, 196, 201, 211, 213, 215, 216, 227, 243, 246, 247, 258, 268-270
— bridge, 40, 47, 58, 124, 132, 200, 208, 226
— — old stone of, used on tow-paths, 221
— measure of, 59, 60
— Pool of, 183
— Stone (*See Staines Stone*)
London & Southampton Rly., 218
Longleat, 256
Lower Mowsham's, 134
Lower Rudge's weir, 262
Lushill, 163

Magpie island, 96
— bucks at, 96
Maidenhead, 45, 50, 99, 100, 123, 132, 136, 149, 191, 243, 276
— bridge, 97
— mill, 45
Mansion House, 236
Mapledurham, 124, 142, 183
— flashlock or weir, 51, 55, 95, 104, 173, 176, 187, 264
— lock, 156, 189
— mill, 45
Marlborough, 162
Marlow, Great, 36, 44-46, 132, 141, 148, 164, 183, 211, 243, 249, 270, 276
— bridge, 46, 276
— flashlock or weir, 36, 46, 50, 52-54, 96, 104, 173, 187
— lock, 140, 156, 158, 185, 266
— mill, 54, 242
— St. Peter's street, 276
Marsh flashlock or weir, 50, 54, 96, 104, 173, 187, 266, 269
— lock, 156
— mills, 17, 45, 54
Marston Maisey, 163
Maybush inn (New Bridge), 275
Medley weir, 3, 7, 176
Medmenham abbey, 96
— weir, 96

Medway, River, 16, 19, 24, 30, 31
Merton (Surrey), 34
Mill End, 132
Molesey, 136, 207, 214, 220, 254
— lock, 208, 220, 244
— — accident at, 220
Monkey island, 126
Monk mill, 197, 262
Mortlake, 32, 126
Moulsford, 260, 276
— *Beetle and Wedge*, 276
— flashlock or weir, 94, 140, 264

New Bridge, 24, 172, 243, 246-248, 275
Newbury, 112, 167
Newditch weir (Shifford), 171
New lock (*See also Hurley*) flashlock or weir, 50, 54, 132
— — weir (Grafton), 60
Newman's bucks, 97
New mill (at Marsh), 45, 242, 266
— flashlock (? at Marsh), 104
Newnton (Ridge's) weir, 263
New River, 144
New Were, 59, 60
Norcot Scours, 276
Nore, the, 260
Normandy, 217
Northmoor lock, 161
North Stoke, 38
— mill, 39
— weir, 55
Nuneham Courtenay, 56, 62
— flashlock or weir, 56, 74, 88, 89, 93, 264
— railway bridge, 67

Odney weir, 245
Old Barge House, 211
Old Eye, 263
Old Man's weir, 262
Old Nan's weir, 152, 171, 176, 262
Old Windsor church, 98
— lock, 161, 188, 244

T

Oliver's (Strand) ait, 202
Orkney Arms, 127
Osney lock, 156, 159, 181, 216
— weir, 264
Ouse, River, 13, 26
Overithwartwere, 33
Oxford, 5, 9, 13, 15-17, 19, 21, 22, 26-28, 37, 45, 55, 58, 59, 62-66, 69-72, 74, 75, 77, 79, 82, 83-89, 93, 101-103, 107, 115, 120, 123-126, 138, 139, 142, 147, 148, 152, 160, 161, 163, 164, 174, 175, 180, 188-191, 194, 195, 197, 198, 211, 216, 227, 242, 243, 246-248, 251, 268-271, 275
— castle mills, 58
— city archives, 106
— freemen claim free navigation, 216, 217
— Grandpont, 275
— mayor of, 85, 217
— mill at, 242
— schools, 72
— university, 9, 37, 66, 68, 71, 74, 79, 80, 85, 89, 103, 107, 114
— — archives, 65, 78, 116, 266
Oxley (Chertsey) mills, 206

Pangbourne, 120, 137, 140, 243, 276
Parrott's paygate, 203
Paternoster Lane, 32
Patrick stream, 95
Penton Hook lock, 98, 198, 201, 207, 209, 235, 251
— lockkeeper, 213
— pleasure tolls below, 247
Petersham, 35
— lane, 215
Pinkhill lock, 156, 159, 246
— weir, 147, 172, 176, 197, 262
Port Meadow, 176
Poulter's Horsing, 148
Purley ferries, 156
— (Mapledurham) lock, 156
Putney, 92, 214
— (Fulham) bridge, 202, 229

Queenhithe, 60, 99, 100, 112
Queen's ait, 97, 276

Radcot, 64, 243, 246, 248, 269, 270
— bridge, 27, 140
— traffic terminus, 269
Rayleigh, 269
Ray (Rea) lock (Boulter's), 50, 54
— mill, 242
Reading, 55, 59, 72, 100, 112, 115-117, 123, 126, 127, 129, 138, 140, 143, 152, 154, 159, 161, 162, 166, 182, 191, 205, 237, 243, 268, 269
— common landing place, 115
Rewley weir, 264
Richmond, 48, 177, 191, 200-202, 208, 210, 213, 221, 226, 237, 258
— lock, 98, 254
— — early suggestion of, 126
— palace, 47, 48, 201
Riddlespool, 97
Ridge's (Cock's) weir, 262
Romney lock, 156, 165, 180
Rotherfield Pypard, 17
Rudge's weir (below New Bridge), 172, 176
— (Tadpole), 262
Rushey lock, 156, 197, 246, 248
— (Rudge's) weir, 171, 176

St. Aldate's, 75
St. John's bridge, 140, 171, 275
— flashlock or weir, 171, 176, 262
— lock, 156, 197, 246
Sandford, 62, 85, 88
— flashlock or weir, 56, 172, 176, 187, 264, 265
— lock, 67, 72, 73, 75, 77-81, 86-88, 93, 156, 181, 196, 265
— mill, 45, 79, 81, 82
Sansom's ford, 248
Sawbridge island, 148
Searle's wharf, 132
Seven Springs, 34, 111

Index of Places

Severn, River, 13, 23, 26, 38, 102, 166, 268
Sheen monastery, 49
Shepperton, 24, 34, 112, 136, 137, 148, 200, 201, 207, 208, 215, 221
— lock, 208
— lockkeeper, 245
— weir, 216, 245
Shifford, 159
— flashlock, 147, 171, 176, 262
— lock, 251
Shillingford, 120, 124, 276
— hotel wharf, 276
Shiplake, 132
— lock, 96, 126, 133, 135, 156, 207
— mill, 45
— weir or flashlock, 51, 55, 173, 187, 264, 270
Shire Oaks, 202
Shotover and Stowood Forest, 70
Siddington, 111
Skinner's weir, 176, 197, 262
Sonning, 95, 152, 175
— bridge, 264, 276
— ferry, 156
— flashlock or weir, 51, 55, 95, 104, 130, 173, 176, 187, 264
— lock, 96, 126, 133, 145, 156, 207
— mill, 45
— weir stream, 246
South Bridge, Oxford, 73
— wharf at, 73-75, 86, 88
Southmill weir, 55
Spade Oak, 132, 148
Stadbury (Shepperton), 147, 148
Staines, 10, 15, 25, 30, 33, 40, 44, 47, 48, 69, 92, 98, 99, 112, 114, 126, 132, 133, 136, 149, 162, 165, 166, 168, 190-192, 194, 199-201, 204, 206-208, 211, 213, 215, 216, 228, 232, 234, 242, 243, 274
— barge to, 112
— bridge, 25, 33, 34, 60, 92, 103, 117, 124, 266
— mill at, 242
— Stone, 20, 93, 98, 113, 117, 124, 142, 183, 190, 237

Staples Inn, 205
Stevens' aits, 203
Stour, River (Suffolk), 133
Strand-on-the-Green, 32, 35, 167, 210, 212, 215, 260
— (Oliver's) ait, 202
Streatley, 25, 55, 276
— bridge, 229
— mill, 45, 55, 276
— weir, 55
Sunbury, 112, 136, 159, 202, 207, 215
— flats, 206
— lock, 207, 208, 245
Surley Hall, 134
Sutton Courtenay, 56, 62, 76, 94, 102, 120, 172, 275
— bridges, 156
— flashlocks, 51, 56, 75, 79, 94, 176, 264
— lock, 67, 77, 78, 82, 84, 85, 103, 173, 190
— mills, 45, 51, 56, 76-78, 81, 94, 103, 242, 275
— pool, 85, 94
— unnamed weirs in, 56
Swale Cliff, 23
Swan inn (Pangbourne), 276
Swiffin's weir, 172
Swift Ditch, 13, 56, 67, 71, 78, 80, 83, 93, 94, 102, 174, 265
— flashlock or weir, 75, 77, 87, 88, 264
— house at, 80, 81, 87
— lasher, 77, 82
— lock, 67, 73, 75, 77, 78, 80-82, 84, 86-88, 93, 102, 264

Tadpole bridge, 275
— weir, 147, 159, 176, 262
Tangier mill, 242
Taplow, 97
— Court, 133
— mill, 45, 151
— — stream, 133, 254

Teddington, 35, 59, 201, 208, 226, 252
— lock, 198, 207, 208, 215, 219, 220, 227, 228, 236, 247, 252, 254, 255
— weir, 209
Temple flashlock or weir, 50, 54, 96, 173, 187
— lock, 133, 156, 244, 249, 266
— — island, 240
— mill, 45
Tenfoot weir, 147, 171, 176, 262
Thames, River, above Lechlade, 4, 64, 162-164, 194, 247, 251
— — expenditure on, 161, 163
— affected by enclosures, 215
— alive, 260
— before locked, 46
— below Boulter's, 148, 149, 151
— below Staines, 158, 199-235
— condition if abandoned, 194
— continuous highway, 19
— diversions of channel, 13, 96
— division into districts, 124, 243
— families associated with, 49, 137
— grown up, 246, 249
— as highway, 99, 252, 258
— keeping peace on, 184
— pollution of, as sewer, 39, 150, 191, 231, 250
— at Port Meadow, 176
— preservation for pleasure, 252
— reservoirs to supply, 83
— royal river, 13
— salmon in, 25, 28, 111, 226
— its source, 34, 111
— surveys of, 57, 92, 101, 107, 139, 242
— tidal bed and soil dispute, 221-225
— tidal revenues barred to the upper River, 249
— traffic, decline of, 182, 188-191, 194, 219
— — increase of, 247
Thames Ditton, 35, 136, 227, 237
Thames Head, 111
Thames weir, 171, 262

Thorn, 71
Thorpe, 207
Thrup (Abingdon), 13
Tidenham-on-Severn, 17
Tower of London, keeper of, 14
Trent, River, 13, 26
Trewsbury mead, 260
Trinity House, 225, 234
— of Deptford Strond, 234
— Square, 236
Trout inn wharf (Tadpole), 275
Trowlock ait, 59
Twickenham, 49, 151, 200, 201, 203, 211, 212, 255
— weir at, 49

Victoria Embankment, 221, 223, 226

Wallingford, 16, 22, 55, 56, 94, 99, 100, 107, 116, 120, 121, 123, 135, 148, 152, 185, 243, 268, 269, 276
— Allhallows parish, 56
— bridge, 85, 94, 98, 264
— canal wharf, 276
— flashlock, 51, 56
— *George* inn, 116
— mill, 56
Walton, 34, 58, 112, 136, 158, 221
— bridge, 206
Wargrave, 54
— landing place, 275, 276
— weir at, 51, 54
Water Eaton, 163
— weir at, 38
Water Oakley, 97
Weirs mill, 240, 242
West (Eaton) weir, 147, 171, 262
Westminster, 25, 123, 214
Weybridge, 112, 136, 201, 208, 214, 215
Wey, River, 215
— navigation, 123
Whitchurch flashlock, 51, 55, 94, 173, 176, 187, 264
— lock, 140, 156
— mill, 6, 45, 276
— "turnpikes," 104, 264

Index of Places

Whitstable Flats, 23
Windsor, 10, 99-102, 107, 112, 123, 125, 132, 134, 136, 148, 150, 151, 191, 193, 211, 220, 242, 243, 269, 276
— bridge, 97, 147, 266
— carpenter, 151
— coal wharf, 276
— park, towpath at, 231
Winney Weg's weir, 171, 262
Witney, 216

Wittenham, Little, 264
— flashlock or weir, 51, 56, 104
Wittenham, Long, 56
— Maddy, 85
Woolwich, 101
Wye, River, 23, 38
Wykewere, 35
Wytham, 197

Yantlet Creek, 15, 188, 199, 239

General Index

Abingdon, Lord, 107, 172
Ackerley, Lieut. Chas. Hy., 101
Acts of the Privy Council, 31, 47, 58
Adams, 80
Admiralty, the, 40, 234
— first lord, 225
Allecia, 13, 269
Allen & Skinner, 188, 230, 231
Allnutt, Zachary, 161, 205-207.
Ancient Laws and Institutions, 12
Andrew of the Exchequer, 16, 269
Anglo-Saxon Chronicle, 268
Annual Register, 204
Appelworth, Henricus de, 269
Arnold, Dr., 185
Ashby, Joseph (miller), 156, 173
Authorities of Conservancy, 9, 40-43, 199
Avalagum Thamisiae, 16
Ayray, Henry, 63

Badcock (bargemaster), 120
Bagnall, Rd., 100
Baker, Mr., 173
Ball, John, 138, 139
Ball, Mr., 79, 80
Banckes, George, 51, 56
Barentyne, Thos., 29
Bargee, word not used, 101
Bargemen, misdemeanours of, 76, 85, 86, 105, 106
— religion and, 169

Barges, compensation for lost, 137
— crews of, 136
— dimensions, etc., of, 53, 62, 109, 118-120, 135, 171-173, 177, 273
— draught of, 125, 129, 134, 135, 143, 158, 177, 183, 206, 208, 216, 254
— expense of navigating, 113, 126, 127, 136, 152
— extent of trade, 121, 136, 228
— as letter carriers, 100
— machines for rowing, 117, 118, 122
— overloading of, 137, 138, 154, 216
— precedence of, 244
— rate of travel, 152, 177, 183, 186, 251
— smaller proposed, 119
— to be towed from mast, 182
— to various places, 99, 100, 112, 119, 120
— undermanned, 190, 191
— Western, 58, 59, 100, 101, 200
— working at night, 220
Barry, Francis, 107
Barton, Richard, 55
Bathurst, C., 127, 174, 261, 262
Battie, Dr. Wm., 201
Batting, Jas. (lockkeeper), 156
Baylie, Richard (Vice-Can.), 74
Baynes, —, 202, 210
Beches, de, 24, 25
Beckley, Wm. (lockk'per), 87, 156
Bed and soil of Thames, ownership of, 32

General Index 287

Belcher (bargemaster), 120
Belloc, H., 139, 260
Benson, Thomas, 49
Bereford, Wm. de, 20, 22
Bertie, —, 115
Binnell, Robert, 110, 111
Birch, W. de G., 14, 15, 24, 60
Bishop, James (lockkeeper), 156
— John, 45, 47, 49, 52, 54, 92-94, 96, 99, 105, 121, 272
Blackmanne, Wm., 51
Bligh, General, 227
Blount family, 51, 55, 173, 187
Board of Trade, 192, 240, 255
— of Works, 232-234
Boat-letting to novices, 236
— slides, 237
Bodleian library, 65
Bodley, Sir Thomas, 65
Bonde (bargemaster), 57
Bondholders, State protection for Thames, 219
Boner, Alexander (waterbailiff), 31, 32
Bossom family, 181
Boston, Lord, 254
Boucher, Mr., 237
Bowde, Mr., 50, 54
Bowen's *Map*, 135, 261, 263
Bowles, C., 261, 262
Bowthe (bargemaster), 57
Boydell, J. & J., 17
Bradfield, Rd. (lockkeeper), 156
Braye, John de, 25
Bridges, pontage toll on barges, 261
Brindley, Jas., 126, 149
Brocks, Thos. (lockkeeper), 156
Brodewater, Robert, 51, 56
Brookland, W., 116
Brown, —, 180
Browne (bargemaster), 57
Browning, Robert, 95
Brynty, John (or Brynkys), 50, 54
Buckingham, Earl of, 201
Bucks, defined, 121
Buisshope, Jacobe, 51, 56
Burstal, Captain, 236

Bury, George, 80, 81
Butler, Thomas, 50, 54
Byrde, Robert, 51

Cables, towing, 46, 53, 87, 106, 148, 165, 229
Cambell, Sir James, 91
Campbell, R., 240
Canals, General Union, 185, 186,
— preferred to River, 146, 150, 151
— projected, 122, 126, 128, 151
— to be turned into railways, 186
Carpenter, ignorant (Windsor), 150, 151
Carriers Cosmographie, 99
Catholics, 38
Cecil, Wm., Lord Burghley, 40, 42, 45, 50
Chancellor, the Lord, 66
Charles I, 69-71, 91, 98, 100
Charles II, 102
Chestehunte, Walter de, 25
Chilburye (bargemaster), 51
Child, Thos. (lockkeeper), 156
Clark, Charles, 185
Clarke (Radcot), 171
Clayton, Sir Wm., 173
Clerk of the Market, 42
Coal dues, 213
— — to aid navigation, 128, 130, 142
— sole freight, 230
Cobbett, Wm., 92
Coddesdon (bargemaster), 57
Collet (bargemaster), 57
Collins (bargemaster of Abingdon), 120, 139
Collins (of Swift Ditch weir), 87
Collyer (bargemaster), 57
Commission of 1695, 106, 108, 109, 114, 261
— 1730, 85, 86, 109, 115
— 1751, 113-117, 123, 127, 130, 261
— — minutes burnt, 117
— — orders of, 171-173
— 1770 (See *Thames Commissioners*)

288　The Thames Highway

Commissions of Sewers, 42, 44, 103
— negligence of, 21, 22, 40, 43
— petitions for, 163, 164
Common in running water, 20
Commonwealth, 100, 168
Comptroller of the Household, 48
Conservancy, court of, 117
Considerations (Allnutt), 205-207
Convocation of Oxford University, 65, 73
— Accounts, 68, 72, 79, 80
— Book of the Chest, 68
— Register, 68
Coombe (Combe), W., 17
Cordrey, Geo., or Cawdrey (lock-keeper), 156
Cornish, C. J., 6, 92
Cosmo III, Travels of, 101
Cottrell, Hughe, 54
— Rd., 51, 55
County Councils, riparian, 256
Cranborne, Viscount, 60
Crawford (bargemaster), 120
Cromwell, Thomas, 38, 39
Crosby, the, 210-212
Crown jurisdiction, 9, 221-224, 232-234
— *v.* City of London, 221-225, 231-235
— tolls, 15, 16
Culley, Nicholas (bargemaster), 103
Customs, Commissioners of, 213
Customs of Old England, 138
Cutler (bargemaster), 57

Dabnet, Clement, 56
Daily News, 252
Danby family, 86, 156, 172, 187, 240
Danes, the, 268
Darvill, Mr. (Windsor), 193
Dead animals in River, 253
Deane, Mr., 173
Debois, Mr., 76

Derby, Earl of, 51, 55
de Ros, Lord, 227
Domesday, 242
Dominicans, 28
Dorchester, Lord, 70, 71, 91
Drayton, Sir John, 17, 269
Dredging, 19
— a method of, 205
Dunch, Edmund, 63
Dunch, Wm., 51, 56
Dysart, Earl of, bargeway, 215
— paygate, 121, 203

Edington, Robert, 205
Edward the Confessor, 12
Edward I, 19, 22, 59
— *Year Book* of, 20
— II, 22, 26
— III, 23, 24, 26, 27
— IV, 33, 35
— VI, 49, 61
Eliot, Lord John, 163
Elizabeth, Queen, 39, 41, 42, 44, 47-50, 52, 54, 55, 57, 258
Elmes, Anthony, 50, 54, 96
Elsee, C., 173, 187
Elson, John, 51
Elstone, Richard, 56
Embankments a nuisance, 197
England's Improvement, 101
Equilibrium gates, 205
Essay to Prove, 110-113
Exchequer, the, 16, 42, 49
Exhibition of 1851, 188
Extracts from Navigation Rolls, 127, 174

Farmer, Richard, 73-75, 77, 79
— Thomas, 50, 52, 54
Ferries, establishment of, 247
— free to navigation, 187
— hostility to, 167
Fettiplace, Edmund, 51, 56, 63
Fisheries, affect navigation, 31, 117, 146
— originators of weirs, 5, 6

General Index   289

Fishermen, 34
Flashes, description of, 195, 196
— rate of travel, 175, 176
— regulation of, 126, 147, 152, 157, 169, 175, 176, 195, 207, 249, 250
— requisite for navigation, 7, 44, 128, 129, 189, 207
— to be abolished, 183, 189
Flashlocks (*See also* Weirs), 7, 82, 121, 129, 140, 141, 177
— late use of, 131
— method of passing, 7, 8, 83, 90, 91, 121, 154, 251
— older than pound locks, 2, 144, 145
— payments to owners, 162, 175, 182, 187, 197, 262-7
— purchase of, 124, 142, 144, 145, 190
— register of, 170-173, 187
— rights reserved, 125
— tolls abolished, 242, 246
Flexman, John (lockkeeper), 156
Floods, delay traffic, 146, 183
— of 1774, 200
— prevention of, 250
— railway embankments cause, 250
Ford, John, 50, 54
Foster, A. J., 186
Freights, rates of, 99, 100, 116, 118, 131, 132, 135, 154, 206, 268, 270
Frewyn, Robert, 51, 55
Fry of fish, commercial value, 3, 4
— destruction of, 3, 28, 29, 34, 41, 92
Fuller, Mr., 173

Gardener (bargemaster), 120
Gas works pollute Thames, 231
Gearing, Eliz. (lockkeeper), 156
— Richard (do.), 156
Geddes, Alex. (lockkeeper), 156
General Letter Office, 100
Gentleman's Magazine, 117, 126
George II, 85, 113, 116
George, Robert, 51, 56

Gibbons, Daniel (lockkeeper), 156
Globe, the, 213
Gnill (bargemaster), 57
Godden, Miss G. M., 170
Golafre, John, 26, 27
Gold, George, 49
Good, Richard, 63
Gordon, John, 215
Gore, Hon. C. A., 233
Gould, Caleb (lockkeeper), 156
— John (do.), 156
Government refuse toll, 160
Graham, Wm., 191
Grain (bargemaster), 120
Grave, J. W., 187
Green & Brown, 187
Greye (bargemaster), 57
Griffiths, Roger (waterbailiff), 110, 111, 127, 261, 262
Grissell, Mr., 237
Grover, Mr. 134
Gull, defined, 121
Gvylden (bargemaster), 57

Hale, T., 104
Hall, S. C., 59, 120
Hall, Thomas (lockkeeper), 95, 156
Harcourt, Lord, 172
Harris, Oxford gaoler, 151
Hart, Mrs. (Eaton), 171
Hatfield Papers, 59
Hatt, 86
Hauliers, 177, 202
Haweis, daughter of Wilfrid, 18
Headington stone, 66
Henry I, 14
— II, 19, 217
— III, 15, 18, 59, 269
— IV, 17, 29, 32
— VI, 30
— VIII, 38, 39
Hewett, John, 202
Hewit, Widow (lockkeeper), 156
Heywoode, Rd., 50
Hicks, Berkeley, 180, 181
Higgs (bargemaster), 120

U

Highways suffer through defects of navigation, 41, 43, 66, 102
Hill (bargemaster), 57
— Mrs. (lockkeeper), 86, 156
Hillary, Roger, 25
History of Prices, 268
History of the Exchequer, 16
Hodges, Chas., 181
Holland, Dowager Lady, 173
Honey, Thos. (or Hooney), lockkeeper, 156
Honyball, Thos., 49
Hooper (bargemaster), 120
— Nicholas (bargemaster), 103
Horses, number used in towing, 147, 148, 203
Houghton, John, 80
Houseboats, 177, 202, 257
House of Lords MSS., 262
Humpherus, Hy., 100, 170
Hundreds to destroy weirs, 38
Hunt, Thos., 137
Hyde, Sir Hy., 63

Ilande, Robert, 51, 54
Inland Cruising, 68
Islands interrupt towing, 164, 165

Jackson, George (lockkeeper), 156
— Joseph (do.), 156
James I, 60, 63, 65, 69, 82, 84, 85, 102, 217
Jaques, or Jacques (bargemaster), 120, 121
Jennyngs, Rd., 49
Jess, James, 64
Jessopp, James, 63
John de London, 19
John, King, 15, 16, 18, 19
Jones, Roger, 65
Jurisdiction over River, 9, 12, 255
— — local, 10
Justice, Rd., 51, 56

Keen, Thos., 181

Keep, Thos., 156
Kempe, Sir Nicholas, 68, 69, 79
Kennet and Avon Canal Co., 173
Kidels, 16-18, 23
King, Mr., 173
King & Davis, 177
King's Bench, 105
Knappes, Harry, 51, 55
Knight, Wm., 49
Knowles, Sir F., 49

Lafford, Wm. (Keen Edge), 156
Landing places, 247, 274-276
Langford, Wm. de, 25
Langham, Mr., 172
Lansdowne MSS., 35, 40, 43, 49, 270
Larchyn (bargemaster), 57
Lasyngby, Elizabeth, 32
Launches, 187
Leach, Stephen, 192, 213-215, 225
— Stephen W., 225, 229, 236, 251
Leech, Wm. (lockkeeper), 156
Leonard, James (bargemaster), 120, 137
Lisle, Lady, 38
Lockhouses, 133, 134, 154
— damp situation of, 218
— sites refused, 134
Lockkeepers, allowances to, 218
— appointment of, urged, 145, 160
— changes of, 248
— checks upon, 168, 214
— duties of, 168, 177, 178, 209, 210, 216, 243, 244
— gratuities to, forbidden, 243
— to live in lockhouses, 154, 209
— not to keep inns, 33
— not to take lodgers, 248
— register of, 155, 156
— repudiate presents, 218
— to be speeded up, 253
— wages, 155-157, 168, 189, 229, 242
— women as, 179, 251
Locks, advertisements at, declined 253, 256

General Index 291

— alarm bells at, 251
— blocked with weeds, 248
— casually regarded, 1
— construction of, 136, 137, 139, 208
— continuous flow through, 155, 244
— cuts, 143, 159
— damage to, 109, 136
— decayed, 182, 194, 225, 239, 248, 249
— dirty condition, 197, 237
— distances to be exhibited, 247
— essential advantage of, 4, 43, 90, 91, 128, 164, 165
— farming of (*See Tolls*)
— gardens, prizes for, 254
— holdfasts in, 231
— hostility to, 207, 208
— modern, first built, 9, 10, 63, 67, 68
— names and keepers' names to be displayed, 216
— other terms for, 2, 70, 126
— prohibited below Boulter's, 124, 132, 149, 153
— register of, 155, 156
— revival of building, 123, 124
— steamboats and, 226
— tickets, 243, 245
— to be kept clean, 244
— to stand empty, 158, 178
— etc., unattended, 152, 167
Lockton, Philip (bargemaster), 103
Locomotive, steamboat, 226-228
Loder, C., 171
London, Corporation of, 47, 48, 59, 61, 69, 91, 92, 104, 105, 117, 123, 124, 132, 136, 139, 142, 146, 153, 165, 168, 170, 174, 175, 177, 182-186, 198, 202, 207, 210, 213, 216-219, 221, 222, 225-236, 238, 256
— — inspectors, 213, 214
— — jurisdiction over Thames, 10, 14, 15, 18, 24, 27, 32, 33, 35, 40, 42, 44, 59, 60, 69, 91, 110, 112, 132, 133, 165, 190, 199-235, 272

— — — suggested termination of, 221
— — *Letter Books*, 17, 25, 27, 31, 33
— — Navigation Committee, 133, 157, 164, 167, 200, 210, 212, 225
— — — engineer, 210
— — — financial position, 216, 219, 225, 230, 232, 233, 253
— — — records, 263
— — — refuse to pay toll, 157
— — shallop, 174, 175, 184, 211
— — surrender to Crown, 232-235
— — threat to supersede Thames Commissioners, 166
— — works of, 158, 165, 166, 225, 230
— County Council, 255
— Lord Mayor of, his views of the River 202, 210-212
London Pamphlets, 149
Longford (bargemaster), 120
Lonsdale, Lord, paygate, 204
Louthe, Roger de, 25
Loveden, E. Loveden, 166, 171
Lovelace, Mr., 50, 54
Lucan, Lord, 208
Lucas, Farmer, 134
Lucy, Wilfrid de, 18
Lybbe Powys family, 95
Lynche (bargemaster), 57

Madan, F., 72
Madox, Thos., 16
Magna Charta, 16-18, 23, 35
Malet, Robert, 20
Maria Wood, 210-212
— — Company, 212
Marlborough, duke of, 191, 262
Mary Tudor, 49
Mathewe, Rd., 50, 54
May, D., 187
— (bargemaster), 120
— Mr. (Sonning), 173
Mayow, Edward, 86
Merry, Harry, 50, 54

Metropolitan Water Board, 255
Mills, allowed tolls on barges, 8
— between Wytham and Lechlade, 196, 197
— connection with locks and weirs, 5, 53
— control stream, 128, 130, 242
— defence of, 52, 53
— as generating stations, 6
— none above Godstow, 160
— not admitted under City jurisdiction, 160, 209
— as nuisances to traffic, 8, 9, 52, 82, 90, 196
— protected, 240, 242
Millers, affect lock tolls, 153
— as lockkeepers, 146, 160
Mollyners, John, 56
Monasteries, 38, 39
Monte Acuto, Wm. de, 22
Mooring rights, 274-276
More, C. J., 254
Morland, J. T., 116
Motor craft, 68
Murray, C. S, 187
Mylne, Robert, 144-147, 149, 151, 152, 160, 263
Myddleton (bargemaster), 57

Naturalist on the Thames, 6, 92
Navigation, abandoned, 192, 193
— Barges, City of London, 200, 202, 210-212
— — — expenses of, 210, 211
— condition in 1865, 193
— districts open, 246, 248
— interested parties, 3
— limitations of, 35, 36, 44
Navy, 98, 272
Netting, prohibited, 237
Newell, Mr., 173
New Inventions, 104
Noctinavigation, 103

O'Brien, M., 133
Ordnance Office, 161
— *Surveys*, 23

Ordric, Abbot, 13
Orkney, Lord, 187
Ovens, John, 56
Overton's *Map*, 261, 262
Owen, S., 136
Oxford Books, 72
Oxford-Burcot Commission, 9, 10, 62-89, 92, 101, 102, 104-106, 114, 143, 261, 271
— locks, etc., well built, 78
— neglect by, 69, 70, 84
— overridden, 85, 86
— sale of works, 87-89
Oxfordshire, Natural History of, 82

"Pair of Sculls," 247
Panting, Robert, 79
Parker, Richard, 216, 217
Parliament, 9, 24-26, 29, 34, 37, 60, 63, 65, 69, 123, 127, 128, 142, 147, 150, 162, 166, 182, 183, 207, 217, 219, 242, 270
Parsons, Messrs., 167, 168
Patent Rolls, 261
Pearman, J., 187
Peart (lockkeeper), 220
Pembroke, earl of, 33
Penny Encyclopaedia, 17
Penycook, John, 34
Pepys, Samuel, 100
Perfect, Mr. (? Southby), 171
Petermen,-nets,-boats, 92
Phelps, Geo. (lockkeeper), 156
Phillimore, Dr., 187
Phillips, J. S. (Abingdon), 172, 174, 187
Photographs, 10, 11
Pincestre, Stephen de, 19
Pinke, Dr., 79
Pither, Jas. (lockkeeper), 156
Pitman family, 156, 173, 187
Pitts, Mrs. 56
Pleasure tolls, 125, 179, 189, 192, 220, 243, 247, 254
— — exemption from, 201, 218
— traffic, tax on, 245
— — precedence of, 254

General Index

Pleydell, —, 115
Plot, Dr. Robert, 82, 83, 102
Plumbridge, Thos. (bargemaster), 143
Pollington, Ralph, 51, 55, 56, 94
Popham, —, 115
Port of London Authority, 255
Poundlocks, term abolished, 244
Powell, Edmund (lockkeeper), 78
— Edward, 257
Present State of Navigation, 118-121
Prince, Daniel, 118
Privy Council, 40, 44, 47, 91, 234
Punch, 212
Purvis (of Dunbar), 225, 226
Pycheford, Geoffrey de, 19, 20
Pye, —, 115
Pyecroft, —, 190

Quaint (bargemaster), 120

Railways, 137, 185, 198, 219
— competition of, 123, 151, 181, 186, 188, 225, 230
Rancklyn (smith), 80
Ravenstein, E. G., 201
Ray, Richard (lockkeeper), 156
Reasons for Preferring Canal, 150
Reddnapp, Thos., 49
Refreshments, notices forbidden, 243
Remembrancia, 92
Rennie, John, 205
Restaurants, floating, 256, 257
Richard I, 14, 18, 19, 33, 199, 233
— II, 29
Roberts, Wm., 51, 55
Robertson, H. R., 249
Rogers, Prof. J. E. Thorold, 268-273
Rookes, John, 256
Rosewell (Marlow), 96
Royal rivers, 9, 12, 13, 36
Rudge, — (lockkeeper), 156
Rush, John (bargemaster), 103

St. John's College, 172
St. Leonards, Lord, 237
Salmon, 25, 28, 111
— Embankment fishery of, 226
Salter (Caversham), 55
Sampson, John, 31
Sanders, —, 156
Sappin (bargemaster), 120
Savory (bargemaster), 120
— (lockkeeper), 220, 221
Sawde (bargemaster), 57
Sawyer, Widow, 51, 56
Scrope, Rd. etc., 28, 50, 54
Searle, Joseph (bargemaster), 152
Seebohm, Frederic, 17, 23
Sewage, 191, 197, 253
— prohibited in Thames, 241, 250
Sharp, Mr., 202
Shebbeare, Mr., 231
Shoal (steam barge), 227
Shooting on Thames, 248, 250, 252
Small, Wm. (lockkeeper), 156
Smyth, Richard, 51, 55
Snell, F. J., 138
Somers, Sir John, 84
Somerset, duke of, 49
Southby (? Perfect), 115, 171
Spenlove, Mr., 172
Spiering, Hugo, 70-72
Stane Street, 193
State of the Thames, 150, 152
State Papers Domestic, 69, 273
Steam traffic, 133, 137, 167, 187, 204, 217, 224, 227, 234
— — west of London Bridge, 226
— vessels, 204, 210, 211
— — damage by, 226, 227
— — demand free navigation, 217
— — lines of, 188, 215
— — speed of, 188, 226-228, 236, 237
— — tolls on, 227, 228, 236, 243
Stevenson, J., 14
— R. L., 95
Stone, J., 187
— Jonius, 64
Stonehouse, Sir George, 80
Stoner, Francis, 50, 54

Stonor, Sir Walter, 38
Storer, A. M., 156
Stow, John, 30, 35, 43-45
Strange, John, 180
Strides across locks, 133
Stringer, Christopher, 75
Stripling Thames, 2, 275
Strype, John, 43, 45, 52
Styles, Mr. (proctor), 65
Sunday traffic, 53, 169, 170, 184, 185, 228
Susanna, barge, 185
Swann, J. (Sandford), 172, 187
Swan-upping, 202
Symonds, Rev. Rt., 171

Taillour, Wm., 33
Tailor, Harry, 50, 54
Tatham, Colonel, 204, 205
Taunt, H. W., 92
Taylor, John, 54, 61, 72, 77, 92-99, 105, 112
Thame Isis, 72, 92
Thames (W. Westall), 177
Thames Commissioners, The, 33, 87, 88, 114, 122-200, 205, 216-219, 225, 229, 231, 239, 240, 242, 249
— — authority disregarded, 138, 139
— — bond holders of, 240, 241, 253
— — disputes with City of London, 166, 174, 175, 207
— — financial position, 142, 143, 154, 155, 161, 182, 183, 189-194, 219, 253
— — reduction of staff, 194
— — supersession, 190, 192, 193, 198
Thames Conservancy, 1857, 190, 192, 212, 224, 233, 234, 236-239
— — 1866, 114, 193, 198, 199, 239-256
— — criticised, 248, 249
— — financial position, 247-249, 253

— — jurisdiction modified, 255
— — launch, 246
— — museum, 246
— — praised, 249
Thimble, Mr., 69
Throckmorton, Sir C., 171
Tide, range of, 25
Timber from men-o'-war, 140, 141
— as staple freight, 273
Times, the, 169, 191, 241, 247, 249, 250
Tisdale, Thos., 51, 56
Tollgates, 200, 201
Tolls, 8, 13, 14, 76, 81, 82, 84, 85, 88, 98, 103, 104, 113, 116-118, 125, 127, 130, 135, 136, 143, 162, 165, 171-173, 177, 182, 187, 200, 201, 203, 208, 209, 214, 215, 219, 242, 243, 245-248, 261-267.
— City collection of, 214
— evasion of, 143, 215, 244, 245
— exemptions, 201, 203, 215-217, 243, 269
— farming of, 88, 153, 155-157, 180, 181, 219
— imperfectly collected, 179, 180, 214
— method of distribution, 162
— not uniform, 129, 153
— etc., purchased by City of London, 200, 201
— reduction of, 186, 225, 229
— right to, acknowledged, 18, 24
— to be State guaranteed, 219
— suspended, 188, 189
Tolson, Dr., 68
Tomkins, John (bargemaster), 103
— (lockkeeper), 86
Towing, 58, 82, 106, 109, 110, 134
— by horses, 58, 191, 201, 231, 252
— — prohibited, 201
— by steam, 167, 187, 188, 228, 229,
— charges, 134
— through water, 203
— unemployment relief, 131
Towpaths, 137, 153, 164, 165, 185, 202

General Index

— damage by steamboats, 226, 228
— to be free, 66, 88
— interruptions of, 153
— prohibited, 133, 153
— as public highway, 59, 276
— suggestion to close, 231
Treasury, first lord, 225
Trees as obstruction, 44, 45
Trink nets, 30, 31
Trows, 59
Trullock, Thos., his weirs, 51, 56
Truss, Charles, 146, 200, 210, 213
Turner, Mr., 173
Twang (bargemaster), 120
Two Reports (Oxf. 1811), 161, 163

Upton, John, 49

Vanderstegen, Wm., 150, 152
Victoria, Queen, 223, 233, 234
Voyage, definition of, 148, 171

Walters, Widow (lockkeeper), 156
Wane, defined, 160
Ward, Mr., of Marlborough, 162
Warde (bargemaster), 57
Warrants disregarded, 138
Waterbailiffs, 34, 91, 104, 117
Water Companies, 240, 241
Watermen's fares, 112
— *History of*, 100
Waters (bargemaster), 120
Webb (bargemaster), 120
Weirs, (*See also flashlocks*)
— abuse of for fishing, 5
— advantage of, 4, 17, 43, 53
— cause floods, 5, 157
— construction of, 7, 49, 53, 113, 121, 160, 175, 189
— increased height of, 118, 119
— the ancient locks, 2
— original motive for, 5, 6, 108
— as nuisances, 34, 50, 52, 56, 57, 101, 108
— persistence of, 57
— prescriptive right to, 19, 196
— purchase of, 240
— separate ownership of, 145

— under public control, 242
— various kinds of, 35
Weir streams, right of navigation, 246
Wells, Wm. & Mrs. (lockkeepers), 156, 171
Welshe (bargemaster), 57
Westall, G., 67
— Wm., 177
Westcott, George, 50, 54
Weston, Robert, 50, 54
Wethered, Rev. F. T., 249
Whisler, Wm., 51, 55
White, a carpenter, 79
Whitworth, Richard (or Robert), 149
Whysler, Hugh, 51, 55
Whyte, Wm., 49
Wildgoose Thos., 60
William III, 105
William, son of Andrew, 15, 16, 269
Williams, T. P. (Temple), 173, 187
Wilmott, Edward, 51, 56
Winches, 8, 36, 178
Winchester, marquess of, 49
Windsor, Constable of, 22
Winter, Joseph (lockkeeper), 156
Wodcocke, John, 30
Wolley, Robert, 54
Wolsey, Cardinal, 37
Wood, Anthony à, 14, 17, 68, 83
— Oliver, 49
Woods & Forests, H. M., 221, 231-234, 237, 238
— first commissioner, 225, 233
Worsers, 59
Worth, de, 24
Wren, Sir Christopher, 144
Wright, Messrs., 173, 187
Wyat (bargemaster), 120
Wyatt (lockkeeper), 86
Wydmore, John, 51, 55
Wylforde, Nicholas, 51, 55
Wyllyams (bargemaster), 57
Wyllys, 51, 55
Wynter (bargemaster), 57

Yarranton, Andrew, 101, 102,

THE STRIPLING THAMES

. A BOOK OF THE .
RIVER ABOVE OXFORD

Cr. 8vo., viii.+496 pp., 64 Illustrations and full Indexes
Price, 8/6 net

—

THE little Thames of lonely reaches, of endless level meadows, a Thames almost drowsy with solitude. He casts a wide net, to which a trace of the smoke-farthing custom comes as little amiss as the greatness of the Throckmortons, and a pretty way of laying a table in a country inn as well as the fine old rood of Down Amney church. The best is that he does not fail expectation when one comes with him to this or that point in the river which has given the sharpest impression on one's own journeys—the strange sullenness of Shifford reach, as if some lowering ghosts of Alfred's day still haunted the spot where once they held a Parliament; the wonderful freshness of the wind about Eynsham; the young loveliness of the river at Pinkhill lock. And that, after all, is how one judges such a book in the end.—*Manchester Guardian.*

OXFORD constitutes the sharpest of divisions in the experience of the river; for one man who knows the Thames above Oxford there is certainly a hundred who know the river at some point or points below that town. The book grows more personal and more lively as it approaches the Springs of Thames. There is a very beautiful passage upon the little rivers of the Upper Valley that come down from the Cotswold, ending with a sentence that lingers in the ear: " . . . And I too brood over the silver tributaries, *ancillas Tamesis*, and the villages set like jewels upon their banks, whose charm and interest my lifetime will be too short fully to explore and describe." That is very charmingly said. Another passage that must be mentioned even in this short notice is the very excellent description of Ashton Keynes, especially this sentence: " . . . its host of little bridges, the peculiar, the perennial delight of Ashton Keynes."—*Morning Post.*

IT is a delightful thing to read a book by a genuine enthusiast, especially if the subject is not itself of a dryasdust nature. Mr. Thacker is an enthusiast, and "The Stripling Thames: a Book of the River above Oxford," is concerned with one of the freshest holiday lands in England. The book is one which every one who knows the country between Oxford and the Cotswolds will gladly linger over. It is full of all sorts of old, forgotten things, quaintly and sometimes uncritically collected, and discussed with a happy garrulity. All who read it will surely wish to go where Mr. Thacker has been.—*Athenæum.*

www.ingramcontent.com/pod-product-compliance
Lightning Source LLC
Chambersburg PA
CBHW031422150426
43191CB00006B/353